Becoming Literate in the City

Literacy is one of the most highly valued cultural resources of contemporary American society, yet far too many children in the nation's cities leave school without becoming sufficiently literate. This book reports the results of a 5-year longitudinal study in the city of Baltimore, Maryland, tracing literacy development from prekindergarten through third grade for a sample of children from low- and middle-income families of European and African heritage. The authors examined the intimate culture of each child's home, defined by a confluence of parental beliefs, recurrent activities, and interactive processes, in relation to children's literacy competencies. Also examined were teacher beliefs and practices, and connections between home and school. With its broad-based consideration of the contexts of early literacy development, the book makes an important contribution to understanding how best to facilitate attainment of literacy for children from diverse backgrounds.

Robert Serpell was born in England and received his Ph.D. from the University of Sussex. His theoretical and applied research in Africa, Britain, and the United States has centered around the sociocultural context of children's cognitive development. He was Professor of Psychology at the University of Maryland, Baltimore County, for twelve years and is currently Vice Chancellor at the University of Zambia.

Linda Baker is Professor of Psychology and director of the doctoral program in Applied Developmental Psychology at the University of Maryland, Baltimore County. She received her Ph.D. in cognitive psychology from Rutgers University. Her research interests include early literacy development, motivation for reading, metacognition, and parental influences on educational achievement.

Susan Sonnenschein is Associate Professor in the Applied Developmental Psychology program at the University of Maryland, Baltimore County. She holds a Ph.D. in developmental psychology, a master's degree in educational psychology, and certification as a school psychologist. Her research focuses on children's literacy and language development, with particular attention to parental influences.

Becoming Literate in the City

The Baltimore Early Childhood Project

ROBERT SERPELL
University of Zambia

LINDA BAKER
University of Maryland, Baltimore County

SUSAN SONNENSCHEIN
University of Maryland, Baltimore County

CAMBRIDGE
UNIVERSITY PRESS

PUBLISHED BY THE PRESS SYNDICATE OF THE UNIVERSITY OF CAMBRIDGE
The Pitt Building, Trumpington Street, Cambridge, United Kingdom

CAMBRIDGE UNIVERSITY PRESS
The Edinburgh Building, Cambridge CB2 2RU, UK
40 West 20th Street, New York, NY 10011-4211, USA
477 Williamstown Road, Port Melbourne, VIC 3207, Australia
Ruiz de Alarcón 13, 28014 Madrid, Spain
Dock House, The Waterfront, Cape Town 8001, South Africa

http://www.cambridge.org

First published 2005

Printed in the United States of America

Typeface Palatino 10/13.5 pt.   *System* LATEX 2$_\varepsilon$ [TB]

A catalog record for this book is available from the British Library.

Library of Congress Cataloging in Publication Data
Serpell, Robert.
    Becoming literate in the city : the Baltimore early childhood project /
Robert Serpell, Linda Baker, and Susan Sonnenschein.
        p.   cm.
    Includes bibliographical references and index.
    ISBN 0-521-77202-8 – ISBN 0-521-77677-5 (pb.)
        1. Early childhood education – Maryland – Baltimore – Longitudinal studies.
    2. Minorities – Education – Maryland – Baltimore – Longitudinal studies.
    3. Literacy – Maryland – Baltimore – Longitudinal studies.
    4. Home and school – Maryland – Baltimore – Longitudinal studies.
    5. Education, Urban – Maryland – Baltimore – Longitudinal studies.
    I. Baker, Linda.   II. Sonnenschein, Susan.   III. Title.
    LB1139.27.M25S47   2004
    372.21'0975'6 – dc22   2004045706

ISBN 0 521 77202 8 hardback
ISBN 0 521 77677 5 paperback

Contents

Preface

Far too many children finish school in contemporary American society without becoming sufficiently literate for successful participation in the economy. The problem is so widely acknowledged in the United States that discussion about its source and solutions is not confined to the halls of academia, but is also widespread in the newspapers, on radio and television, and in state and national legislatures. Although difficulties with academic progress are not limited to children from any particular sociocultural group, the problem is greatest for children from low-income families and children of African and Hispanic heritage.

Our goal when we began planning our study in the early 1990s was to follow a group of children attending public school in a large metropolitan area from prekindergarten through their first few years in elementary school. We were particularly interested in documenting socialization practices in children's home environments. We expected to find different patterns of socialization characteristic of the home environments of children being raised in families from different social addresses. What skills and dispositions did children from different sociocultural groups bring to the task of learning when they entered school? What were the expectations and instructional practices of the teachers in whose classes these children were enrolled? We expected that much of the variance in patterns of school performance would be accounted for by variations in the match between socialization practices experienced by children at home and what was expected of them at school. Although our study was not designed as an intervention, we expected findings from it to inform subsequent interventions.

The study described in this book, the Early Childhood Project, has been a truly egalitarian collaborative effort on the part of the three authors. Different particular components have been led by each of us at various times, and a number of separate reports have been published under our names arranged in various orders. However, we have maintained a commitment throughout to the eventual integration of all the strands into a single book. Forging consensus on the text presented in this volume has been a protracted and sometimes challenging task spread over several years. At the end of the day, we do not regard the order of names on the title page as anything more than an arbitrary ordering.

A work of this scope could not have been undertaken without financial assistance and support from others. The University of Maryland, Baltimore County (UMBC), provided funds for our pilot work as well as funds to assist with data analysis and interpretation at the end of the project. Funds provided by the National Reading Research Center (contracted by the Office of Educational Research and Improvement; PR/Award no. 117A20007) and the National Institute of Child Health and Human Development (R01 HD29737-0A1) enabled us to conduct the study. The opinions expressed in this book are ours and do not necessarily reflect those of the funding agencies.

The Early Childhood Project provided the focus of work over a period of more than 10 years for a research team comprising faculty and students of the UMBC Psychology Department centered in, but not confined to, the graduate program in Applied Developmental Psychology. We are profoundly grateful to the many graduate and undergraduate students who assisted in the conceptualization and implementation of this study, as well as the documentation and interpretation of our findings. Many of the graduate students involved in the Early Childhood Project completed master's theses or doctoral dissertations within the framework of the study. Graduate students included Dorothy Adamson, Adriana Amari, Hibist Astatke, Diane Schmidt Bates, Yolanda Vauss Berry, Marta Caballeros, Evangeline Danseco, Marie Dorsey, Sylvia Fernandez-Fein, Hemalatha Ganapathy, Adia Garrett, Victoria Goddard-Truitt, Linda Gorham, Brenda Haynes, Susan Hill, Angela Katenkamp, Kirsten Mackler,

Akintunde Morakinyo, Faith Morse, Kimberly Munsterman, Olena Prachenko, Beverly Pringle, Deborah Scher, Zewe Serpell, Dewi Smith, Helen Williams, Patricia Tenowich, and Sharon Teuben-Rowe. Undergraduate students who participated in the data collection and analysis included Sharon Adar, Keshet Burt-Hedrick, Suzanne Bosking, Kai Brown, Yvonne Bush, Jennifer Childs, Lee Custer, Laurie Fairall, Elyse Grossman, Julie Grossman, Kris Hardwick, Veronica Jayachandarah, Jennifer Kaupert, Kelly Kern, Eun Kim, Will Lamb, Bridget LaPorte, Linda LaVeque, Tracy Michaels, Gail Morrow, Stacey Robotham, Laurie Shaw, Erika Smith, Nicole Talley, Shirley Villagaray, and Teniko White.

In addition, we are indebted to the contributions of Dr. Abdeljalil Akkari, who spent a year attached to the project as an adjunct assistant professor, and Dr. Elyse Foorman, who spent a sabbatical semester with us. Also, we were fortunate to have on the team Theresa Rose, whose secretarial and interpersonal skills played an important role in holding the whole enterprise together.

We also want to thank the administrators of the Baltimore City Public School System for providing us access to their staff and students. Our greatest gratitude is to the many children and parents who graciously provided us access to their lives and gave generously of their time and attention to discuss with us their experiences, hopes, and concerns about the process of becoming literate.

At the time the data collection phase of our study concluded, the children were completing third grade. We plan in the near future to revisit these children, who are now in high school, and their families, to document how the early socialization practices and literacy competencies described in this book relate to their subsequent development.

1

Early Appropriation of Literacy in Sociocultural Context

Becoming literate involves the gradual assumption of ownership of a system of meanings that enables people to communicate through written texts. Human societies have generated a number of such systems over the course of history. These include not only languages and scripts, such as those in which the present text is printed, but also a wide range of structured activities, such as reading for entertainment, studying at a university, publishing a newspaper, sending E-mail, and so on. The social functions of these various activities collectively define the cultural practice of literacy, and the appropriation of the system of meanings informing that practice is a prerequisite for full membership in a literate society.

The importance that industrialized societies place on children becoming literate is reflected in the hours that children are expected to spend in school. Becoming literate is regarded as an essential part of growing up. Nevertheless, many children in literate societies such as the United States struggle to learn to read, and a sizable percentage fail to master all but the most basic skills (U.S. Department of Education, 2001). The demographic profile of the group of children who fail to become literate includes an over-representation of children growing up in low-income families and children of African or Hispanic heritage.

Adults in industrialized societies who do not achieve individual literacy are seriously marginalized in many ways. However, this was not always the case in America, nor is it true of a number of contemporary communities around the world. Human societies have often organized themselves without the practice of literacy. This fact, sometimes overlooked in the modern, industrialized world, has implications for understanding both the cultural practice of literacy and the social and psychological processes through which individuals are inducted into it. It means, for instance, that a person, whether child or adult, may be intelligent without being literate. It also means that the processes of literacy learning and socialization are not part of humankind's biological heritage, but a product of cultural, social, and historical factors.

The longitudinal study of early literacy socialization that we present in this book took place in the city of Baltimore, Maryland, on the eastern seaboard of the United States. We followed the lives of a cohort of children enrolled in the city's public schools for the 5 years from 1992 to 1997, from the age of 4 when they entered prekindergarten through the end of third grade at the age of 9. When we started our study, the Baltimore City Public School System, like school systems in other large urban areas, was struggling with limited success to provide its students with a good education. For example, 63% of students who should have graduated with the class of 1994 reportedly failed or dropped out prior to graduation (Baltimore City Public Schools System, 1999, section 8.2).

The children in our study came from low- and middle-income families of European American and African American heritage. Much of our focus was on the home environments in which these children were raised. We examined the *intimate culture* of each child's home, defined by a confluence of parental beliefs, recurrent activities, and interactive processes. We explored the relation between that intimate culture and the child's literacy development during the 5 years of our study. Because we did not want to place parents with low levels of individual literacy on the defensive, we deliberately cast a wide net and gave our study a general name, the Early Childhood Project. Our account of the children's literacy development also includes an analysis of the important cultural institution of school, one of whose explicit functions is to cultivate individual literacy.

The concept of literacy has three complementary facets. It is a dimension of personal development, an educational goal of the school curriculum, and a cultural resource of contemporary American society. We discuss the relations among these three facets, portraying education as a developmental opportunity, schooling as a social institution, and socialization and teaching as cultural practices. In the life of a child growing up in the city of Baltimore, becoming literate involves acquiring cognitive skills, participating in the social activities of both the family and the institution of school, and appropriating a set of cultural resources that are widely used across many settings.

The theoretical framework of the Early Childhood Project was designed to integrate several strands of theory that emerged in the early 1990s from somewhat separate intellectual traditions: (1) a systems view of the context of human development (Bronfenbrenner, 1979, 1989); (2) the eco-cultural niche of child development (Gallimore, Weisner, Kaufman, & Berheimer, 1989; Super & Harkness, 1986); (3) cultural beliefs regarding the nature of caregiver responsibility and effectiveness (Goodnow & Collins, 1990; Miller, 1988; Sigel, 1985); (4) literacy as a cultural practice requiring skills (Heath, 1983; Scribner & Cole, 1981; Street, 1984); (5) participatory appropriation as an account of children's cognitive socialization (Lave & Wenger, 1991; Rogoff, 1990; Serpell, 1993a, 1993b; Vygotsky, 1978); and (6) emergent literacy (Sulzby & Teale, 1991). We discuss each tradition in the sections that follow. Next, we turn to an analysis of the cultural institution of school and how, over the course of history, it has assumed such a critical function in the promotion of individual literacy. We then propose an integrative synthesis of these various strands of theory in terms of children's developmental journeys at the interface between the cultures of home and school. The chapter ends with an overview of the plan of the book.

THE SOCIOCULTURAL ECOLOGY OF HUMAN DEVELOPMENT

The early theoretical notion that context served simply as external stimulation has given way to the more complex perspective of a system of social activity, informed by a system of cultural meanings (Serpell, 1993b, 1999). This theoretical shift has methodological implications. Such discussion acknowledges the common humanity of researchers, parents, and teachers and their responsibility to co-construct or negotiate a shared understanding of possibilities for the enhancement of children's developmental opportunities (Serpell, 1994).

Systems-oriented views of human development highlight the interdependency of human actors and focus on dyads and groups as self-sustaining units over and above what each individual brings to social interaction (Bronfenbrenner, 1979; Sameroff, 1983). Development, according to a systems perspective, consists of changes in the way that a child participates in social activities. An important dimension of that change is from a peripheral role to a more central one (Lave & Wenger, 1991). The developmentally more advanced person's participation earns him or her greater legitimacy, and he becomes more fully integrated into the social system that hosts the activity. For example, the less developmentally advanced child might quietly listen to his mother read a story, whereas the more advanced child might interject comments on elements of the story. As the child comes to participate more actively in reading interactions, he increasingly becomes acknowledged as a member of the community of literate practice, one whose opinions about the storybook count, because he has shown an understanding of the medium in ways that are intelligible to other members of the literate culture. In later phases of development, the child will graduate to the status of a full-fledged reader, who can extract meaning from print without assistance and can participate more equally in discussions of the content of the text with other members of the literate community.

Another theme of the systems view is that social behavior is embedded in a set of relationships that are interdependent. For example, included within Bronfenbrenner's (1979) ecological systems theory are microsystems, such as the child's family or school class; the mesosystem, representing interactions among different microsystems; and the macrosystem, representing societal norms and cultural values or mores. The behavior of an adult sharing a storybook with a child is informed not only by the immediate context, the structure of the text, and the child's reading skills, but also by her enduring relationship with the child as parent, school teacher, or family friend. That dyadic relationship in turn is informed by a set of enveloping constraints, such as the family of which they are members, the neighborhood in which they reside, and the society of which the neighborhood is a constituent part. The dyadic relationship between the child and his school teacher is similarly informed by a set of enveloping, nested systems.

Thus, human development is deeply embedded within a system of social activities and cultural meanings. The development of a child between the ages of 4 and 9 involves growing complexity as a person, increasing competence in many different domains, and progressive incorporation into a particular society and its culture. The process of becoming literate involves not only growth of individual competence, but also, by the same token, induction into new forms of participation in society and a new range of understandings of the culture. From this induction flows a growing authority to interpret actions and events within the society's system of cultural meanings.

For instance, as a child becomes more literate, she is not only able to decode the words printed on a greeting card and to sign her name on it, but she also comes to understand what it means to send such a card to a friend to invite him to a birthday party or to console him when he falls sick. This understanding enables the child to express her feelings about the occasion through a purposeful choice among various cards with different inscriptions on display in the store. A parent or teacher who acknowledges this child's emerging competence to use the resources of literacy for authentic communication will respect her choices as legitimate. In this way, literate adults welcome the child into the community of literate practices.

At the outermost, macrosystemic level of American society, the pervasive significance of literacy for the American way of life is represented in many ways. The nation's written constitution, laws, and regulations are a recurrent frame of reference in civic affairs. Governmental and commercial activities alike are administered through bureaucratic organizations that rely heavily on written documentation. Citizens are expected to articulate their relations with those organizations in writing, often by completing forms that require entry of information in specified spaces. In the nation's most prominent religions (Christianity, Judaism, and Islam), religious texts serve to define the principles of moral conduct and are sometimes cited in public gatherings to buttress moral arguments. The power and prestige attached to science and technology are closely tied to the information systems in which they are documented, with heavy emphasis on the authority of publication in print. Despite the ascendancy of radio and television, the print media retain an enduring preeminence for the dissemination of political and economic news. Thus, whether in commerce, economics, law, politics, religion, science, or technology, that which is written is often definitive in contemporary America. The importance of literacy in the world into which American children of the 1990s will grow was acknowledged in various ways by each of the families we studied in the Baltimore Early Childhood Project.

Formal education is conceptualized at the level of the American macrosystem, as in most other contemporary societies, as a means of transmitting the accumulated wisdom of the culture to the next generation and as a strategic societal mechanism for the preparation of a workforce to participate productively in the national economy. The individual process of becoming literate is generally construed in American culture as the foundation of formal education. Indeed, the terms *educated* and *literate* have become virtually synonymous in contemporary usage as descriptors for an adult person. Thus, becoming literate is imbued with social significance because it represents the beginning of a journey along a pathway toward effective incorporation into the larger social system. The process is also imbued with cultural significance because it provides a major form of access to the system of meanings that informs social activities. Ideally, through participating in the cultural practices of literacy, the developing child gradually appropriates a distinctive system of meanings (D'Andrade, 1984), not only coming to understand how those meanings inform the practices of literacy, but also eventually deploying the system as an interpretive resource to explain to herself and others why one course of action is more appropriate than another.

Embedded within the macrosystem, and responsible for the concrete instantiation of its principles, are various institutions, some of which are specialized for the maintenance, transmission, and cultivation of literacy, such as schools and libraries. Opportunities for the developmental appropriation of literacy also arise in other contexts of life in an American city. The demand for individual literacy is a feature of everyday transactions in stores, clinics, and family homes. Although these contexts are less explicitly specialized than schools for the structural support of literacy development, their implicit orientation may also be a powerful influence on how children approach the demands of that developmental task.

THE ECOCULTURAL NICHE OF CHILD DEVELOPMENT

The concept of the developmental niche focuses on the structure of the context within which a child is raised. Super and Harkness (1986, 1997) advanced the concept as a way of articulating "the interface between child and culture" and identified three components of the niche: (1) "the physical and social settings in which the child lives," (2) "customs of child care and child rearing" (which we refer to as *cultural practices*), and (3) "the psychology of the caretakers" (which we refer to as *ethnotheories of caregiving*).

Gallimore et al. (1989) described the notion of activity settings as another means of conceptualizing the cultural context of children's development. A cultural practice such as literacy is made up of recurrent activities, including shared storybook reading, making a shopping list, or searching a newspaper for advertisements of commercial products. Each activity is culturally defined in terms of its participants; the nature, timing, organization, and location of the tasks; and the meaning the tasks have for the participants (see also Tharp & Gallimore, 1988). Technological artifacts, such as paper and pencils, books, or computers, also often serve as defining features of a cultural activity.

Figure 1.1 illustrates in schematic form the relations among the cultural practice of literacy, the various activities that instantiate that practice, and the process of guided participation through which a parent facilitates the child's appropriation of culture. Every cultural practice provides a guiding framework of rules that the novice must assimilate. In the case of the literate activity of shared storybook reading, key constructs include the story and its elements, such as the protagonists, the setting and the plot, the text and pictures in the book, the pages, and the cover. Key rules include how to hold the book so the pictures are the right way up, how to turn the pages one at a time, and how to take turns reading or commenting on the book (Ninio & Bruner, 1978). Literate adults know these constructs and rules and share an implicit theory of how they fit together. As these adults follow the rules, they demonstrate a script for the participating child

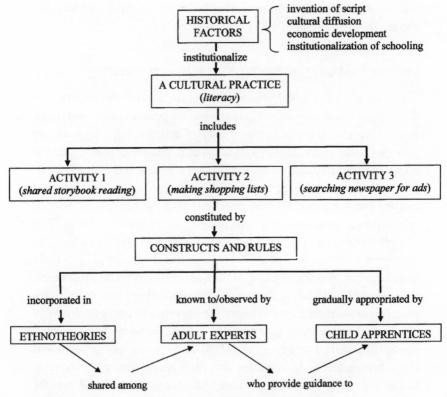

FIGURE 1.1. The appropriation of cultural practices through participation in activities with guidance by experts in light of their ethnotheories.

to follow; as the child participates in the activity, he gradually appropriates the rules, using them as a framework for interpreting the unique contents of different stories in various books.

Once a practice is acknowledged by a community as an identifiable element of its cultural repertoire, it acquires certain properties that facilitate communication. Parents and teachers familiar with shared storybook reading as a "packaged" cultural routine can draw on it as part of their stock of higher-order categories for exchanging views and experiences (e.g., "You should read more often to Johnny," "Try including some more advanced books in your bedtime story sessions," "Have you thought of getting his father to read him stories sometimes?"; Serpell, 2001).

Children's Everyday Experiences Within the Niche as Facilitators of Literacy Development

Researchers have long been interested in the effects of the home environment on literacy development. Early research documented relations between social address variables, such as socioeconomic status or parent education level, and children's literacy, but did not explicate the source of such relations. A second wave of research, recognizing the limitations of status variables as indices of the environment, focused more on characteristics of the environment itself, such as availability of print materials in the home and frequency of reading. More recent still is direct observation of the literate activities within the home. Rather than relying on quantifications of material resources or on parental reports of literacy-related behaviors, researchers have begun to document the variety and scope of literacy events within the home through detailed ethnographic descriptions and microanalysis of parent–child interactions during such events. This changing emphasis is leading to a better understanding of the role of the family in literacy development and how this role varies across different sociocultural communities. The shift of attention from status variables, such as parental occupation, to process variables, such as the nature of shared reading activities, also provides a clearer indication of how intervention should be designed to induce change.

When the Early Childhood Project was conceived, researchers had identified a number of print-related home experiences associated with positive literacy outcomes, such as frequent reading with children and exposure to a wide range of print materials (e.g., Guthrie & Greaney, 1991; Morrow, 1988; Scott-Jones, 1991; Sulzby & Teale, 1991). A growing number of researchers were also beginning to document that other sorts of opportunities within the niche could be helpful, such as parent–child conversation and oral storytelling (e.g., Heath, 1983; Snow, Barnes, Chandler, Goodman, & Hemphill, 1991). The Early Childhood Project sought to extend our understanding of the literacy-promoting resources available at home, even to those children whose families lacked the financial means to purchase a wide array of cultural artifacts.

Demonstrations that certain home experiences correlate with literacy development are informative, but they leave unanswered important questions about the nature of the experiences in which children are immersed during the course of their daily lives. Qualitative research methods are better suited to addressing such questions, and indeed several ethnographic studies completed in the 1980s revealed the variety and scope of the literacy activities in homes of families from diverse sociocultural backgrounds (e.g., Anderson & Stokes, 1984; Heath, 1983; Taylor & Dorsey-Gaines, 1988; Teale, 1986). However, none of these studies examined in detail many of the psychological variables that are critical to the appropriation of literacy, including the beliefs and values of responsible adults in the child's environment and the processes of adult–child interaction during experiences affording opportunities for literacy learning. Moreover, they neglected the motivational and affective dimensions of shared reading and learning to read. Our study sought to overcome these limitations with the design of a detailed inventory of home resources and activities and a series of in-depth interviews probing parental ethnotheories, as well as analysis of directly observed representative interactions in the setting of children's homes. We describe our various methodological tools in Chapter 2.

CULTURAL BELIEFS REGARDING THE NATURE OF PARENT RESPONSIBILITY AND EFFECTIVENESS

The study of cultural beliefs or ethnotheories has its roots in anthropology, and the literature is rich with hypotheses about how culture informs this aspect of the developmental niche. A limitation of anthropological research, however, is a failure "to make clear exactly what individual natives really believe, since these studies focus primarily on collective representations of various kinds, such as myth and ritual" (D'Andrade, 1990, p. 108; see also Jahoda, 1982). Within psychology, in contrast, research conducted prior to the 1990s on parental beliefs was often guided by little or no theory, giving rise to isolated investigations of unrelated beliefs rather than more programmatic research (Miller, 1988). As a consequence, the origins of the beliefs and the processes controlling the relationship between beliefs and behavior remained poorly understood.

In designing the Early Childhood Project, we were sensitive to such concerns. We drew on the suggestions of Miller (1988), who called for future research in this area to pay special attention to studying parents' actual beliefs, as opposed to the beliefs that psychologists think they should have, to studying beliefs comparatively, to conducting longitudinal studies of how beliefs develop and change, and to conducting more cultural comparisons but "measuring differences in experience directly rather than inferring differences from group membership" (p. 281). We also drew on Goodnow and Collins (1990), who stressed the need for further research on the processes involved in the change of an individual parent's ideas over time. They noted the value of focusing such research on major developmental transitions, where "the changes in children are highly visible, and the implications of the change are likely to be significant to both parents and children and to the relationship between them" (p. 97). One such transition is marked by the entry of children into formal schooling. In the Early Childhood Project, we documented parents' changing ideas as their children made the transition from prekindergarten to elementary school.

Ascertaining parental beliefs can be difficult because parents may have many different beliefs about their children, and these beliefs may not always be readily available for conscious reflection. For example, Rodrigo and Triana (1995) examined how the various components of a belief system are represented in memory and how they are deployed in making practical judgments and formulating expectations of behavior. The authors were critical of the notion that ethnotheoretical, lay beliefs about child development and socialization are represented in an individual's memory in the form of structurally organized schemas, and concluded that it is the "structure of information presented" that is crucial for the elaboration of inferences about actions.

Among explanatory schemas that may form part of a parent's beliefs, one type of particular interest to us is the notion of a developmental goal for the child, toward which the parent construes his or her socialization practices as oriented. We recognize that there may be considerable variation among parents in how deliberately their practices are focused on molding or nurturing a certain direction of development. Hallden (1991), for instance, reported that two contrasting themes coexisted for many of the contemporary Swedish parents she interviewed: an Aristotelian concept of "the child as being" whose development is a natural process directed by inner drives and for whom parents should be available as a resource, and an alternative concept of "the child as project" whose development the parent should actively strive to influence by serving as an introducer or mediator. Parents may invoke either of these contrasting models "in order to understand and come to grips with various problems" (p. 339) that arise in the context of caregiving.

Research has also revealed that parents often have seemingly incompatible beliefs, beliefs that are incompatible with practices, and beliefs that are, at best, only weakly related to children's outcomes. For example, in several studies, parents of children attending American schools were asked about their perceptions of the significance of schooling (Laosa, 1984; Okagaki & Sternberg, 1991; Stevenson, Chen, & Uttal, 1990). Low-income parents of African or Hispanic heritage tended to endorse academic goals even more highly than middle-income parents. Yet, the pattern of academic achievement of those low-income minority group children is relatively weak. One explanation for why children of parents with high academic goals for their children do not consistently achieve academic success is that "goals are not always accompanied by a knowledge of how to achieve them. Parental hopes and expectations, for example, are often not accompanied by an accurate knowledge of how to make them achievable" (Goodnow, 2002, p. 444).

Another explanation for inconsistencies between parental beliefs and children's outcomes is that parental endorsement of the goal of academic success in response to a simple direct question may conceal a more complex underlying pattern of beliefs and behavior. For instance, parents may send their children double messages by advocating adherence to the school's standards in their direct comments on the child's behavior at school, but criticizing those standards as irrelevant or oppressive when reflecting on their own everyday experiences in the local community or at work (Ogbu, 1990). Parents may have more than one goal for their child and these goals may be weighted differently, with the most highly weighted goals (not necessarily those tapped by the researcher) getting the most attention. In addition, parents of minority cultural groups and/or economically oppressed social groups may tend to exaggerate the degree to which they agree with the philosophy that informs the school system. This may occur partly out of hopeful optimism that things will turn out better for their children than they did for themselves, partly because these parents do not perceive clearly the areas in which their personal and cultural orientations differ from that of the school teachers and partly because there exists in contemporary American society a strong public cultural theme that schooling is a major route for upward social mobility. All these factors may create a social desirability response bias that is difficult for researchers to get beyond when interviewing parents of lower socioeconomic status.

Another example of incompatible parental beliefs comes from the work of Serpell (1977, 1982), who used semi-structured interviews with caregivers in a rural African community to explore adult perceptions of the most valuable attributes of child behavior. Although many parents in these Zambian Chewa villages endorsed the principle of enrolling their children in school, they apparently had other, more highly valued goals as well. Parents, for instance, generally attached greater importance to social responsibility than to intellectual alacrity. Yet, both parents and teachers in Zambian primary schools recognized that intellectual alacrity was more relevant to academic success than social responsibility. Serpell concluded that the indigenous formulation of intellectual development in relation to moral development and socialization differed in important respects from the formal educational model of cognitive growth that informs the primary school curriculum. This discrepancy generated grave difficulties for students, parents, and teachers in integrating the cultures of home and school (Serpell, 1993a).

In light of the various issues discussed previously, the project that we present in this book was designed to analyze the processes of cognitive socialization in context and to delineate the interactive processes through which the child explores and gradually appropriates the cultural resources of the environment. We documented with a unique combination of methods the implicit models held by parents in four contrastive sociocultural groups. We examined the stability and changes in each parent's models as his/her child progressed through the early years of formal schooling, the extent to which the models were shared with other parents in the same and other sociocultural groups, and the particular ways in which the models were related to observed patterns of interaction. Furthermore, our sampling

strategy provided the opportunity to examine how these processes
were instantiated in different sociocultural contexts. As the project
evolved, we were also able to explore the relations between various
aspects of parental beliefs and later developmental outcomes for their
children.

LITERACY AS A CULTURAL PRACTICE REQUIRING PARTICULAR COGNITIVE SKILLS

Our view of literacy as a system of meanings embedded in particular
cultural practices calls for an account of development at the interface between sociocultural and psychological aspects of cognition.
Vygotsky's (1978) theoretical perspective has been widely invoked
in the contemporary literature on cognitive development and education for this purpose. Not only did he maintain that social interaction
is an important mediator of cognitive development, but he also advanced a particular formulation of that mediating interface. Technological devices, such as writing and mathematics, evolve as products
of cultural history and also mediate the cognitive activity of individuals. We have adopted the neo-Vygotskian conception of literacy
as a cognitive tool with both a cultural history and a developmental
empowering and structuring potential (Cole & Griffin, 1980).

Scribner and Cole's (1981) comparative study of literacy in different scripts within a single society showed how, in addition to its
formal properties as a system of representational meaning or mode
of encoding information, literacy can be viewed as characteristic of
a set of practices. The cultural practices of literacy are constituted by
recurrent activities in which a particular technology and particular
systems of meaning are directed toward socially recognized goals.

Viewing literacy as a set of cultural practices helps us understand
how groups of people can be literate in different ways. Within what
Heath (1983) termed the mainstream subculture of literacy, individuals engage on a daily basis in distinctive "types of uses of reading," including instrumental, news-related, recreational, critical/
educational, social-interactional, and confirmational activities, as
well as distinctive "types of uses of writing," including memory aids,
reinforcement or substitutes for oral messages, social-interactional,
financial, and expository activities. Members of other American

subcultures also engage in literate activities, but these are character-ized by different types of uses of reading and writing with different patterns of cognitive demands and opportunities for cognitive devel-opment (Nerlove & Snipper, 1981). The relative importance of differ-ent forms of engagement with text (Wells, 1990) in the early phases of a child's socialization may thus vary across different sociocultural contexts (Serpell, 1991).

PARTICIPATORY APPROPRIATION AS AN ACCOUNT OF CHILDREN'S LITERACY SOCIALIZATION

The concept of guided participation provides an explanatory account of one type of process through which literacy is fostered at home. As Rogoff (1990) discussed, a child and a more competent adult or sib-ling sometimes engage in a collaborative process whereby the more competent person provides a supportive structure and facilitates the child's appropriation of new skills. In Rogoff's view, children acquire their competence in the cognitive domain of literacy through a form of apprenticeship, with or without the benefit of explicit instruction.

Adults who deploy the cultural resources of literacy in their daily lives serve as models of competence that the "apprenticed" child strives to emulate. Children's participation in the activities that call for literate skills is phased by adults in accordance with social norms and modulated in the light of estimates by adults of the child's com-petence. Studies of mother–child interaction in problem-solving tasks suggest that mothers are indeed sensitive to the competencies of their children, offering more assistance if their child appears to need more and offering less if the child needs less (e.g., Baker, Sonnenschein, & Gilat, 1996; Freund, 1990). Studies of storybook reading interactions reveal a similar patterning, with parents providing qualitatively dif-ferent kinds of scaffolding as their children develop (Sulzby & Teale, 1991).

One aim of the Early Childhood Project was to acquire a better understanding of children's developing literacy skills as they ob-serve and interact with more knowledgeable others both at home and at school. Wells (1986) identified a number of ways in which children's home experiences in the preschool years foster language and later literacy skills. In discussing how children learn language, he emphasized that the talk in which young children engage is not an end in itself but is goal directed to achieve other purposes, such as communicating their needs and desires. Similarly, we believe that at least some of the child's learning about literacy at home may occur as the child engages in literate activities for purposes other than explicit learning, such as looking at two boxes of cereal and deciding which to choose.

Our emphasis on the child's appropriation of literacy as a mechanism by which children become literate builds on a broad trend in research and practice away from the concept of reading readiness (National Association for the Education of Young Children, 1998; Sulzby & Teale, 1991). This changing conceptualization is indicated by the coining of the expression *emergent literacy*, reflecting the notion that children begin to appropriate a broad base of literate knowledge even before formal schooling begins. "An emergent literacy perspective ascribes legitimacy to the earliest literacy concepts and behaviors of children and to the varieties of social contexts in which children are becoming literate" (Sulzby & Teale, 1991, p. 728).

ASSESSING LITERACY COMPETENCIES IN THE EARLY YEARS

Influenced in part by cross-cultural studies of human development, psychologists have acknowledged the importance of studying behavior within different contexts because the skills a child displays in one situation may differ from those displayed in another (Rogoff, 1998; Serpell, 1976, 1979). For example, although a child might not demonstrate certain skills when observed in the laboratory, he may demonstrate them when observed within the familiar structure of the home. More recent research has accorded increasing attention to early manifestations of how children construe the practices of literacy and their social contexts (Neuman & Dickinson, 2001). Studies of these phenomena have established the feasibility of measuring several indices of early literacy, including concepts about print and its uses, phonological awareness, and narrative production. The design of our project included a wide range of observations and assessments of these indices of early literacy appropriation. Moreover, as we explain in Chapter 2, we paid special attention to ecological validity by tailoring these tasks to reflect the prior experience of each individual child in order to minimize the impact of varying degrees of familiarity as a source of extraneous variance in our assessments of children's competencies.

As the children grew older and became familiar with the shared environment of the school classroom, we also assessed their competencies on tasks that form part of the school curriculum and are widely used by educators and researchers. We now turn our attention to the institution of school, which carries a special authority in the domain of literacy because it is generally regarded as the principal site of literacy learning.

THE CHARACTER AND ORIGINS OF CONTEMPORARY FORMAL EDUCATION

Contemporary American public schools constitute a distinctive cultural institution, differing from other schools, both from earlier models of public schooling in the course of American history and from other contemporary types of school, including public schools in other societies, and various types of private schools in the United States. They share, however, a number of design features with an emerging international model of "institutionalized public basic schooling," which has been strongly influenced by the practices of Western formal schooling in the mid-20th century (Serpell & Hatano, 1997).

The cultural tradition informing those practices includes the following premises: a primary goal of the curriculum is to impart a commitment to objectivity and rationality; the children enrolled are in a formative stage of intellectual and moral development; and focused, explicit instruction holds the key to enabling children to acquire essential academic competencies. In addition to these premises, the paradigm is characterized by hierarchical organization of the curriculum, an emphasis on advance preparation of children for future cognitive challenges, standardized instructional targets, group instruction, regular scheduling of activities, and age-grading of classes. Some of these characteristics have arisen over the course of history, not so much from philosophical or pedagogical ideals, but more from considerations of organizational efficiency and administrative convenience (e.g., the need to manage a large number of children brought together in one place for instruction). These factors, extrinsic to the explicit agenda of education, nevertheless have become so profoundly institutionalized that they now define to a large extent what most public elementary schools are like as contexts for learning.

As early as the 18th century, a challenge to the dominant tradition of European education was advanced by the French philosopher Rousseau, which has continued to influence Western educational thinking, under the theme of "child-centered education." Rousseau contended that education should be a natural outgrowth of the child's development rather than a set of contrived experiences. Childhood, he argued, is a qualitatively distinct period of life that demands freedom for the child's personality to express itself. The educational process should be centered on nurturing personal developmental tendencies, not on the content matter of particular domains nor on the teacher's authority and convenience. Rather than providing systematic instruction, the role of the teacher should be that of facilitating the child's natural curiosity about the world. This humanistic theme of child-centered education was taken up in Europe by Pestalozzi and later in the United States by the influential educational philosopher and reformer, Dewey. It remained well represented in the training of teachers for the hands-on task of teaching within most public elementary schools in the United States at the end of the 20th century. Thus, although the institutional framework of schools emphasized hierarchy, standardized schedules of activity, and predetermined normative outcomes, teachers were encouraged to follow the guiding principles of respect for the child as a whole person, emotional support for each individual's unique needs and interests, and nurturance of open-ended learning through experience.

The most thorough application of child-centered educational principles has been in the institution of the kindergarten, a concept pioneered by Froebel in 19th-century Germany. The preservation in English of the German term *kindergarten* (literally a garden for children) serves to highlight both the principle of respect for the child as a whole person, whose organic development should be nurtured like a plant, and the importance of play as an opportunity for learning about the natural environment through exploration. This conception of how children develop intellectually was further elaborated by

Piaget, whose theory has had a large influence on the education of American teachers, especially those preparing to work in early childhood education. The importance of play for children's learning was noted by several of the prekindergarten and kindergarten teachers in the Early Childhood Project.

AN INTEGRATIVE FORMULATION

To recapitulate, the perspective that we have synthesized from the various sources cited previously views the context of human development as a complex of incompletely overlapping, partly interdependent systems of social and cultural organization. Within this complex, the development of each child is viewed as embedded within an eco-cultural niche, characterized by a particular constellation of material resources, recurrent activities, and modes of co-constructive participation in those activities, informed by the implicit theories of child development and socialization held by his or her principal caregivers. These caregiver ethnotheories are an important resource for intersubjective understanding among the parents, other caregivers, and children in a given cultural group, because they provide the framework within which the responsibility and effectiveness of individual acts are evaluated in the course of everyday life. Literacy is viewed in our analysis as a cultural practice that specifies and regulates particular recurrent forms of activity, participation in which requires particular cognitive processing skills, contextual knowledge, and strategies for matching the skills deployed to the context.

Although public schooling as a shared cultural resource is designed to be equally accessible and valuable to all sectors of the society, in practice, some sociocultural groups have consistently fared better in the system than others (e.g., National Assessments of Educational Progress, 1990–2000). We believe that two sets of factors have interacted to determine these differential school success rates: variations in the cognitive repertoires that children bring to school and variations in the educational practices to which the children are exposed in school. Our perspective on the presence of ethnic and socioeconomic inequalities in schooling is similar to one that Laosa (1984) termed "the developmental, socioculturally relativistic paradigm," which "calls for understanding behavior from the varied perspectives of the different groups" (pp. 62–63).

A major focus of our investigation was to document microsystemic interaction between the child and parents and patterns of learning opportunities available to the child within the eco-cultural niche of his or her home and neighborhood. We also recognize, however, that as the child enters school, additional variables come into play that reflect macrosystem inequities. To some extent, the transition from preschool to elementary school is marked for all children by an element of cultural discontinuity. Children of minority cultural groups, however, are more likely to encounter dissonant mixed messages regarding the value attached to certain forms of behavior that were adaptive in their home environment. Moreover, the strategies available to such children for dealing with this additional layer of cultural complexity vary, depending on the status of their family's ethnic group relative to the dominant cultural norms of society (Ogbu, 1990).

THE PLAN OF THE BOOK

Reflecting the theoretical framework of the study, our exploration of the contexts for literacy development was broadly based. Accordingly, we named the project the Early Childhood Project and characterized it as an investigation of factors affecting children's transition from home to school. Methodologically, this formulation enabled us to begin our interactions with the children's parents, many of whom had limited levels of formal schooling and therefore may have harbored some feelings of inadequacy in the domain of literacy, without a primary focus on literacy as such. Our elicitation of information concerning the home resources, recurrent activities, and caregiver beliefs relevant to the child's appropriation of literacy thus took place in the context of a broad range of questions about cognitive, emotional, moral, and social development. Details of the procedures followed in the project for recruiting families, for interviewing them, and for eliciting, observing, and measuring the behavior of children in various situations are presented in Chapter 2, along with a broad characterization of the city of Baltimore, where the project was situated. Chapter 2 also provides an overview of the competency profiles that we documented over 3 to 5 years for the children who participated in the project. Figure 1.2 provides a conceptual guide to how the various factors influencing the process of becoming literate in sociocultural context are discussed in Chapters 2 through 8 of the book.

Chapter 3 presents an account of our findings on the literacy development opportunities afforded by children's daily lives at home. We propose that each family home is characterized by its own intimate culture, within which a particular set of meanings are defined and promoted for the development of literacy. We analyze what parents told us about the socialization goals they held for their children with respect to literacy and other domains of development, as well as their conceptions of how best to intervene to nurture development. We also report on what we learned about family routines and the meanings attached to them by parents. We present three different cultural themes about the meaning of literacy development that were reflected in the socialization practices reported by parents and the interpretations they offered of those practices. Two of the themes, which we term the *skills perspective* and the *entertainment perspective* on literacy socialization, form a recurrent strand of analysis throughout the remainder of the book. As we discuss, the entertainment perspective proved to be a significant predictor of children's developing literacy competencies.

Chapter 4 focuses on co-constructive processes during children's participation in literacy-relevant activities. We consider children's shared storybook reading with a parent or older sibling at the start of kindergarten and with a parent in first grade. We examine peer interactions during a rhyming game and during a writing task. We also document parent–child interactions during a writing task that occurred when the children were in third grade. Unlike many studies of shared reading, we analyzed the type of talk that occurred and the social/affective quality of the interactions. As we discuss, the social/affective quality of storybook reading interactions predicted children's subsequent reading motivation and the frequency with which they read age-appropriate texts, which, in turn, predicted their reading competencies.

Chapter 5 provides an analysis of children's early literacy development over the 5-year period sampled by the project. We begin by describing children's competencies prior to formal schooling within

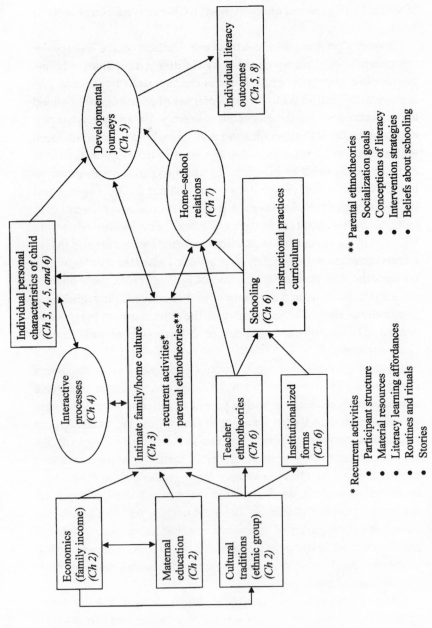

FIGURE 1.2. An integrative schema for the book.

Individual literacy outcomes *(Ch 5, 8)*

Developmental journeys *(Ch 5)*

Home–school relations *(Ch 7)*

Individual personal characteristics of child *(Ch 3, 4, 5, and 6)*

Interactive processes *(Ch 4)*

Intimate family/home culture *(Ch 3)*
- recurrent activities*
- parental ethnotheories**

Schooling *(Ch 6)*
- instructional practices
- curriculum

Teacher ethnotheories *(Ch 6)*

Institutionalized forms *(Ch 6)*

Economics (family income) *(Ch 2)*

Maternal education *(Ch 2)*

Cultural traditions (ethnic group) *(Ch 2)*

* Recurrent activities
- Participant structure
- Material resources
- Literacy learning affordances
- Routines and rituals
- Stories

** Parental ethnotheories
- Socialization goals
- Conceptions of literacy
- Intervention strategies
- Beliefs about schooling

three broad strands of literacy development: orientation to print, narrative competence, and phonological awareness. We then consider how development within these strands proceeds over the primary grades, in conjunction with the development of basic skills in word recognition and reading comprehension. Consistent with much research since the mid-1990s, we show that children from poorer families did not perform as well as children from wealthier families on many of our indices of early literacy. We also show that home literacy experiences and parental beliefs about how literacy is acquired are associated with children's subsequent competencies and orientations toward reading.

Chapter 6 begins with a brief history of the Baltimore City Public School System within the broader context of education in the United States. We then present information culled from our teacher interviews, including teachers' views of themselves as professionals, their assessments of the students' academic competencies, and their expectations of these children's academic future. We discuss two in-class observations: first-grade teachers' storybook reading and the use in kindergarten of a play literacy center to foster children's engagement in literacy activities. We show that teachers have well-articulated theories of how children learn and develop, and there are some ethnicity-related differences in the nature of these theories. Teachers' assessments of their students' literacy competencies were fairly accurate with respect to growth over the year and performance relative to classmates. However, teachers often failed to situate their students accurately relative to national norms.

Chapter 7 compares parents' and teachers' beliefs about children's schooling. The chapter addresses two general questions: (1) Do parents and teachers share a similar set of beliefs about children's academic development and the role that each plays in children's school success? (2) Do parents and teachers view the focal children in a similar manner? As we discuss, many parents may need more direct guidance from teachers than is currently provided about how to assist their children. The chapter concludes with a description of an action research project in which teachers explored different means to improve their interactions with their students' parents.

In Chapter 8, we review our findings and discuss how they are related to the contemporary research literature on early literacy development. We advance our views on the implications of our findings for public policy and professional practices in the field of education and for the many parents and families in the United States and elsewhere who express a desire to learn from research what are important principles for the design of an effective strategy to support their child's early development of literacy.

2

Growing Up in Baltimore

The Early Childhood Project

This chapter provides an overview of the methods and data analytic strategies of the Early Childhood Project, the longitudinal research project described in this book, and to provide background information about Baltimore that situates the study in context. We begin with a historical and sociological account of the people of Baltimore. We then describe the rationale of our sampling strategy and present a detailed description of our sample. The chapter also presents the methods of inquiry and analysis of the Early Childhood Project. We describe our approach to developing measures of competency in various aspects of literacy, indices of the ecocultural contexts of the children's homes, and interpretive accounts of social interactive processes. We describe the data analytic procedures, and explain how and why we mix qualitative and quantitative methods. The chapter closes with a summary of the literacy achievement of the children at the end of the Early Childhood Project in relation to city, state, and national achievement norms for third graders.

THE CITY OF BALTIMORE

Baltimore is Maryland's largest city, covering a land area of 81 square miles (209 square km), and its main economic hub. Baltimore is an inland port and major Atlantic seaboard city located on the upper reaches of Chesapeake Bay. The city was the site of the country's first important railroad terminal and was a leading manufacturing center, known in particular for shipbuilding and airplane production. The manufacturing base began to fail in the 1950s and 1960s, accompanied by a period of urban decay in the city center.

Like many northern metropolises in the late 20th century, Baltimore experienced a "structural transformation" from "centers of production and distribution of material goods to centers of administration, information exchange, and higher-order service provision" (Kasarda, 1986, p. 303). This macroeconomic change in the labor market contributed to a precipitous decline in labor force participation by African American males, especially younger ones, who were increasingly dropping out of public high schools without graduating, or graduating with very low levels of literacy. Their disadvantage in the changing labor market was further exacerbated by the expansion of participation by women during this period, and by the bulge in the adult population flowing from the post–World War II "baby boom." Between 1970 and 1984, Baltimore lost 73,000 (or 39%) of a total of 187,000 industrial jobs with a mean educational requirement of less than 12 years, and gained 15,000 jobs requiring some higher education. This pattern of polarized redistribution of employment opportunity was shared to varying degrees by eight other major cities in the United States, especially those in the Northeast (Wilson, 1987).

Another salient dimension of Baltimore City as a macrosystem has been defined by the changing relations between people of European and African extraction. As Olson (1991) put it, "much of the history of Baltimore is dominated by the social dynamics of race" (p. 57). In the 19th century, the extreme division between black and white institutionalized in the form of slavery was challenged by the American Civil War. The state of Maryland declared itself on the side of the Union, but the tenuous commitment of Baltimore's white population led to the city's occupation by federal troops throughout the war. Following the war and the Emancipation Proclamation in 1870, the African American community came to play a critical role in city politics, initially within the Republican party of Abraham Lincoln and emancipation, but eventually shifting its primary allegiance to the Democratic party under the reform politics of Franklin Roosevelt in the 1930s.

Migration from the south at the end of the 19th century precipi-
tated a rise in the size of Baltimore's African American population,
and in the face of resistance by European Americans to integration,
a segregated Black neighborhood emerged in Old West Baltimore.
Building on its 19th century tradition of political activism, the African
American community of Baltimore established a reputation for cultural assertiveness and became a nationally renowned center for jazz
performances in the 1940s and 1950s. Yet, as we discuss further in
Chapter 6, residential and educational segregation between the White
majority and the rapidly growing Black population of the city (24%
in 1950, 60% in 1985) remained a source of tension that reached crisis
proportions during the civil rights era of the 1960s.

An exodus of middle class, European American families from cities
such as Baltimore in the wake of school desegregation in the 1950s was
followed by an intensification of poverty and crime, which has become a hallmark of "inner-city" conditions across the United States.
Wilson (1987) cited statistics for the 50 largest cities of the United
States (including Baltimore), showing that in just one decade "the
number of persons living in poverty areas (i.e., census tracts with a
poverty rate of at least 20 percent) increased by more than twenty percent from 1970 to 1980, despite a 5% reduction in the total population
in these cities during this period" (p. 46). The demographic profile of
most of the inner-city neighborhoods afflicted by this concentration
of poverty, drug addiction, and violent crime comprised a predom-
inance of African American, female-headed households, of young
people ages 14 to 24, of unemployment, and of long-term depen-
dency on public welfare subsidies.

Various interpretations of the processes underlying this marginal-
ization of inner-city neighborhoods have been proposed, including
the constructs of "ghettoization" (Clark, 1965), "culture of poverty"
(Lewis, 1966; Moynihan, 1965), and "underclass" (Auletta, 1982).
Wilson (1987) argued that, in addition to the history of racial op-
pression emanating from the institution of slavery, a complex of contemporary economic and social factors converged in the 1970s and
1980s to isolate concentrations of "truly disadvantaged" families in
neighborhoods characterized by a sustained pattern of social dislo-
cation. Among these was a massive exodus of middle-class African

Americans, who opted to relocate to the suburbs, citing both rising crime statistics and declining quality of public schooling as major reasons for their move.

Revitalization efforts began in Baltimore in the 1980s, with major renovations of the downtown and waterfront areas. Tourism now brings in more than $1 billion annually. Manufacturing today is still one of the largest industries in Baltimore, employing 13% of its residents, according to 1990 census figures. The other four largest industry sectors were retail trade (14%), health services (13%), public administration (10%), and education services (8%). The Baltimore City Public Schools System (BCPSS) is currently the city's third-largest employer, with more than 11,400 employees, of whom about 60% are African American (BCPSS, 2002, section 9).

Demographics of the City in the 1990s

The demographic information we present about the city of Baltimore is based primarily on the 1990 census data. We use these data rather than those from the more recent 2000 census because they more accurately characterize the city at the inception of the Early Childhood Project in 1993. Data drawn from the 1990 census on household income in Baltimore indicate that 17% of households had annual incomes less than $10,000 and 18% from $10,000 to $20,000. The federal poverty level for a family of four in 1990 was $12,700. The average household income in the city was $28,217. Forty-three percent had incomes from $20,000 to $50,000, 18% from $50,000 to $100,000, and 3% higher than $100,000.

Families in the Early Childhood Project were not asked to provide us with income information. We believed that such a question was too intrusive and might interfere with our establishment of a trusting and collaborative relationship. However, we acquired information from the Baltimore City Public Schools System as to whether children at the participating schools qualified for free or reduced lunch. We used that information as a selection criterion for the project. Families we designated as low income qualified for and received free or reduced lunch; those we designated as middle income did not receive free or reduced-price lunches. In 1993, the household income for a family of four that made them eligible for free lunch was $18,655 (130% of the federal poverty level of $14,350) and for reduced-price lunch $26,547 (185% of the federal poverty level). Thus, entitlement to free or reduced-price lunch places a family roughly in the bottom one-third of family incomes for the city, and probably the bottom 10% to 20% of the income range of Baltimore families with four or more members. It is important to note that families can choose not to apply for free or reduced-price lunches. Thus, it is possible that we inadvertently recruited a few families from the schools serving middle-income neighborhoods whose income levels were in fact low enough to make them eligible for free or reduced-price lunches, but who chose, perhaps for reasons of pride, not to apply.

The population in Baltimore in 1990 was 743,000. The population has been steadily decreasing from a high of 950,000 in 1950, as more and more families moved to the suburbs, as discussed previously. In 1990, according to the census, the percentage of Baltimore residents classified as black was 59% and white 39%. Fewer than 2% of the population comprised Hispanic, Asian, and other races/ethnicities. The proportional representation of children attending public schools in Baltimore does not reflect the representation in the population at large, given that many wealthier European American families choose to send their children to private schools. Thus, for the Early Childhood Project, it was necessary to oversample the European American families to achieve more balanced numbers at each of the four social addresses we sought to represent. Enrollment in the Baltimore City Public Schools system in 1990 was 119,264, of whom the majority were classified as black. An additional 17,364 children (15% of the total) attended private schools.

The census data on education level of Baltimore adults indicated that 15% had less than a ninth-grade education, 25% started high school but did not complete it, 28% graduated from high school, 18% had taken some college courses but did not earn a degree, 9% had a college degree, and 7% a graduate degree. The distribution of education levels of parents participating in the Early Childhood Project was as follows: 8% less than ninth grade, 18% some high school, 36% high school graduate, 20% some college, 10% college graduate, and 8% a graduate degree. The percentages reported in the census data for all Baltimore adults (including those who are not parents) were similar to the parents in the Early Childhood Project at the upper education levels, but a smaller percentage of parents in the Early Childhood Project did not complete high school (26% vs. 40%).

Baltimore is divided into nine planning and police districts, identified by geographic area (e.g., Southeast, Central, Northeast). The 11 neighborhood schools attended by children participating in the Early Childhood Project are spread throughout the city, located in seven of these nine districts. The schools themselves are located within 10 different city neighborhoods. Four of these neighborhoods, those populated by the middle-income participants in the project, are in the northern part of the city. These neighborhoods have a more suburban character, with wide streets, large houses, and parklike settings. One of the neighborhoods was originally part of Baltimore County, a suburban jurisdiction that surrounds the city. Another of the neighborhoods was originally established as a summer community to which city residents could escape. The other six neighborhoods sampled in the project shared many of the features cited previously from Wilson (1987) as characteristic of American inner-city poverty areas in the 1980s.

THE PARTICIPANTS IN THE EARLY CHILDHOOD PROJECT

Selection of Schools/Neighborhoods

The participants in the Early Childhood Project were recruited in two separate waves, the first in the winter/spring of 1993 and the second in the summer/fall of 1994. The study was initiated as a research project of the National Reading Research Center through a contract with the U.S. Office of Educational Research and Improvement. Because the budget was relatively small, we were unable to recruit the full complement of families at the outset of the project. With additional funding secured from the National Institute of Child Health and Human Development (NICHD) in 1994, we were able to expand the sample.

We describe in detail the procedures used during recruitment of the Wave 1 families. Participants in the project were drawn from the residential neighborhoods served by six public elementary schools in Baltimore City. As already noted, one of the salient sociocultural characteristics of the city is a rather high level of *de facto* residential segregation between the African American and European American segments of the population. This "social reality" is reflected in our sampling frame.

The Baltimore City Public School System (BCPSS) made available to us their computerized data on the proportion of students in each grade at each school qualifying to receive free and reduced lunch, which was our index of their family's income. Through analysis of these data, we generated four lists of schools, each fitting one of the following sets of descriptive criteria:

1. *Low income African American*: student population 86% or more African American, and 86% or more qualifying for free lunch
2. *Low income European American*: student population over the past 3 years 75% or more European American, and 75% or more qualifying for free lunch
3. *Low income, mixed ethnicity*: student population over the past 3 years ranging between 33% and 66% African American, the remainder being European American, and 75% or more qualifying for free lunch.
4. *Middle income, mixed ethnicity*: student population over the past 3 years ranging between 33% and 66% African American, the remainder being European American, 60% or more paying for lunch.

In groups 3 and 4, the criteria also stipulated that there be no more than a 15% difference between the ethnic groups in rate of qualifying for free lunch or paying for lunch.

Two schools located in two different neighborhoods were selected as having each of profiles 1 and 2, and one each with profiles 3 and 4. Schools were excluded from consideration as research sites if they were involved in other ongoing major research/intervention projects, or if the principal expressed a reluctance to participate when approached. All the schools in the lower-income neighborhoods received supplementary funding through Chapter 1/Title 1, a federal program designed to assist schools serving large numbers of children living in poverty.

Recruitment of Families

Considerable attention was given to planning a recruitment strategy given our understanding of some of the difficulties that can arise in securing the participation of low-income families in social science research projects. For example, because we believed that some of our potential parent participants might have limited literacy skills and that they might be unable or unwilling to respond to a letter sent home from school with their child, we set up opportunities for face-to-face contact. In addition, because we believed that some of the prospective participants might be more comfortable learning about the project from someone of similar ethnicity, we systematically included one or more black graduate research assistants in the teams assigned to conduct recruitment visits at the predominantly African American schools and white graduate research assistants in the teams visiting the predominantly European American schools. (We use the terms black and white advisedly here because the student team included blacks who were not African American and whites who were not European American.)

The investigators met with the prekindergarten teachers at the six schools to talk with them about the project and to enlist their assistance in recruiting families. Working with the teachers, we generated a list of children eligible to participate in the project, based on the following sampling criteria and balance considerations:

- Each child should have an older sibling living with him or her at home.
- There should be equal numbers of male and female participants from each school.
- There should be equal numbers of African American and European American children from the balanced-ethnicity schools, and in schools that are predominantly one ethnicity, all children should be of that ethnicity.

- Children should not have any already identified developmental disabilities.
- The economic status of the child's family should be comparable to that of the majority of the families served by the school (as indexed by lunch ticket status).
- Children should live within the official catchment zone of the school.

Only the first of these criteria warrants explanation. We decided to select only later-born children in order to limit the variance in the child's home environment with respect to parenting knowledge, experience, and attention. This selection criterion also afforded us the opportunity to explore the influences of older siblings on the child's appropriation of literacy.

Recruitment proceeded in a variety of ways. Brief letters were first sent home with the potential focal children (12 to 16 at each school), informing parents that their child had been selected for participation in the Early Childhood Project and inviting them to meet with us over refreshments at the school to learn more about the project. Informal meetings were held at each school at the time parents dropped their children off for school or when they picked them up. In addition, we also arranged to be at the prekindergarten classrooms on several other occasions. The teachers introduced us to individual parents of focal children, and we gave them some general information about the project at that time. Follow-up appointments were arranged with those parents who expressed interest in learning more about the project and/or who agreed to participate.

The initial recruitment process stretched over a 3-month period beginning in January 1993. All the focal children recruited in Wave 1 were born in 1988 and were therefore eligible to begin kindergarten in 1993–1994. Although kindergarten attendance is mandatory in the state of Maryland, prekindergarten attendance is optional and indeed is not available in all schools. However, approximately 90% of the Baltimore elementary schools have prekindergarten programs, most of which are federally funded.

Recruitment of Wave 2 families followed similar procedures as for Wave 1, beginning in the late spring of 1994 when children were in kindergarten and continuing into early fall when children began first grade. We recruited at three of the original six schools, a process that yielded 14 new families. In several cases, parents who agreed to participate reported hearing positive things about the project from friends and neighbors. We also identified a number of potential schools that would enable us to increase the proportion of middle-class families within the sample. In our original planning of the Early Childhood Project, we did not intend to recruit comparable numbers of families from the four social addresses we were sampling because they were not proportionally represented in the population of Baltimore. However, in response to the strong advocacy of reviewers of the proposal submitted to the National Institute of Child Health and Human Development, we decided to oversample the middle-income families in order to be able to examine more systematically the similarities and differences associated with income and ethnicity. Once the children were in kindergarten and first grade, we were no longer constrained by whether a prekindergarten program was available (schools serving middle-class families were not eligible for state or federal funding for prekindergarten programs). Families were recruited at three additional schools serving predominantly middle-income families and at two additional schools serving mixed ethnicity low-income families. Principals and teachers again provided us with the necessary information to enable us to invite only those families that met our selection criteria.

Characteristics of the Participating Schools

Table 2.1 provides information about the participating schools, showing the characterization as serving middle- or low-income neighborhoods or serving primarily African American, European American, or mixed ethnicity neighborhoods. Also shown in the table are statistics the Maryland State Department of Education used to characterize schools (Maryland School Performance Report, http://msp.msde.state.md.us). These include demographic information regarding yearly attendance rates and withdrawal rates, averaged across the 5 years of the Early Childhood Project. The table also provides information about the performance of children on the Maryland State Performance Assessment Program (MSPAP), a performance assessment

TABLE 2.1. Demographic and Achievement Data for Participating Schools

School	Income	Ethnicity	Mobility	Attendance	MSPAP	CTBS	MSPAP Quartile		Recruited		
							City	State	Wave 1	Wave 2	Retained
B	Low	AfAm	25	95	9	18	1	1	6	6	11
A	Low	AfAm	25	93	6	24	1	1	4	2	4
F	Low	AfAm	24	92	7	31	4	2	–	4	3
D	Low	EurAm	19	95	13	41	3	1	5	–	2
C	Low	EurAm	23	93	7	36	2	1	8	4	7
E	Low	mixed	29	92	3	18	2	1	8	–	6
H	Low	mixed	21	95	22	31	4	2	–	6	6
G	Middle	mixed	21	94	17	45	4	1	9	–	7
I	Middle	mixed	6	96	33	74	4	2	–	10	9
K	Middle	mixed	9	96	43	62	4	2	–	4	3
J	Middle	AfAm	15	94	10	29	2	1	–	5	5
City	–	–	20	94	12	29	–	–	–	–	–
State	–	–	12	95	37	54	–	–	–	–	–

Notes: Income information is based on whether the majority of children qualify for free lunch at the school in 1993 at project inception. Ethnicity is based on whether there is a clear majority of children in one ethnic group or another in 1993. Mobility is based on the average percentage of children withdrawing from the school over the 1993–1997 period corresponding to the project duration. Attendance is based on the average percentage of children in attendance over the 1993–1997 period corresponding to the project duration. The state satisfactory percentage is 94%. MSPAP scores are the percentage of children scoring satisfactory in reading in third grade, averaged across 1995–1997. The state goal is 70% satisfactory. The CTBS figures are the percentile reading scores of 4th graders taking the test in 2000. City and state rank in quartiles is based on the MSPAP scores in reading, math, and writing for Grades 3 and 5 in 2000 (total number of elementary schools in the city is 121 and in the state 830). Wave 1 and Wave 2 corresponds to the number of families recruited from each school in each recruitment wave of the project. Number retained is the number of children still participating in the project at the end of third grade, 1997.

35

administered to all students in the state between 1993 and 2002 in
Grades 3, 5, and 8. The table presents the percentages of third-grade
students receiving a score of "satisfactory" on the reading portions of
the assessment, averaged across the years 1995 to 1997. Scores on the
MSPAP were not reported at the level of the individual child, only
at the school level. Children throughout the state were also required
to take the Comprehensive Test of Basic Skills (CTBS) in Grades 2
and 4.

School-level data were available beginning in the year 2000; thus,
what is shown in the table are the data for children who were in Grade
4 two years *after* the Early Childhood Project cohort was in Grade 4.
Scores are expressed as national percentiles on the Reading portion of
the test. City- and statewide data are provided on all these indicators
for comparative purposes.

Table 2.1 also provides information drawn from another source
that ranks all the schools in Maryland based on MSPAP performance
(www.psk12.com). A composite figure is used, based on the percentages of children scoring Excellent in Grades 3 and 5 on reading, math,
and writing. The website lists the actual ranks of the schools, but to
preserve anonymity we report instead quartile rankings, both at the
city level and at the state level. Schools listed as being in the fourth
quartile were in the upper 25% of all schools, schools listed as being in the first quartile were in the lower 25% of all schools, and
so on.

Table 2.1 indicates that two of the middle-income schools (I, K) had
consistently high levels of performance on achievement measures,
and in fact were above the statewide averages. The fact that neither
of these schools approached the state's goal of 70% of the students
receiving a score of satisfactory on the MSPAP illustrates that this
criterion was set extremely high. The neighborhoods served by these
schools are in the northwestern part of the city and are regarded
as highly desirable residential areas. The low withdrawal rates at
these two schools attest to the stability of the neighborhoods. The
other two schools serving middle-income neighborhoods (G, J) are
in less affluent parts of the city, and they did not differ substantially
from some of the low-income schools on many of these indicators.
Nevertheless, there were some low-income schools (A, B) that ranked

consistently low on the achievement indicators. These schools also had mobility rates of 25% or more.

Attrition and Student Mobility

As with many urban areas, Baltimore experiences a high degree of student mobility. As shown in Table 2.1, the citywide average withdrawal rate was 20%. (The rates for new admissions each year were comparable.) Within the Early Childhood Project sample, 13 children changed schools during the course of the study, but their families stayed with the project. We were given permission at the outset to follow the children to different schools within the city to administer our competency assessments, which we did for nine of the children (two low-income European American families, seven low-income African American). We also retained as participants four families that had moved to nearby suburban neighborhoods (three low-income European American families, one middle-income European American). Fifty-two of the children remained at their original school for the entire duration of the project.

Some degree of attrition is to be expected in longitudinal projects, especially those that make fairly substantial demands on participants' time. Table 2.1 shows the number of families who completed the first set of interviews in each wave of the project, 40 in Wave 1 and 41 in Wave 2. (An additional 13 families agreed to start the first step of the interview process, the diary, but then decided to withdraw from the project before providing usable data. Therefore, we do not consider these families as having been fully recruited.) At project's end, we retained 63 of the 81 families, resulting in an overall retention rate of 78%. This compares favorably with the retention rate of other similar longitudinal studies, such as that of Leseman and de Jong (1998), who had a 73% retention rate over 3 years. (The parents in one family at School G decided to withdraw after completing the first round of interviews because of the time commitment. However, they gave their permission for us to continue to assess their twin children for the entire duration of the project, which we did.) Some of the families we lost had moved out of the area, others chose to discontinue participation for other reasons.

Demographic Characteristics of the Participating Families

Demographic information was obtained from parents during the first home visit. The information included the focal child's birth date; the names, birth dates, and relationships of other children living in the home; the names and relationships of other adults living in the home; and the names of any others in the neighborhood significant to the child. Additional demographic information pertaining to parental age, occupation, and education was obtained during a subsequent visit with the parents. We intentionally delayed asking for this information until some degree of rapport had been established with the families. Table 2.2 provides demographic information about the participants by social address, indicating numbers recruited in each of the two waves, numbers of boys and girls in the sample, ages of children and parents, educational levels of parents, numbers of children and adults living in the household, and numbers of households headed by a single parent (just less than one-half of our sample). In the Early Childhood Project, all these single parents were mothers. The table shows that in about one-third of these cases (or one-sixth of our sample), the mother was the only adult in the household. Table 2.2 also indicates the number of families who remained active participants in the project through the spring of 1997.

Age and education information was available for only 66 of the mothers and 40 of the fathers. Mothers in the two middle-income groups were significantly older than mothers in the two low-income groups, but the ages of the fathers did not differ significantly. Educational levels of mothers and fathers differed with social address. For mothers, the low-income European American group had the lowest levels of education, whereas the middle-income European American group had the highest. The two groups of African American mothers had education levels intermediate to those of the European American groups. For fathers, the middle-income European American group had completed significantly more years of education than fathers in the other three groups, which did not differ.

Mothers were asked whether they worked for pay or as a volunteer, and whether they themselves attended school. If so, they were asked to describe the activities and to indicate approximately how many hours per week they devoted to them. Responses differed

TABLE 2.2. *Demographic Information for Early Childhood Project Families and Children by Social Address*

	African American Low Income	European American Low Income	African American Middle Income	European American Middle Income
Recruited				
Wave 1	14	17	5	4
Wave 2	13	9	9	10
Gender				
Boys	15	11	8	11
Girls	16	17	9	5
Age				
Child	4.43 (0.29)	4.43 (0.27)	4.32 (0.65)	4.60 (0.29)
Mother	30.23 (4.47)	30.25 (6.17)	37.90 (8.66)	36.84 (5.18)
Father	35.23 (7.79)	33.89 (6.75)	41.11 (9.78)	38.50 (4.99)
Education				
Mother	11.62 (1.69)	9.95 (1.88)	13.00 (0.82)	15.00 (2.91)
Father	11.70 (1.06)	11.00 (1.94)	13.22 (2.95)	16.82 (1.94)
Household residents				
Adults	1.86 (0.76)	1.93 (0.67)	2.58 (1.16)	1.94 (0.25)
Children	3.31 (1.28)	3.21 (0.92)	2.91 (1.16)	3.19 (1.11)
Single mother households				
Alone	10	7	1	1
With other adults	5	2	2	2
Retained in ECP	23	16	11	13

Note: Wave 1 families were recruited when the children were in prekindergarten, in 1993. Wave 2 families were recruited when the children were in late kindergarten/early first grade, in 1994. Age is calculated as of January 1993. The number retained is the number of children/families who remained with the project until the spring of 1997. Parental education is reported in years of schooling completed, with 12 = high school graduate, 16 = college graduate. Household residents include all adults living in the household and all children, including the focal child, reported as means.

considerably in relation to social address. The low-income mothers were far more likely than the middle-income mothers to report that they participated in none of these activities (44% and 66% for the low-income European American and African American mothers, respectively; 0% and 11% for the middle-income European American and African American mothers, respectively). The percentages of mothers working full time (greater than 35 hours per week) showed less variability (39% and 19% for the low-income European American and African American mothers, respectively; 42% and 56% for the middle-income European American and African American mothers, respectively). The low-income mothers reported jobs in daycare, stores, hospitals, schools, and utilities. The middle-income mothers reported jobs in state and federal government, community service organizations, consulting, and teaching in higher education. Low-income mothers were less likely to report volunteer activities than were the middle-income mothers (6% and 19% for the low-income European American and African American mothers, respectively; 83% and 42% for the middle-income European American and African American mothers, respectively). The volunteer activities mentioned were in school, community, and church.

OVERVIEW OF RESEARCH APPROACHES IN THE EARLY
CHILDHOOD PROJECT

General Procedures for Working With the Families

To build rapport with the families, it was decided that each family would be seen by the same graduate research assistant on each visit. In most cases, the assigned research assistant was the one who made the initial contact at the school. Thus, each research assistant had responsibility for families in a particular neighborhood. There was one research assistant per school for the schools that were predominantly one ethnicity; there were two research assistants per school for the mixed ethnicity schools. For almost all families, the research assistant was of the same ethnicity as the parent. The exceptions typically occurred in the middle-income African American families where a European American research assistant sometimes was assigned because of personnel constraints. However, in these cases a second member of the research team, usually an undergraduate assistant who was African American, accompanied the primary research assistant on at least the first few visits with the families. Thus, at least one member of the visiting team was of the same ethnic appearance as the family. All but one of the graduate research assistants were female. The male research assistant was accompanied by a female on the home visits.

Each of the three principal investigators had primary responsibility for overseeing the project activities at specific school/ neighborhood sites and worked closely with the primary research assistants in their contacts with the families. The full research team met weekly to review progress, to ensure procedures were standardized through group training and role playing, and to discuss special circumstances that arose.

With the increased funding that enabled us to expand our sample, we also expanded our team of research assistants. To illustrate, consider the 1995–1996 academic year. Four students were funded as full-time research assistants (20 hours per week), and these students had responsibility for visiting 10 to 12 families each. Eight additional students worked on the project for the research experience and had responsibility for visiting 3 or 4 families each. Among the 12 research assistants, all were female; 6 were African American, 5 European American, and 1 Asian. Ethnicity matches continued to be made when feasible.

Whenever a research assistant left the project, she contacted her assigned families to let them know and to introduce them to the research assistant who would replace her. When possible, both students visited the family on the next visit to make the transition go as smoothly as possible. The new research assistant read through the family records collected to date to familiarize herself with the family before visiting. Most of the research assistants worked on the Early Childhood Project for 2 or 3 years; one was with the project for its entire duration. In fact, six families she met on recruitment when the children were in prekindergarten were visited regularly by her until the project's end when the children were in third grade.

During an initial visit with the family, the research assistant described the study in more detail, obtained informed consent for the participation of the child and the primary caregiver, and collected demographic information about the family. Informed consent included permission to audio- or videotape interviews and observations, to obtain information about the child from school records, and to assess the child's literacy competencies at their schools. When the appointment was made, the parents were asked whether they preferred to meet in the family's home, the child's school, or a neutral location in the neighborhood. Approximately 75% of the parents recruited in Wave 1 chose to meet in their homes; the remainder chose to meet at the school. By the second interview, most of the parents were comfortable enough to have the research assistant visit them at their homes, and by the third visit, all interviews took place at the participants' homes unless an exceptional circumstance arose. All of the Wave 2 families were willing to have the first visit take place in their homes.

In most families, the child's mother identified herself as the primary caregiver and therefore served as our primary respondent. However, in four families, the father was identified as the primary caregiver and served either as primary respondent or as co-respondent. (One of these families withdrew during the first year of the project; the other three were retained.) In a few of the families, grandmothers also played a role in the interview process during some of the home visits. One mother died during the project, and the grandmother became the primary respondent.

The budgets from the funding agencies included sufficient funds to provide the families with honoraria for their participation. When the Wave 1 families were recruited, we budgeted $100 per family, payable in four $25 installments over the course of the project. When supplemental funding from the National Institute of Child Health and Human Development (NICHD) was received, the reviewers recommended that we increase the honorarium to build in greater incentive for continued participation. Accordingly, the honorarium was increased to $195, payable to the Wave 2 families in three installments of $50 (upon completion of the diary), $65 (at the end of their second year), and $80 (after the final home visit). The Wave 1 families were switched to a comparable schedule. We also provided the children with their choice of a small gift or a check for $5 at the end of the project to thank them for their participation. Other efforts were also made to maintain rapport and contact with the families between visits. For example, the research assistants often sent birthday cards to the focal children they visited. We also provided the families with copies of the videotapes we made during some of the interactive home activities.

Scheduling problems sometimes arose, primarily because some families did not have telephones. This meant that research assistants needed to stop by the homes to arrange a convenient interview date. Many times multiple visits were needed in order to find someone at home. As the children grew older, we sometimes sent messages home with the children. The research assistants learned to accommodate to the uncertainties of working with families whose day-to-day lives were often challenging and stressful. These uncertainties sometimes meant that home visits intended to be conducted close together in time could not be.

Overview of Methods

The Early Childhood Project was designed to chart the emerging competencies of literacy in children being raised in different eco-cultural contexts. Our research design called for a wide range of observations of the behavior of the children and their parents over a period of 5 years. We observed them in both structured and unstructured situations, using a variety of measures, some of which were used by earlier researchers and some of which were developed in the course of this project. The environmental variables we measured were conceptualized as interdependent features of a highly redundant system, which we term the *eco-cultural niche of development* (following Super & Harkness, 1986, and Gallimore et al., 1989). The eco-cultural niche can be described in terms of its recurrent activities, material resources, modes of guided participation and co-constructive learning, and caregiver ethnotheories. The emergent competencies of literacy were assessed longitudinally in a variety of contextually appropriate ways.

Parents were interviewed once or twice during each year of the Early Childhood Project. These interviews provided detailed documentation of recurrent activities related to literacy development

(through a diary and an ecological inventory) and information regarding parental ethnotheories of child development in general and
literacy development in particular. Some of the interview questions
were asked each year of the project, others were asked only once, and
still others were asked in response to previously asked questions.
Quasi-naturalistic observations were made of the parent, focal child,
and siblings as they engaged in selected recurring activities with the
potential for fostering literacy development (storybook reading, language play, and writing). Teachers were interviewed to explore their
theories of emergent literacy and the ideas and expectations that informed their interactions with their students and their families.

Three sets of measures were used to characterize each child's emergent literacy skills. One set consisted of contextually sensitive measures tailored to the literacy experiences documented in the lives of
individual children. Included here were measures of knowledge of
the purposes and processes of reading, knowledge of the functions
and uses of various types of functional print such as calendars and
grocery lists, oral narrative production, recognition of words in environmental context, and storybook reading. A second set of measures
tapped more conventional skills underlying the development of literacy, such as phonemic awareness and letter knowledge in the early
years of the project and word identification, reading comprehension,
and writing in the later years. A third set included children's scores
on school-administered standardized tests and teacher evaluations.
The competency measures were first administered in late spring of
1993, with subsequent testing in the spring of 1994, 1995, 1996, and
1997. For Wave 2 children, the first round of competency testing took
place in the fall of 1994.

DATA COLLECTION PROCEDURES

A major task at the beginning of the Early Childhood Project was the
development of a method for documenting the actual experiences of
children within their homes and communities. We carefully considered several existing measures of the home environment, but decided
that none of them suited our purposes. The strategy adopted in the
Early Childhood Project was to ground our analysis of variations
in the niche of children's development in a close examination of the

accounts given to us by those responsible for its management (i.e., the parents). Thus, our procedures for collecting information about the child's home environment differed from inventories such as Caldwell and Bradley's (1984) HOME both in the amount of detailed information that we collected with respect to the particular domain of literacy, and in the degree to which our data collection strategy was sensitive to local cultural variation. The procedure began with a diary of recurrent activities, followed by a more structured elicitation regarding the child's participation in specific activities with literacy-fostering potential (the ecological inventory), followed in turn by open-ended and structured questions designed to reveal caregiver ethnotheories about child development in general and literacy development in particular. Care was given to the development of elicitation techniques that would be meaningful and nonthreatening to our diverse group of respondents. We emphasized that our purpose was to learn about the family's approach to child-rearing rather than to impose or advocate an "expert" point of view. These approaches were field tested the year before the Early Childhood Project got under way with families in Baltimore with similar social addresses.

In the sections that follow, we first describe the diary and ecological inventory approaches in some detail. We then describe in more general terms the procedures for parent and teacher ethnotheory interviews, observations of selected recurrent activities, and child competency assessments. Further details can be found in subsequent chapters where the relevant findings are discussed.

Diary of Recurrent Activities

The first step in our efforts to document the characteristics of the environmental niches in which children in our sample were being raised was to ask the parents to keep a diary of their child's daily experiences. The diary served as our entry point into the child's life and was described as such to the parents. Parents were asked to report each activity the child engaged in, who else participated, what materials were used (e.g., type of toy), and how long the activity lasted. The respondents were free to define their own focus, but we offered them a framework for organizing their entries (activities surrounding getting up, breakfast, morning, lunch, afternoon, dinner, evening, going to bed). Parents were asked to keep the diary for 1 full week, ideally on 7 consecutive days.

Parents were given the option of keeping their diary by speaking into an audiocassette recorder or by writing in a notebook. The audiorecording option was included for the benefit of parents who might feel uncomfortable about their literacy skills or who might find it less burdensome than writing. A spiral notebook was left with the parents who chose the former option; a small tape recorder and tape were left with those who chose the latter. The research assistant contacted the parent a day or two after the visit to ensure the parent understood and was adhering to the instructions for keeping the diary. Encouragement and appropriate feedback were given. The diaries were reviewed by the research assistant and one of the principal investigators in order to identify themes and activities for follow-up discussion with the families. (Further details about the diary procedures appear in Baker, Sonnenschein, Serpell, Fernandez-Fein, & Scher, 1994; Baker, Serpell, & Sonnenschein, 1995; and in Chapter 3.)

The Ecological Inventory

Our conceptual framework for documenting the ecological context within which young children gain experience relevant to their emergent literacy took as the primary unit of analysis a culturally defined recurrent activity in which the focal child participates. The instrument used to record information about the child's recurrent activities is referred to as the ecological inventory. Based on the work of Baine (1988) and Gallimore et al. (1989), it served as a checklist for systematically reviewing with the respondent each of several distinct types of literacy-related activity in which the focal child participated. Our rationale for the particular range of recurrent activities included in the inventory was grounded in a review of the research literature on factors influencing the development of specific knowledge and competencies associated with early literacy (Morrow, 1988; Sulzby & Teale, 1991). Each activity had the potential to influence one or more of the following domains of development: (1) orientation toward print; (2) general knowledge of the world; (3) narrative competence;

and (4) phonological awareness. The activities were organized on the inventory within five general categories characteristic of a child's everyday experience: games and play activities; meal-time activities; TV and radio activities; recurrent outings; and reading, writing, and drawing activities.

The ecological inventory was administered four times during the course of the Early Childhood Project. Most of the specific items on the ecological inventory appeared each year, but some additional items were added to reflect the growing range of the children's experiences and competencies. For example, we asked about children's independent reading of chapter books in Grades 2 and 3 only, recognizing that this was a more likely recurrent activity for children at that age.

The first ecological inventory for each family was administered under conditions that differed somewhat from the remaining inventories. It built upon the diary describing the child's activities. During the home visit that followed diary collection, the research assistant went through the ecological inventory form systematically with the parent. First, the games and play activities mentioned in the diary and recorded in advance on the form were read to the parent. Any clarification needed about these activities was obtained at this time. The parent was then asked to describe other ways in which her child plays frequently at home, in the family, or in the neighborhood. Any information obtained through this questioning was added to the inventory form.

The parent was then asked how often and with whom the child engages in specific game-related activities deemed relevant to emergent literacy. These activities appeared as a checklist on the inventory form. The frequency estimates for each activity were obtained and recorded using a 4-point scale, ranging from "never, not at all" to "very often, i.e., almost every day." Information about the co-participants was obtained and recorded according to the age range of the others involved. Coding categories were (1) young child (the principal co-participants are children the same age or younger than the focal child); (2) older child (the co-participants are older than the focal child; (3) adult (the principal co-participants are considered adults by the parent); (4) alone (the child does not engage in the activity with others); and (5) combination (the ages of the co-participants vary). Parents were asked to give an example of a specific activity in each category if it had not been provided spontaneously in the diary or elicited in the previous questioning (e.g., the name of a specific board game the child played).

Each activity category of the ecological inventory was completed in essentially the same manner as the play-related activities (i.e., review the activities from the diary, ask if any other activities occurred, document the frequency and co-participants of specified activities). Additional questions on the inventory form were asked and answers recorded (e.g., questions dealing with specific aspects of the child's interaction with video and audio media).

Subsequent ecological inventories were administered in a similar manner, but the interviews did not begin with reference to diary activities. Information acquired from the diaries and ecological inventories is presented in Chapter 3. The way in which participation in selected activities relates to other variables is discussed in Chapters 3, 4, 5, and 7.

Parent Ethnotheory Interviews

To the extent possible, our interview method involved a series of steps through which we engaged the child's parent in conversations about the child that were grounded in ostensible, recurrent activities of the child's everyday life. We drew on information provided to us in the diaries they kept, in their responses to ecological inventory questions, and to responses provided in previous interviews.

To ensure all information provided by the parent was captured, interviews were audiotaped with permission. The interviewer recorded information on the interview schedule during the visit, but the primary source of information for subsequent analyses came from transcriptions of the audiotapes. The interviews ranged in length from 45 minutes to 2 hours, with an average length of about 1 hour. For some of the home visits, the interviews immediately followed the administration of the ecological inventory. For other visits, the interviews took place after observations of recurrent activities. Specific questions that were asked are discussed in Chapters 3 and 7 in conjunction with the findings.

Teacher Ethnotheory Interviews

Teachers were interviewed to determine the ideas and expectations that informed their interactions with their students, with some questions identical to those asked of the parents. In addition, the teachers were asked to comment specifically on the strengths of the children participating in the study and on their perceptions of the parents. We adopted a similar analytic process for the study of teachers' ethnotheories as the one we used for parents, asking teachers their views about how children learn and develop. Teachers were interviewed in one in-depth session. In a previsit telephone call, we informed teachers about the general topics for discussion. Key elements of the interviews were comparable to those in the parent interviews. Topics included elicitation of a hierarchy of goals, factors affecting attainment of stated goals, and the discussion of relative importance of home and school to the child's development in each domain mentioned in the parent interview (literacy, numeracy, etc.). In addition, we questioned each teacher about the daily schedule of activities, skills being fostered by the activities, her philosophy of teaching, her judgments of strengths and weaknesses of each focal child, and her expectations of and for the families.

Teachers were interviewed at a time convenient to them by the principal investigators, typically at the end of a school day in their classrooms. The interviews lasted approximately 60 minutes. The interviews were tape recorded, and a transcript was created for further analysis. The interview protocols were similar across the 4 years during which interviews were conducted (prekindergarten, kindergarten, Grade 1, and Grade 2), but some questions were added and others deleted in accordance with the changing experiences of the children. Teachers received a $25 stipend during the year of their participation as a token of our appreciation. Specific questions that were asked are discussed in Chapters 6 and 7 in conjunction with the findings.

Observations of Co-Constructive Activities

We observed the nature of the child's literacy appropriation as the child interacted with more competent others in several different contexts. We had three selection criteria in deciding which activities to observe: (1) the activity had to be relevant for literacy development; (2) the activity had to be recurrent (defined as occurring at least one time per week) for the focal child; and (3) it had to take place in interaction with a more competent "other" who was a frequent participant in the child's life. Our rationale for the third criterion was based on the theoretical premise that children gradually appropriate literacy competencies through interactions with more competent members of their eco-cultural niche.

One of the co-constructive activities that we observed was storybook reading involving the focal child and a family member who read regularly to that child. Another co-constructive activity was language play involving the focal child and an older sibling playing. As indicated by Zukow (1989), many children growing up in low-income families in the United States and elsewhere around the world spend much time playing with and being cared for by older siblings. Thus, to get a representative sample of literacy-fostering opportunities afforded to these children, we believed it important to focus on the nature of the child–sibling interaction.

Pilot work conducted in the summer of 1992 with members of communities comparable to those in the Early Childhood Project indicated the difficulty of eliciting an interaction, other than storybook reading, that appeared to be comparable in level of involvement or in tone to more spontaneously occurring activities. Although focal children were reported in the diaries to engage in many literacy-relevant activities, we had difficulty getting the child to engage in these activities on demand. They were either unwilling to do so when asked or tended to perform for the camera in a stilted manner. Therefore, we opted to take advantage of the children's tendency to perform for the camera, by having that be the stated purpose for their task participation with siblings.

The first observations took place when the Wave 1 focal children were in kindergarten. This observation included language play and writing in collaboration with an older sibling and storybook reading with either the parent or an older sibling (whoever the child most frequently read with at home). The second observations took place when children were in the second half of first grade. Both

Wave 1 and Wave 2 children were included. This observation again entailed shared storybook reading, but this time the focal children had the opportunity to participate in the reading. In about one-half of the dyads, the mother alone took responsibility for reading; in the remaining dyads, the child took shared or primary responsibility. The third observation took place when the children were in third grade. Here, parents and children were asked to write about a memorable event they had experienced. All interactions were video- and audiotaped and subsequently transcribed. Further details about the procedures are provided in Chapter 4 in conjunction with the findings.

Assessing Children's Competencies

During each year of the project, children were given competency assessments at their schools. In prekindergarten through Grade 2, the assessments were divided across two sessions lasting approximately 25 minutes each. The Grade 3 testing was completed within one session of about 35 minutes. Breaks were provided when it seemed appropriate. Children were tested individually by a graduate student member of our research team who was not involved in home visits to the child's family and who was usually of the same ethnicity as the child. Testing sessions were approximately 1 week apart. Each child received the tasks in the same predetermined order. Children who had moved to another school during the course of the project were tested at their new school or at another locale convenient to the family such as the public library.

Table 2.3 provides a listing of all of the competency measures that were administered throughout the project. Descriptions of the measures are presented in Chapter 5 in conjunction with the findings.

The Baltimore City Public School System agreed to make available to us all scores obtained on standardized tests during the course of the project. These include the Boehm Test of Basic Concepts administered to 5-year-olds and the CTBS administered in Grades 2 and 4. Unfortunately, the data provided to us were too incomplete to be very useful and will not be considered further in this volume. Teacher assessments of each child's progress were obtained during

TABLE 2.3. *Measures of Children's Competencies*

Type of Task/Measure	Grade Administered				
	Pre-K	Kind.	Gr. 1	Gr. 2	Gr. 3
Orientation to print/functional uses of print					
Environmental print	x	x			
Letter identification	x	x			
Functions of print	x	x	x		
Concepts about print	x	x	x		
Calendar use			x	x	
Mail sorting			x	x	
Coupon completion			x	x	
Phonological awareness					
Nursery rhyme knowledge	x	x	x		
Rhyme detection	x	x	x		
Alliteration detection	x	x	x		
Rhyme production	x	x	x	x	
Alliteration production	x	x	x	x	
Phoneme elision			x	x	x
Narrative competencies/listening comprehension					
Storybook "reading"	x	x			
Storybook comprehension (simple)	x	x			
Storybook comprehension (complex)			x	x	
Personal narrative production	x	x			
Retelling of shared experience	x			x	
Retelling of storybook (complex)				x	

Reading competencies			
Woodcock-Johnson Word Identification	x	x	x
Woodcock-Johnson Word Attack	x	x	x
Woodcock-Johnson Vocabulary			x
Woodcock-Johnson Passage Comprehension			x
Story editing (error detection)	x		x
Expository passage comprehension		x	x
Expository passage oral reading fluency		x	x
Production of familiar event schema (writing)		x	
Reading motivation and conceptions			
Motivation for Reading	x[a]	x	x
Conceptions of Reading		x	

Note: The measures administered to Wave 1 children in kindergarten were administered to the Wave 2 children at the beginning of first grade. All other assessments were administered in the spring.

[a] The Motivation for Reading assessment was given only to Wave 1 children at the beginning of first grade.

interviews with the teachers when the children were in prekindergarten through Grade 2. The Grade 3 teachers were asked to complete a written evaluation of their students, but too few teachers returned the questionnaires to allow meaningful conclusions.

APPROACHES TO DATA ANALYSIS

Our theoretical framework drew upon the concepts and methods of various disciplines, and our approach to data analysis used both qualitative and quantitative techniques. Two complementary types of data analysis were conducted: (1) quantitative analyses of patterned relations among selected indices of environmental and competency variables; and (2) qualitative case studies and narrative interpretive accounts of individual changes in behavior over time, social interactions, and personal or cultural explanations of these phenomena. In broad terms, the quantitative analyses treated niche characteristics as antecedent variables and competencies as outcome variables. Rather than adopting a simple cause-and-effect model, however, we sought to document children's developmental pathways.

One of the most ambitious goals of the Early Childhood Project was to build bridges between the qualitative research methodology of ethnography and the quantitative methodology of experimental psychology. We view these two approaches to data collection as not only complementary, but also mutually informative. Our research approach was field based, driven in large part by the information provided to us by the children's parents, their teachers, and the children themselves. Thus, rather than generating a specific hypothesis about a particular aspect of literacy development and constructing a circumscribed measure to test that hypothesis, we formulated general questions consonant with our theoretical perspective and systematically collected data to address them. The data we collected were used as sources for more specific hypothesis testing.

This methodological approach has an advantage over more traditional hypothesis testing approaches in terms of greater ecological validity; the researcher is less likely to overlook important characteristics of the natural environment and experiences of the research participants because of preconceived ideas and expectations. As noted in Chapter 1, several theorists and researchers, in lamenting the lack of ecological representativeness of much data that has been collected, have urged researchers to ensure what is being tapped by their measures truly represents actual practices and beliefs of respondents (Goodnow & Collins, 1990; Miller, 1988). In our project, we began by identifying recurrent practices and experiences characteristic of the focal child's home and school environments. From there we determined the meanings attributed by the parents to these practices, as a means of understanding parents' beliefs. We also determined what literacy and literacy-related abilities the children possessed. Our methodology thus represents an interweaving of the qualitative research tradition of ethnography with the quantitative research tradition of experimental psychology.

Because the Early Childhood Project does not have an experimental design, it is not possible to draw firm cause-and-effect conclusions from the data. However, the longitudinal nature of the project permits us to make some tentative inferences about causality. Measurements collected earlier in time can more plausibly be posited as causes of later ones than concurrent measures. We expected at the outset that some of the influences would be causal, as in the effects of home experiences on phonemic awareness, but we also expected that some influences would be bidirectional. For example, parental beliefs about the importance of literacy may lead them to purchase books for the child, which in turn may influence the child to engage in more frequent literate activities. This interest on the part of the child will motivate the parent to purchase more books for the child and create an even richer literacy environment. Because of the close contact we maintained with individual families over time, we were in a good position to detect such bidirectionality.

One of the major strengths of our research design is the opportunity it afforded to provide detailed ethnographic information about the contexts in which low-income and minority children develop. Much of the data on normative literacy development at the time the Early Childhood Project was conceived came from investigations of white middle-class children. In recognition of the fact that lower-income and minority children were understudied in developmental research, in 1994, the NICHD issued a call for proposals for researchers to conduct the kinds of in-depth analyses we undertook in the Early Childhood Project.

Prospective Correlations and Predictions: Some Methodological Alternatives

How should we approach the search for clusters of variables that are influential on the developmental appropriation of literacy? In the chapters that follow, we explore several different types of analysis. No single one of them appears to us to be definitive. Rather we seek by juxtaposing them to generate a multidimensional picture.

One approach that we explored might be termed *retrospective empirical validation*. This consists of identifying groups of children with distinctive profiles of change over time in performance on measures of literacy and then going back (retrospectively) to compare them with respect to their patterns of home experience in earlier years. In Chapter 5, we present one such analysis of two groups of low-income children. One difficulty encountered in this approach is disambiguating the direction of causation, but the longitudinal design of our study affords some unique opportunities to compare the validity of competing explanations.

Another approach is *atheoretical exploratory factor analysis*. In this case the data for all the children are combined and subjected to factor analysis in search of clusters of variables that co-occur. We have made a number of forays along these lines. Our most extended application of the exploratory factor analytic approach has been to ratings on family routine scales adapted from Fiese's work, discussed in Chapter 3. When this type of analysis generates clusters of variables that hang together empirically, a tentative theoretical label can be applied to each factor based on an inspection of the content of those items that "load" most heavily on it. These factors can then be examined prospectively for their predictive validity with respect to various competency outcomes.

Each approach considered here, retrospective empirical validation and atheoretical, exploratory factor analysis, may contribute to our understanding of how the various influences on children's literacy appropriation are organized. But, as we have noted, each also has certain limitations. A third approach is the *interpretive elaboration of life journeys.* The idea here is to construct an internally coherent account of the sequence of experiences in the life of an individual child that cumulatively contribute to the child's profile of literacy in Grade 3. Or, putting it differently, this formulation, grounded in the interdisciplinary field of cultural psychology, aims to generate interpretations of the development of persons-in-context (Cole, 1996; Valsiner & Lawrence, 1997), in terms of participatory appropriation of cultural practices and the system of meaning informing them. The character of these longitudinal profiles is driven by an analysis of the reports by the child's parents and teachers, and by our observations of the child in various contexts over that period, seeking explanatory connections among these through a process of idiographic interpretation rather than relying on statistical correlations among aggregated data. The descriptive elaboration of family intimate cultures in Chapter 3 constitutes a first step in the direction of implementing this strategy.

Conventions for Reporting Statistics in This Book

Our intended audience for this book includes not only researchers in the fields of early literacy and child development, but also educators and policy makers. To increase the accessibility of the book to readers without statistical expertise, we decided to omit detailed descriptions of the statistical procedures used to analyze our data. Similarly, we decided to provide statistics, such as correlation coefficients, in footnotes only. Some of the data presented in this book are published in scholarly journals where full reports of statistical procedures are provided. Interested readers may consult the original sources. Other findings are reported more fully in technical reports, which are available via ERIC (the document reproduction numbers are included with the citations in the reference list). Still other findings are reported for the first time in this book. Readers who would like additional information, including statistical details, are invited to contact us.

Because the Early Childhood Project is primarily concerned with examining relations between and among variables, many of the statistical analyses are correlational in nature. We report bivariate correlations, where we examine the degree of relation between two variables.

For example, we examine the degree to which children's motivation for reading is related to their reading achievement. We also report partial correlations, where we examine the strength of a relation between two variables, taking into account the influence of a third or fourth variable. For example, we examine the relation between reading comprehension and frequency of independent reading in third grade, while controlling for first-grade word recognition (see Chapter 5). We also use multiple regression techniques where we examine the relative contributions of a number of different variables to a particular outcome. For example, we examine how parents' views about the most effective way to help their children learn to read, children's early orientation to print, and children's early phonological awareness predict children's subsequent reading achievement (see Chapter 5).

Another statistical procedure we use frequently is analysis of variance. This procedure is used to determine whether groups of participants differ significantly from one another. In a true experiment, participants would be randomly assigned to different treatment groups. However, in the Early Childhood Project, our groups are defined by pre-existing sociocultural group membership, and hence this is a quasi-experimental analysis. Researchers sometimes use an analytic design where ethnicity and income level are considered as two separate factors with two levels each (income level: high and low; ethnicity: African American and European American). We have chosen instead to consider our participants as members of one of four sociocultural groups, jointly defined by ethnicity and income level. When we find a statistically significant difference among the four groups on a particular variable, such as phonemic awareness, we conduct Tukey's Honestly Significant Difference (HSD) follow-up tests to determine exactly which groups differ from one another. In the text, we will simply report whether statistically significant differences were found among the groups, with F ratios provided through footnotes. Note that because this is not a true experiment, we cannot say that it was membership in a particular group that caused the difference, but rather that the difference was associated with group membership. In other words, quasi-experimental analyses should be interpreted in the same way as correlational analyses.

The third type of analytic strategy we use frequently are nonparametric tests of association, such as chi square. We use this approach when we want to find out whether particular response patterns happen more often with one group of participants rather than another. For example, we ask whether parents and teachers differ in the responsibilities they assign to the home and school for teaching children to read (see Chapter 7). A contingency table is created showing the numbers of teachers and the numbers of parents who indicated more responsibility to the home, more responsibility to the school, or no difference. Chi-square analyses will allow us to determine whether the frequencies differ among the cells. The results of chi-square analyses are reported in the text, with specific values provided in footnotes.

All correlations, group differences, and tests of association that are reported as statistically significant in this book met at least the minimum alpha criterion of $p = .05$. Researchers today often discuss their results in terms of effect sizes, an indication of the strength of the statistical relation. In accordance with Cohen's (1987) "rules of thumb," effects are reported as moderate in size in cases where the magnitude is such that it "would be apparent to an intelligent observer," small where the effect is "real but difficult to detect visually,"and large where the effect is "the same distance above a medium effect as small is below it." In the case of the correlation coefficient r, this means that a value of about .10 is described in the text as a low or weak correlation, a value of about .30 as moderate, and a value of about .50 as large or strong. When reporting the outcomes of multiple regression analysis, we consider an effect small when it accounts for 5% to 10% of the variance, moderate when it accounts for 10% to 25%, and large when it accounts for more than 25%.

Much of the information we collected from the participants in our research was qualitative in nature, consisting of discursive responses to open-ended questions. Another important source of information came from observations of interactions between parents and children or between siblings. In both contexts, we needed to devise systems for interpreting the data, for characterizing the kinds of things respondents talked about or did. These coding schemes were always co-constructed by members of the research team, and once they were applied to the data they were checked for reliability. For all coding schemes described in the book, reliability was determined by having a second independent rater code 15% to 20% of the responses. The minimum inter-rater reliability considered acceptable was .80.

A LOOK AHEAD AT THE LITERACY OUTCOMES OF CHILDREN IN THE EARLY CHILDHOOD PROJECT

In this section, we summarize the levels of literacy achieved by the sample at the end of third grade, as indexed by the children's reading scores on the Woodcock-Johnson Tests of Achievement – Revised (Woodcock & Johnson, 1989/1990). This test is widely used in educational research and practice, and it has good psychometric properties. We describe these assessments in detail here because they constituted our primary outcome measures at the completion of the project, and they are referred to throughout the book in relation to other indices. Four different reading subtests were administered, the first two in Grades 1, 2, and 3, and the remaining two in Grade 3 only. The items on the tests become progressively more difficult, with administration terminating if the child misses five consecutive items.

The Letter-Word Identification subtest calls for the child to identify words that appear in large type in a test booklet. The published version of the test calls initially for identification of 12 isolated letters. This portion of the task was not administered to children in the Early Childhood Project because their letter identification was tested separately. For purposes of comparison with national norms when the children were in Grade 3, 12 points were added to the child's raw scores.

The Word Attack subtest measures the child's skill in applying phonic and structural analysis skills. The child is asked to read aloud pseudowords. Following the developer's instructions, a Basic Reading Skills composite score combining the word identification and word attack scores was created for some of the analyses reported in this volume.

The Passage Comprehension subtest calls for the child to read short passages and supply missing words in a cloze procedure. The child must state the word that would be appropriate in the context of the passage. The first five items, which have accompanying pictures rather than text, are not typically administered to children who are already reading. Following administration instructions, we had children begin the task with item 6. (If a child was unable to succeed with item 6, the easier items would have been administered, but this was not necessary for children in the sample.) A score of 5 was added to the raw score to allow comparison with national norms.

The Reading Vocabulary subtest calls for the child to read words and supply appropriate meanings. In Part A: Synonyms, the child states a word similar in meaning to the word presented, and in Part B: Antonyms, the child states a word that is opposite in meaning to the presented word. A Reading Comprehension composite score was constructed from the Vocabulary and Passage Comprehension subtests, following the developer's instructions, and was used in some of the analyses reported in this volume.

The children's scores on the Woodcock-Johnson ranged from well above the national average to extremely low levels, bordering on eligibility for special education services. (In fact, a handful of the students were subsequently referred for such services in the years following the conclusion of the Early Childhood Project.) To situate our study in a broader context, Table 2.1 compares the average performance of students in schools attended by our sample, on the CTBS and the MSPAP, with two larger frames of reference: all Baltimore public schools and all Maryland public schools.

Table 2.4 provides information about the literacy outcomes of the Early Childhood Project children based on their scores on the four subtests of the Woodcock-Johnson: Word Attack, Letter-Word Identification, Vocabulary, and Passage Comprehension. (See Chapter 5 for a complete discussion of children's literacy competencies at different assessment points throughout the project.) The data are reported as mean grade equivalent scores of children in each sociocultural group at the end of third grade. The Woodcock-Johnson test was normed on a representative sample of children from across the United States, and the grade equivalent scores were derived from these norms. Because the children were tested in the ninth month of the third-grade school year (i.e., May), their expected grade equivalent score is 3.9.

Children in the two low-income groups had mean grade equivalent scores at least one grade equivalent below expected levels; the

TABLE 2.4. *Grade Equivalent Achievement Scores of Focal Children in Grade 3 on the Woodcock-Johnson Reading Tests by Social Address*

	African American Low Income	European American Low Income	African American Middle Income	European American Middle Income
Word Attack	2.6	2.1	3.3	4.8
Word Identification	2.6	2.6	3.3	5.0
Vocabulary	2.4	2.3	2.9	5.3
Passage Comprehension	2.9	2.6	4.0	4.9
n	22	15	10	13

Note: Scores on the Woodcock-Johnson are reported as grade equivalents. The expected grade equivalent score on the Woodcock-Johnson is 3.9, based on testing in late spring.

low income African American children scored several months ahead of the low-income European American children on two of the subtests. The middle-income European American children's mean scores were consistently above grade level, with two subtest means reaching Grade 5 levels. The middle-income African American children had more variable scores than the other children; vocabulary was 1 full year below grade level, whereas passage comprehension was 1 month above. On the two subtests of word recognition, the children were 6 months below grade level.

In general, the performance patterns of the children in the Early Childhood Project were consistent with the larger patterns observed at schools serving different types of neighborhoods, as shown in Table 2.1, and with data reported in national assessments such as the National Assessment of Educational Progress (NAEP; www:nces.ed.gov/nationsreportcard/naepdata). For example, the 1998 NAEP assessment results for fourth graders in reading revealed a substantial difference in scale scores for children receiving free lunch vs. not (198 vs. 227, on a 500-point scale). The difference between African American children and those classified as White (i.e., European American) was very similar: 194 vs. 227. The data for the state of Maryland revealed similar patterns: mean scores of students receiving free lunch were 195, no free lunch 225. Mean scores of African American children were 195, and those of White children were 229. Moreover, these achievement gaps persist even

for students from more affluent minority families (www.NCRel.org/
gap/takeon). Thus, when we stand back and inspect the profile of
our study's participants in broader overview, it seems that this sample is quite typical of American children attending public elementary
schools in the 1990s.

3

The Intimate Culture of Children's Homes

In this chapter, we describe the recurrent, literacy-related activities reported and observed within the homes of the children we studied in Baltimore, and we identify some salient organizing themes around which those activities were interpreted by their participants. Our description of the *intimate culture* of family homes in Baltimore brings together findings collected with several of the instruments described in Chapter 2. We adopted two complementary approaches in our interviews with parents over the years: a relatively objective, ecological inventory that generated quantitative indices of the frequency of various types of activity; and a more interpretive exploration of the meanings informing the patterns of activity reported. This exploration was designed to reveal the parent's implicit theory of child development and socialization. The chapter begins with a theoretical orientation to the concept of intimate culture and then offers an account of our findings, starting with a survey of the patterns of child engagement in recurrent activities, followed by an examination of the parents' socialization goals, and beliefs about the best strategies for achieving them, as these were expressed to us in the parental ethnotheory interviews. Next we discuss family routines, based on our adaptation of scales designed by Fiese and her colleagues (Fiese, Hooker, Kotary, & Schwagler, 1993; Fiese & Kline, 1993; Sameroff & Fiese, 1992). At the end of the chapter, we present a synthesis of several indices of intimate culture that have proven to be highly predictive of literacy appropriation in our sample – namely, the family's relative emphasis on two contrasting cultural themes about the nature of literacy socialization.

ECOCULTURAL CONTEXT, HUMAN DEVELOPMENT, AND THE FILTER OF INTIMATE CULTURE

Each child in our study resided in a family home with one or more primary caregivers, or parents, who took responsibility for organizing the child's everyday life. The family home defines the range of persons with whom the developing child interacts at the microsystemic level, and the activities engaged in by those within the home. And it is those particular interactions and activities that filter and mediate the impact of larger cultural formations, by determining how and when any one of them enters into the child's range of experiences. The unique constellation of persons, activities, and meanings that make up the life of a family generates what we term, following Lomnitz-Adler (1992) and Levinson (1996), a particular *intimate culture* (Serpell, 1997, 2001).

An important stimulus for our research project was the endurance of disparities in educational achievement among American social classes and ethnic groups. However, as Bronfenbrenner and Crouter (1983) pointed out, the tendency of social and behavioral scientists to rely on "social address" labels, in terms of socioeconomic status, race, or ethnicity, for comparative analysis of behavioral and cognitive phenomena threatens to obscure the influence on cognitive development of more directly relevant characteristics of individuals and social processes. The politicization of race and class in American society makes it essential to acknowledge these categories when deriving social policy implications from scientific research. But, in our search for understanding, we cannot afford to assume social significance for the categories per se.

Ultimately what matters for a child's literacy development is not the social class or ethnic group to which his or her parents belong, but those parents' particular socialization practices and the beliefs informing them (Snow et al., 1991). Some of those beliefs may well bear a direct causal or interpretive connection with the social address from which a given parent originates. However, there are considerable variations in beliefs and practices across members of a given sociocultural group; many commonalities can also be detected across sociocultural groups. For any particular group of persons, a body of shared beliefs and practices involving a unique subset of uses and understandings of the larger society's technology and institutions can be identified, which constitute the intimate culture of that group. From this perspective, several levels of social grouping can be distinguished. Not only can we identify regional variants of social class and ethnocultural group distinctions within a particular regional instantiation of a class, but even within an ethnically and economically homogeneous social group in a particular region, additional cultural parameters differentiate among particular neighborhoods. Furthermore, within a neighborhood, the cultural context experienced by a particular child differs from one family to another.

Acknowledging the possibility of such a variety of cultural formations enables us to elaborate the notion of cultural group membership beyond the notion of a social address. Rather than portraying what an individual derives from membership as externally defined, we can turn our attention to the interpersonal processes through which members negotiate the understandings that they share. Nevertheless, the larger, less precise categories of African American, or middle class, or American do have some explanatory power for the interpretation of culture. Any particular intimate culture will typically include traces of those larger, incorporating social formations.

One way of focusing on the particular in discussions of culture has been articulated by Geertz (1983) with the concept of *local knowledge* that represents a set of understandings shared by members of a small community. However, in the modern world saturated with telecommunication, "local" does not quite capture the restricted, in-group quality of what mediates between a developing individual and the macroculture. The metaphor of concentric circles often used to depict Bronfenbrenner's (1979) conception of the ecology of human development is both helpful and misleading because of the excess meaning that it carries (Serpell, 1990). The implicitly spatial relationship between the macroculture and a particular neighborhood is violated in many ways by reality. Not only does television programming penetrate into the living rooms of every family, but the members of any urban American family also use commercially standardized products to clean their carpets, to brush their teeth, and to illustrate stories for their children. When they travel around the city they use public transport, whose schedules are bureaucratically determined, buy their daily food and household supplies from stores organized in terms of the macroculture's taxonomy of commodities, packaging, and pricing, and bring these products home to organize their daily lives.

Yet, these invasive macrocultural resources are filtered through the lens of an intimate culture shared by a particular social grouping. To understand this filtering process, we need to delve inside these intimate cultures and examine their architecture. Since Heath's (1983) landmark study, several other investigators have generated rich, descriptive accounts of the literate practices of subcultures other than the middle-class subculture that is so well known to the majority of literacy researchers and educational professionals (e.g., Moll & Greenberg, 1990; Purcell-Gates, 1996; Taylor & Dorsey-Gaines, 1988; Teale, 1986). Each study not only demonstrated that the lives of low-income American families are rich with literacy events, but it also suggested in varying degrees that each subculture constituted a coherent form of literacy.

We turn now to the recurrent literacy-related activities engaged in by children in the Early Childhood Project, and identify some salient themes around which those activities were organized.

RECURRENT ACTIVITIES AND LITERACY-RELATED EXPERIENCES

The design of our study affords us several windows into the intimate culture of each family, including the diary kept by the parents, the ecological inventories documenting the nature and frequency of children's engagement in literacy-related activities, and the parent ethnotheory interviews. We first examine the ecological inventory, which was conducted with a child's parent in the context of a visit to the home. As described in Chapter 2, the inventory was organized in terms of several broad categories of recurrent activities that afford opportunities for the child to learn about literacy. We administered the inventory four times over the course of the study, allowing us to

TABLE 3.1. *Children's Mean Frequency of Engagement in Recurrent Literacy-Related Activities*

	Grade			
Activity	Pre-K	K/First[a]	Second	Third
Storybooks	2.39	2.19/2.35	2.25	1.80
Preschool books	1.25	1.83/1.22	0.97	0.90
Chapter books	–	–	0.98	1.32
Word games	0.83	1.43	1.05	1.30
Board games	0.93	1.33	1.66	1.70
Storytelling	1.50	1.90/1.72	1.61	1.52
Mealtime conversations	2.32	2.90/2.88	2.69	–
Educational television	2.10	2.24/1.60	1.56	1.62

Note: Parents used the following rating scale: 0 = never; 1 = rarely, less than once a week; 2 = occasionally, at least once a week; 3 = often, almost every day. Ratings represent the mean for reading with others and alone.

[a] Parents recruited to the project in Wave 1 were interviewed when their child was in kindergarten; those in Wave 2 were interviewed for the first time when their child was beginning first grade.

trace changes in the relative salience of each type of activity as the child develops, as well as changes in the participant structure of the activities.

Table 3.1 shows the mean frequencies with which selected categories of recurrent activity were reported as children moved from prekindergarten through third grade. Among these, only participation in board games shows a simple trend of steady increase in frequency across the 5 years. Other opportunities for literacy appropriation, such as story telling, storybook reading, and watching educational television shows, varied quite unevenly in reported frequency from year to year. This probably reflects the expanding range of recurrent activities in which children participate at home as they grow older, and complementary shifts in parents' priorities depending on their perceptions of their child's needs and interests.

Frequency of Children's Engagement with Text

The type of text that children read changed as they moved into elementary school. Table 3.2 shows the percentages of children engaging in selected reading activities across the four family social addresses that we sampled. Although few children had *no* interaction with text,

TABLE 3.2. *Percentage of Children Reading Different Types of Text*

	Storybooks			Preschool Books		
	Daily		Not at All	At Least Weekly		Not at All
	Alone	With Others		Alone	With Others	
Prekindergarten						
Low income African American	56	35	8	50	61	33
Low income European American	33	53	0	33	47	55
Middle income African American	100	73	0	75	82	0
Middle income European American	100	54	0	67	38	0
End of kindergarten/first grade						
Low income African American	52		0	65		4
Low income European American	47		0	40		40
Middle income African American	36		0	73		0
Middle income European American	54		0	23		54

	Chapter Books		
	Daily		Not at All
	Alone	With Others	
Second grade			
Low income African American	13	0	26
Low income European American	13	0	73
Middle income African American	18	0	9
Middle income European American	62	15	0
Third grade			
Low income African American	4	0	30
Low income European American	7	0	40
Middle income African American	18	27	0
Middle income European American	69	31	0

middle-income children more frequently engaged in age-appropriate reading activities than low-income children. In prekindergarten, all the middle-income children, but only 45% of the low-income children, engaged in daily storybook reading. By the second and third grades, more middle-income children, particularly European American ones, read chapter books each day than did low-income children. Correspondingly, the frequency with which parents reported reading preschool books or storybooks with their children decreased. Although not reported in Table 3.2, relatively few older children looked at preschool books. No middle-income European American child engaged in this activity after first grade. In contrast, 45% of the middle-income African American third graders still reportedly perused preschool books at least several times a week. By the time the children were in third grade, relatively few read storybooks with others, perhaps reflecting that more children were now reading chapter books.

There were also some other significant differences between the practices reported by middle-income families and those of lower-income families, not all of which flow in a simple logical fashion from differences in the level of material resources at their disposal. Ninety percent of the middle-income parents reported that their child in prekindergarten interacted with at least one type of book every day, and 90% reported that their child went to the library, whereas the corresponding percentages for the low income parents were 52% and 43%, respectively.[1]

Another way of considering the frequency of engagement with print is to consider such experiences in relation to children's subsequent literacy competencies. Table 3.3 disaggregates the frequencies by the child's eventual level of reading proficiency, as measured at the end of our study in the third grade. We selected those children who at the end of third grade were reading on grade level (based on their scores on the Woodcock-Johnson Reading Comprehension Composite) and those children reading between grade equivalents of 1.6 to 2.6. Eleven (2 low income, 9 middle income) of the 62 children who completed the third-grade assessments were in the group of high scorers, and 20 (15 low income, 5 middle income) were in the group of

---

[1] Chi square (1) = 4.60, 6.60, p < .05, .01, respectively, for these two income-level contrasts.

TABLE 3.3. *Percentages of Children Classified as Scoring High and Low in Reading Comprehension Who Read Different Types of Books Each Day*

	Grade							
	Pre-K		K/First		Second		Third	
	SB	ABC	SB	ABC	SB	CB	SB	CB
Alone								
Low scorers	20	0	37	26	65	10	65	10
High scorers	100	50	55	36	40	80	0	73
With Others								
Low scorers			37	32	40	10	45	10
High scorers			64	45	44	20	9	36

Note: We did not distinguish reading alone from reading with others during pre-kindergarten. SB is storybook reading, ABC is preschool books, CB is chapter books. Classification of scorers as high or low was based on the Woodcock-Johnson Reading Comprehension composite in Grade 3. Of the total sample of 62 children, 11 were low scorers and 20 were high scorers.

low scorers. As shown in Table 3.3, children who were on their way to grade-appropriate levels of reading proficiency (i.e., high scorers) were more often reported to engage in storybook and preschool book reading in prekindergarten, kindergarten, and first grade, and chapter book reading in second and third grades, than the group of children who would demonstrate lower levels of reading proficiency (i.e., low scorers).

The differences in the type and frequency of reading shown by the group of high scorers and low scorers is apparent when we consider each child's individual pattern of reading experience over the course of our study. Nine of the 11 children in the high scorers group (82%) reportedly had daily experience reading storybooks and/or chapter books each time we documented reading practices. By second grade, 10 of the 11 children (92%) engaged in daily reading of chapter books, a more developmentally appropriate form of narrative text for this age group than storybook reading. Only 1 of the 20 low scorers (5%) reported consistent daily reading of storybooks and/or chapter books.

High scorers also engaged with more types of printed material each day than did low scorers. This was most apparent when we considered children's independent engagement with text, something that can be viewed as an index of children's interest in reading. High scorers engaged with an average of 2.42 types of printed material each day, whereas low scorers engaged with 1.46 types.

It is difficult to tease apart cause-and-effect relations in this complex of variables. Were children reading "harder" text because they were more skilled readers, or did they become more skilled readers because of the type of reading they did? The longitudinal nature of our study enabled us to conduct analyses to support more causal interpretations of the data. These analyses, reported in Chapter 5, show that the type of reading children engaged in predicted growth in their reading skills from one year to the next.

Television Viewing and Parent–Child Conversation

Watching television is a common activity for many children in the United States, with reported viewing times estimated at between 2 to 3 hours per day for preschoolers and elementary school-age children (Huston, Wright, Marquis, & Green, 1999; Neuman, 1988). Discussing a television program with one's child affords parents opportunities for expanding the child's knowledge of the world and, perhaps, fostering the development of other forms of literacy-relevant knowledge such as vocabulary and awareness of print. Children in the Early Childhood Project watched a wide array of programs, including situation comedies (e.g., in third grade, approximately 77% of the children watched such programs at least once a week and 48% watched them almost every day), educational shows (57% at least weekly, 27% almost daily), dramas (57% at least weekly, 27% almost daily), and news or documentary shows (60% at least weekly, 32% almost daily).

As part of her master's thesis within the Early Childhood Project, Kirsten Mackler (2001; Mackler & Baker, 2001) explored the relations among television viewing practices, conversations about television shows, and children's reading skills. When the children were in third grade, in addition to indicating the frequency with which their children watched various types of television programs, parents also were asked (in those cases where they themselves watched televison with their child) whether they discussed the meaning of the words uttered by characters, the realism of the shows, the motivations of characters, the information presented, and the meanings/morals of the stories. Approximately 80% of the parents reported watching television with their children at least several times a week; 44% of the parents reported doing so almost every day.

Some parents reported that they just watched the programs with their children, without engaging in much discussion, whereas others responded to their children's questions, and some parents initiated discussion by commenting on aspects of the show they considered noteworthy. Sixty-seven percent of the parents mentioned discussing the information presented in the shows, and 69% reported discussing moral issues raised in the shows. Sixty-four percent of the parents discussed how realistic the shows were, and 56% discussed why the characters behaved the way they did. About one-third of the parents said that they explained the meaning of a word heard in the show to their children, typically in response to a question posed by the child. The extent to which parents discussed the programs was not related to social address.

Aggregating Information From the Ecological Inventories

In search of a more integrative picture of children's participation in recurrent activities, we developed two means of aggregating data from the ecological inventories. The first synthesis is based on the types of literacy skills likely to be fostered by an activity. The second is based on which participants engaged in the activities involving print.

Many of the reported activities had a very low frequency of occurrence. Moreover, engagement in a specific activity may not matter as much as engagement in any of a set of activities, each of which fosters a common skill. For example, although storybook reading may help children learn about narrative structure, so might listening to people tell stories or watching dramas on television. Accordingly, three members of the research team independently reviewed all the activities in the ecological inventories and categorized them according to the type of literacy skill each was most likely to foster (Sonnenschein, Katenkamp, Tenowich, & Serpell, 2003). The Word Recognition scale included reading preschool books, playing with educational toys, playing hand clap games, and singing songs. The Story Comprehension scale included pretend play, story telling, and reading story and chapter books. The World Knowledge scale included watching the news or documentaries on television and reading nonfiction books, magazines, and newspapers. The Daily Living Skills scale included going on outings, errands and shopping, and using the TV guide. We summed the frequency of occurrence data to obtain four composite scores. We aggregated the information separately for each yearly administration of the ecological inventory.

To consider the relation between children's activities and their literacy competencies, we correlated children's scores on the activity composites with their scores on three literacy measures – basic reading skills, reading comprehension, and use of functional print (e.g., filling out one's name and address on a form, using a calendar to find the day of the week that one's birthday fell on, sorting envelopes by the address printed on them). The basic reading skills and reading comprehension measures were administered in third grade; the use of functional print was assessed in second grade. The more that children engaged in activities involving story comprehension each year, the higher they scored on the literacy measures.[2] Only during prekindergarten was engagement in activities within the word recognition composite related to subsequent reading skills.[3] Multiple regression analyses confirmed these correlational findings.[4] Examination of the specific activities within the story comprehension composite indicated that much of the variance in reading scores was due to reading storybooks or, as children got older, chapter books. In fact, by third grade, reading storybooks was no longer related to literacy development, but reading chapter books was.

---

[2] All correlations between storyline composite and basic reading skills, passage comprehension, and functional print were significant, with the exception of those computed between the kindergarten/early first-grade activities for Wave 2 children and the outcome measures. Significant correlations ranged from .42 to .63.

[3] The correlation between word recognition activities in prekindergarten and third grade basic reading skills was $r (26) = .44, p = .02$.

[4] Third graders' basic reading skills were significantly predicted by the Story Comprehension composite in kindergarten (Beta: .52), second grade (Beta: .41), and third grade (Beta: .32). The Word Recognition composite in prekindergarten was a significant predictor of second graders' use of functional print (Beta: .39) and of third graders' reading comprehension (Beta: .40). Second graders' use of functional print was significantly predicted by the Story Comprehension composite in kindergarten (Beta: .55), and second grade (Beta: .35). Third graders' reading comprehension was significantly predicted by the Story Comprehension composite in kindergarten (Beta: .45), second grade (Beta: .32), and third grade (Beta: .33).

The second selective synthesis of children's recurrent activities focused on the influence of guided participation (Rogoff, 1990) in literacy-related activities, using data from the ecological inventory completed when children were in second grade. The parent was asked to rate how frequently the focal child engaged in each of several reading, writing, and drawing activities, with either an adult or an adolescent. A composite index was constructed by summing the ratings across 16 items. Within the reading category were preschool books, picture books, storybooks, chapter books, nonfiction books, magazines, newspapers, comic books, word puzzle activity books, and other print materials; within the writing category were writing journals or diaries, letters (correspondence), poems or stories, word games involving writing, and other types of writing, drawing, or coloring. We deliberately omitted from this index items such as "uses a computer" to remove the more obvious bias in favor of families with higher incomes. Nevertheless, this index of reported frequency of engagement by the child in joint literacy activities showed a moderate and significant relation with family income. Higher-income families reported engaging in these activities more frequently than low-income families, with no differences related to ethnic heritage.[5]

In a related vein, when the children were in first grade, we found that the shared reading interactions of middle-income children more frequently included adults than did those of the low-income children (Sonnenschein & Munsterman, 1996).[6] Evidence that adults more effectively guide children's participation in literacy is presented in Chapters 4 and 5. Reading interactions with adults were more pleasant and engaging than those with peers, and pleasant reading interactions were associated with more frequent reading, which, in turn, was associated with better reading scores.

PARENTS' SOCIALIZATION GOALS ACROSS DEVELOPMENTAL DOMAINS

In contrast to the detached objectivity of the ecological inventory, our approach to documenting parents' socialization goals was designed

[5] $r(57) = .41, p < .001.$
[6] Chi square $(3) = 8.08, p = .05.$

to get inside the system of meanings that informs a parent's caregiving practices, by connecting with the parent's everyday understanding. The first step was to invite her to provide us with a relatively spontaneous formulation of the salient activities in the child's everyday life through the diary procedure described in Chapter 2. The instructions on how to maintain a diary were deliberately open ended and left each respondent free to define her own focus. From the initial description of the child's daily life in the diary, we selected a set of recurrent activities in which the focal child engaged with a familiar co-participant. For each of these socially mediated activities, we probed the parent to articulate the personal meaning she attributed to the activity.

Parent Formulations of the Meaning of Their Child's Recurrent Activities

After briefly exploring with the respondent her reasons for buying toys for her children, her views about with whom her own child should be allowed to play, and her beliefs about watching television, we turned to a consideration of six recurrent activities, described by the parent in her own words. These were preselected from the diary (and, in some cases, further elaborated in response to the ecological inventory). For each activity, we asked the parent to give us her own interpretation: "What do you think this activity means to FC (the focal child)? What does it mean to you as her parent?" (For further details see Serpell et al., 1997). Our informants varied considerably in the degree to which they volunteered explicit integrative schemes to situate or reinforce their explanations of what a given activity means to their child and/or to themselves as caregivers. Sometimes they invoked explicit cultural themes in their formulation of explanatory schemas. Three that were frequently invoked were the rejection of violence, the promotion of fun, and the cultivation of motivation for educational success, themes also commonly expressed in various public media (Lightfoot & Valsiner, 1992).

Rodrigo and Triana (1995) suggested that parents' knowledge about child development is generally represented in schematic, prototypical form, stored in their memory as multiple episodic traces of a network of personal experiences, rather than as the well-structured entity that we generally think of as a theory. These episodic traces are only occasionally abstracted at the time of retrieval in order to meet a particular situational demand. This type of incompletely theorized explanation is illustrated in the following account provided by a mother when her daughter was in prekindergarten. Mrs. D[7] expresses an explicit commitment to supporting the pedagogical process that she sees her child going through at school. Mrs. D is a low-income European American woman who dropped out of high school. She contrasts her own attitude with that of her parents when she was a schoolchild. The interviewer invited her to expand on two different types of activity that she described in her handwritten diary: "Mom read them there [sic] Bedtime Story" and "we did her homework."

INTERVIEWER: What does it mean to her when you read Anna a bedtime story?

MOTHER: I dunno, I think she just likes it that I read to her. Cause J (her 14-year-old sister) reads to her but not like I do. I, like, try to express some parts and I just read it on through. I try to make it exciting or whatever, you know. Why make reading boring? Just stops the person from reading. (laughs). That's the way I see it. Cause I know when I went to school, my parents didn't likely give a hoot. If I did my homework, I did it. If I didn't, I didn't. If I went to school, oh well. You know? My kids, no! I know how my parents was and I'm not about...

In this articulation of a personal philosophy, Anna's mother invokes a public cultural theme, that parents should take an interest in their children's progress in school and show their support by attending to homework assignments. Contrasting her own attitude with her parents' delinquency, she advances another explanatory schema to justify her practice of trying to make her reading of bedtime stories exciting: "Why make reading boring? Just stops the person from reading."

---

[7] Mrs. D1. We use here for the first time a referential convention that appears throughout the book. The letter indicates which of the schools listed in Table 2.1 is attended by the focal child. The number indicates the participant number assigned to that family within the Early Childhood Project. To enhance expository flow, we do not include the family numbers within the text itself. Children's names are pseudonyms.

Inference, Tentative Formulation, and Negotiated Specification of Socialization Goals

From the samples of the parents' ideas expressed in response to these questions about the meaning of recurrent activities in the child's everyday life, as well as the extended conversation prompted by the ecological inventory, we extrapolated a tentative formulation of several developmental goals informing the parent's approach to childrearing. Each interviewer met with one of the principal investigators to review in detail the parent's responses to the first interview. Together they searched the responses for expressions of value by the respondent, and inductively derived a set of implicit socialization goals that appeared to inform the meanings she had imputed to the various recurrent activities in her child's everyday life.

For Anna's mother, whose ideas about the meaning of storybook reading and homework were presented previously, the following goals were inferred and discussed with her. The rank order of importance that she eventually assigned to each goal is shown in parentheses.

a. Learn to take care of things (4)
b. Use her imagination (3)
c. Prepare for the future (7)
d. Learn to get along with other people (2)
e. Learn to make her own judgments, choices (5)
f. Learn about the world and other people (1)
g. Become independent (6)

During the second parental interview, the interviewer presented each socialization goal that we had tentatively inferred from the earlier interview. The mother was invited to reject, reformulate, and/or endorse each goal as one she had for her child, and then to add to the list. The process of negotiating consensus about the definition of her goals for her child often involved the mother citing illustrative examples. Thus, with respect to the goal of using imagination, Mrs. D recounted how Anna, faced with a prohibition by their landlord on keeping a cat in the house, had created a fantasy:

So she imagine it, you know, all her cats, that she has. . . . She says they're down the basement. You can't see them because they got invisible cages, when you go down there. So, no wonder I haven't seen them! (laughs). And I hope they don't come out while I'm down there. I might trip on them or something. She said, "Oh no, you won't never trip on them; they'll never come out when you're down there." I said, "Oh, OK." Then, when I'm down there hanging clothes, or something, I'll think "I thought I heard a cat." She goes, "shh ... be quiet, Blackie. Mother can hear you." ... I say "OK."

Parents were also encouraged to add goals that they believed were important, but that had not been identified by the investigator. The resulting list of endorsed developmental goals became our frame of reference for a series of questions designed to clarify the parents' understanding of child development and socialization. The goals expressed by Mrs. D for Anna ranged widely over the domains of social, moral, personal, and intellectual development. When she was asked to place them in rank order of importance, she hesitated at first, then decided to place the intellectual goal "learn about the world and other people" first, the social/moral goal "learn to get along with other people" second, and the personal goal "use her imagination" third. Her account of her investment in her daughter's intellectual development at the age of 4 was phrased in broad terms without explicit reference to mastery of literacy or other specific academic skills.

A Taxonomy of Parental Socialization Goals

We classified the developmental goals endorsed by the parents of our first wave of participants when the child was in prekindergarten into 30 categories, spread across four broad domains. (Examples in parentheses are direct quotes from parents.)

1. Social/moral development, including safety or escape from hazards; rejection of violence; prosocial attitudes, relationships, social skills, tolerance, nurturance; moral, polite, and respectful behavior; wisdom and good judgment (e.g., shouldn't fight or get in trouble; share things with friends; get along with other people; close family ties; learn the Bible).
2. Personal development, including self-esteem, confidence; pleasure, fun, relaxation, happiness; self-actualization; imagination; independence; and responsibility (e.g., feel good about herself; make his own choices; learn responsibility; know that he has something unique to contribute).

3. Intellectual development, including practical, everyday intelligence, competence, self-help skills; communication skills; general knowledge, learning; specific knowledge, learning strategies (e.g., learn widely as much as possible; learn to follow directions; learn about the world; know his address and phone number; develop attention span).

4. Academic development, including academic achievement motivation, motivation to learn, and literacy (e.g., do well in school; enjoy reading; know her school work better; go to college; be motivated to learn; stay in school).

Although these domains display a certain amount of overlap, we were able over a series of discussions to achieve an adequate level of inter-rater consensus in assigning each goal endorsed by our sample of parents to one of the four domains.

Most of the Wave 1 parents interviewed when their child was in prekindergarten endorsed one or more goals in each of the four domains. Eighty-four percent of the parents included at least one academic goal in their rankings. However, parents were significantly more likely to endorse at least one personal or social/moral goal than an academic or intellectual goal.[8] Nevertheless, 64% of the parents who mentioned an academic goal explicitly identified academic achievement as one of their top three goals for their child.

Overall, 76 parents completed the initial series of three interviews about parental goals when their child was in prekindergarten (Wave 1) or entering Grade 1 (Wave 2). The top portion of Table 3.4 shows the distribution of parents' highest ranked socialization goals across the four broad domains in this first round of interviews. Middle-income parents cited a goal in the personal domain as their top priority significantly more often than low-income parents, whereas the low-income parents tended more often to rank highest a goal in the academic domain or the social domain.[9]

We revisited the topic of goals and their relative importance to the parent, and investigated the degree to which a socialization goal expressed at a given point in time represented an enduring or resilient

---

[8] Cochran's Q $(3) = 11.026, p = .012$.
[9] Chi square $(3) = 11.36, p < .01$.

TABLE 3.4. *Percentages of Parents' Top Socialization Goals in Each Domain at Two Interview Points as Function of Income Level*

	Domain			
	Academic	Intellectual	Personal	Social/Moral
Interview 2				
Low-income families	35	12	21	35
Middle-income families	10	10	61	25
Interview 7				
Low-income families	50	0	27	25
Middle-income Families	36	0	46	20

Note: Interview 2 was conducted with Wave 1 parents when their children were finishing pre-kindergarten and with Wave 2 parents when their children were beginning first grade. Interview 7 was conducted with all parents when the children were finishing third grade.

preoccupation. By the time a menu of goals was presented to the parents, they could also see their own "endorsed goals" reflected in the list, and they were informed that the menu represented the goals generated by parents throughout the neighborhoods sampled in the study. This served to build a link between the expression of personal beliefs and shared cultural themes, an issue we address further in later sections of this chapter. A goal was classified as representing an enduring focus for a particular parent if it featured among the informant's Parental Interview 2 endorsed goals and an exactly equivalent or reliably matched goal featured among her Parental Interview 3 selected goals. In the case of Mrs. D, the third interview was conducted 6 months after our first interview with her about socialization goals, when Anna was in kindergarten. Her ranking of the goals was highly consistent with her responses in the earlier interview.

Only 70 of the 210 goals endorsed during Parental Interview 2 were classified as enduring in this way. How then should we interpret the other two-thirds of endorsed goals, those that did not qualify for the designation of an enduring focus? We take the view that although at the time of endorsement, the parent was confident that this was one of her goals, it was not sufficiently enduring and/or salient to be ranked in the top set in the context of the selection that respondents were invited to make in parental interview 3. A further indication of the salience for our respondents of their enduring foci is that 25% of the goals classified as representing an enduring focus were ranked number 1 in the second interview, and 62% were ranked as numbers 1, 2, or 3.

It seems to us inappropriate to regard endurance as a criterion of validity. An endorsement of a goal may be valid for a particular context of elicitation without representing an enduring focus of concern for the respondent that would appear relevant to her across many different contexts and/or on multiple occasions spread over an extended period of time. We have used the term *endurance* to capture the notion that such a focus has to compete for expression with other influences.

In our last and seventh round of interviews with parents in the final year of the project, we revisited the topic of socialization goals and asked the parents first to state what they now considered their most important goals for the focal child, who was now in Grade 3. Next we reminded them of the goals they had stated in parental interview 2 when their child was in prekindergarten (Wave 1) or just entering first grade (Wave 2). For each of their earlier goals, if it was not in the list they had just given us, we asked whether the parent considered it still relevant and important, and if not why not. Then we did the same for the three goals they had ranked highest on the menu presented to them during the third interview. Turning to the goals that were new in their unprompted list in this parental interview, we asked them to explain why these had now become important. Finally, we asked them to restate their considered opinion of what were their top three goals for their child.

Almost two-thirds of the parents who completed the initial series of interviews also responded to this final interview ($N = 50$). Thirty of the families completing both sets of interviews were low-income and 20 were middle-income; there was an even split between children of African American and European American ethnic heritage, and slightly more boys than girls.

The top three unprompted goals at this phase of development (when the focal child was in Grade 3) were reliably assigned to one of the four domains, and they were also compared with the top three goals identified by the same parent in the earlier interviews. In all cases, we were able to match at least one of the respondent's top three goals with one of the specific goals she had emphasized 2 or more years earlier. Moreover, for 38% of the parents, all three of their top-ranked goals at this phase were recognizable as enduring from the earlier interviews. There were no significant differences in this respect between parents of boys and girls, nor among parents in the four sociocultural groups.

The distribution of goals ranked highest at the beginning of this parental interview is displayed in the bottom portion of Table 3.4. The category of intellectual (nonacademic) goals no longer fit any of the parents' top-ranked goals. We interpret this to mean that by the time their children had reached this phase of development, the parents in our sample tended to focus their attention on those intellectual characteristics that are identified by the school as relevant to academic performance. Another striking contrast between the distribution of parental goals in Grade 3 and those at the earlier phase of development is the greater preponderance of academic goals in Grade 3.

A greater emphasis on personal goals among middle-income than low-income parents was still apparent in Grade 3, but was no longer statistically significant. Closer examination revealed that at this phase the relative emphasis placed on these two types of goal by parents at the two income levels varied in different ways according to the gender of the focal child. Each of a parent's top three unprompted goals in Grade 3 was assigned a weight according to its rank, and these were then combined to create a composite weighted unprompted domain emphasis score for each parent with respect to each domain. Analysis of variance revealed a significant interaction between income level and the gender of the child for each of these domain emphasis indices. Lower-income parents placed greater emphasis on academic goals for boys (mean score = 3.00) than for girls (1.80), whereas the reverse was true of middle-income parents (mean for boys = 1.00, and for girls = 2.25). However, low-income parents placed greater emphasis on personal goals for girls (mean score = 2.07) than for boys (1.53), whereas the reverse was true of middle-income parents (mean score for girls = 2.12, and for boys = 3.83).

Because of the relatively small size of our sample when broken down into subcategories, most of the statistical analyses we report in this and later chapters did not include the child's gender as a variable. However, other studies in American schools have reported that boys are generally perceived by their teachers as more at risk for academic failure in the early years of schooling than girls (Sadker & Sadker, 1994). Perhaps low-income parents tend to respond to this challenge by raising the academic stakes for their sons, whereas middle-income parents respond to it by focusing on the need for their sons to attain personal developmental goals such as self-confidence and discipline.

In the case of Anna discussed earlier in this section, Mrs. D began by stating four goals, that she should (1) go to school every day on time; (2) not watch too much TV; (3) do good in school, complete school; and (4) learn to keep her room clean. When reminded of her earlier list of goals, Mrs. D considered them all to still be relevant and important. She explained the new importance of getting to school on time with reference to her having started a full-time job so she now relied on Anna's brother to get Anna ready for school. Her final list of top three goals for Anna were (1) grow up happy and enjoy life; (2) be considerate of others, kind and cooperative; and (3) complete school. Thus, despite her increased concern about Anna's academic opportunities and performance, this mother continued to rank personal and social/moral goals even more highly.

Our finding that parental goals more often emphasized the moral/social and personal domains of development than intellectual and academic skills might not have emerged if we had not gone to such lengths to allow the parents to express their own priorities with minimal constraints. Many other researchers have proceeded directly to the academic domain in their interviews with parents and have reported that across all socioeconomic and ethnocultural groups in America there is a strong consensus among parents on the importance of their child's academic success (e.g., Okagaki & Sternberg, 1991; Stevenson & Newman, 1986). Our data do not contradict this generalization, but they set the enthusiasm for academic development in a broader context, showing that it is only one of a number of socialization goals held by American parents for their children, and not necessarily the pre-eminent one, at least in the early phases of the child's development.

Our method of grounding our data in the everyday lives and discourse of the participating families and communities affords us a greater degree of confidence in the authenticity of the value judgments and interpretations that we attribute to our informants than we could have had if they had responded to prestructured categories designed by us without such intense engagement with them. Building on this grounding, we proceeded over the course of several interviews to explore other features of each parent's implicit theory about child development and socialization, her perception of the responsibilities of home and school, her perception of teachers' goals, and her evaluation of the school's communication strategies with parents. We begin, in the next section, with an analysis of the ways in which parents described and explained their preferred strategies for intervening in the context of their child's home life to promote various aspects of the child's development, including literacy.

PARENTS' CONCEPTIONS OF HOW TO INTERVENE TO NURTURE DEVELOPMENT

Building on the parents' articulation of their goals, we asked them to describe and explain to us the socialization methods they used to help their children progress in five developmental domains: (1) learning right from wrong, (2) learning about the physical world, (3) learning to communicate effectively with others, (4) learning to read and write, and (5) learning about numbers. In each domain the parent was asked, *"What is the most effective way of helping your child learn (domain X)?"* Some interesting contrasts emerged between parents' responses in the domains of morality and literacy. The examples we cite to illustrate the various categories of intervention strategy are therefore all drawn from those two domains.

The coding scheme for categorizing parents' formulations of intervention strategies was developed through a series of inductive steps, interpreting interview responses in light of psychological theories of cognitive development. Three broad categories of intervention strategy were identified:

1. *Proactive intervention:* Defined as deliberate interventions designed to impact directly on the child's behavior, cognition, or motivation. This category included:
   a. *Deliberate instruction* (e.g., "take time out to sit down with them and to study, to plan"; "I try to sit down and talk to her – try to show ... right from wrong.")

    b. *Modeling* (e.g., "by example, because they are read to and they see you writing . . . signing off of cards . . . you read the cards to them," "by example . . . no matter what you do, your children set you up as the example of what's right and wrong: they see everything you do as right. If you vary from what you do, then they consider that, they see that's different and they're gonna ask you – they're gonna question it. . . . ")

    c. *Motivating* (e.g., "encouraging him to write")

2. *In-flight responsiveness:* This expression was adapted from Tharp and Gallimore (1988) to describe an instructional attitude promoting opportunistic responses to the child's behavior as it occurs. We distinguished three types of in-flight responsiveness:

    a. *Differential reinforcement:* interventions that focused on providing positive or negative feedback (e.g., "just teaching them what, from when they start toddling around: 'you can't touch that; that's a No No!' . . . giving them something else they can touch in place of what they can't touch. Don't just say 'you can't do that' and walk away, you know? I don't think that's a good idea – give them something else they can do.")

    b. *Contingent guidance:* guiding the child's responses in the direction of a desired outcome (e.g., "she'll ask me . . . how to spell her sister's name. She already knows that, but she gets mixed up on her sister's name a lot. . . . She gets mixed up on the last letters . . . she'll say 'oh yeah, that's right: A!'")

    c. *ZPD matching:* consciously calibrating a response to the child's behavior, relative to what is construed as the next step in the child's development, based on Vygotsky's (1978) conception of instruction as assisting performance within the learner's zone of proximal development (e.g., ". . . you're writing birthday cards . . . of course, you read the card to them and they begin to identify different cards, you know, first they see the birthday symbols, they're seeing different symbolism, then you point out the letters, you see they begin to think and they enjoy, then they learn how to spell 'happy,' you see what I'm saying, they learn how to spell 'birthday,' because it is something that they're highly interested in. . . . ")

3. *Reliance on the child's experience:* This represents a less directly interventionist stance that relies primarily on the impact of experiences that the child will encounter in self-governed activities in certain settings, a perspective consistent with Piaget's (1971) constructivist theory of cognitive development as driven by exploration, and the related educational tradition of "discovery learning" (e.g., "just being around it, I think, and offering them, having the materials to do it and . . . not pushing too hard. . . . If they enjoy it like he does – he colors, he does all that stuff – it'll just come." "Let them learn from their mistakes . . . because you can tell a child, 'don't do this', and 'do that', and 'do that', and they will not learn until it actually happens . . . they have to do it in order to learn from their mistakes.")

The distinctions among these categories of preferred intervention strategies are drawn in terms of where the respondent lays primary emphasis. In a small number of cases, the parent's explanation explicitly incorporated two different strategic elements, and both codes were assigned. Strategies were differentiated by domain, with more frequent emphasis on in-flight responsiveness (e.g., contingent guidance or differential reinforcement) in the moral domain, and more frequent emphasis on proactive interventions (e.g., deliberate instruction) in the domain of literacy, especially by low-income parents.

Table 3.5 presents the distribution of preferred types of intervention for Wave 1 families. Two types of contrast are apparent: (1) between the two domains of literacy and moral development, and (2) within the literacy domain between the middle- and low-income samples. Proactive intervention strategies were more often preferred for helping children learn to read and write than for learning about right and wrong.[10] When discussing how to foster learning to read and write, low-income parents were more likely to cite forms of proactive intervention than middle-income parents.[11] Parents' intervention strategy preferences for the socialization of literacy were not significantly related to their strategy preferences for the socialization of morality. These ideas about how best to intervene to help a young child to learn and progress toward the goals that their parents cherish

[10] McNemar's test for the significance of changes: Chi square (1) = 3.76, $p = .05$.
[11] Chi square (1) = 3.24, $.10 > p > .05$.

TABLE 3.5. *Percentages of Parents Favoring Each Type of Intervention for Literacy and Morality Development*

	Type of Intervention		
	Proactive Intervention	In-flight Responsiveness	Reliance on Experience
Literacy			
Low income African American	73	13	13
Low income European American	75	8	17
Middle income	29	29	43
Morality			
Low income African American	33	67	0
Low income European American	54	38	8
Middle income	57	43	0

Note: $N = 34$, Wave 1 families.

for them constitute an intermediate, pragmatic level of explanation, generalizing beyond the immediate situation, but not explicitly addressing issues at a high level of abstraction.

The account volunteered by Anna's mother, Mrs. D, in our initial interview with her about the meaning of recurrent activities in her child's everyday life could be taken as implying that, when reading aloud to her child, she was adopting a proactive intervention strategy of motivating. Here is what another mother, Mrs. A,[12] said when asked directly, "What is the most effective way of helping a child of this age to learn to read and write?"

To me the way I would do it, I would (like) sit Amina down and I would write her name out first and then I would tell Amina to make the first letter. She'll pick a book on her own and, you know, she pretend she read but when I sits there and read with her, you know, I points to the word as I read along with her so she'll know how to (you know) identify the word that I am reading. I would think that soon, when she get in kindergarten, Amina she will be able to read and write.

This was coded as an instance of belief in the efficacy of deliberate instruction, a form of proactive intervention. Mrs. A, a low-income

---

[12] Mrs. A1.

African American mother of two, is a full-time homemaker who has never worked outside the home since completing high school. She expressed a wide range of goals for Amina in prekindergarten, among which number 1 was learn to read, and her one enduring preoccupation when Amina was in kindergarten was coded as "learn skills for doing well in school."

Consider, by way of contrast, Mrs. G,[13] a middle-income African American mother of four, who works part-time as a realtor, is trained in secretarial work, and has written a book on her computer, aimed at an audience of young children, that she hopes to get published. When asked about the most effective way of helping a child of this age to learn to read and write, she replied, "let them draw, they're scribbling." This was coded as an instance of reliance on the child's experience. Expanding our focus of attention to the full range of opinions expressed by Mrs. G makes it clear that this is not a case of "laissez-faire." In her diary, at one juncture she wrote:

We have mommy school today we have art. That's our major activity. We always have homework in our major activity & our major activity today is art. I covered the walls of the boys room with tag board and I gave them markers paint, crayons, diff't size markers and fluorescent, lots of color, so they had plenty to work with. They had glue and they could stick things on to the tag board. I covered it w/ 8 sheets of tag board & each of them had a section & they worked well. They wrote things, they drew pictures of people. Jennifer (the focal child in this family) likes to write. Jennifer is a natural journalist I'd say. She keeps a journal at home, she writes things that she does, people that she know....

During the second interview, we asked Mrs. G to explain the concept of "mommy school." She replied:

Mommy school got started when they were infants. I used to exercise them. So we started out with an aerobics class. And so, everything I taught them was a learning thing, and they always wanted to know "When are we going to school?" "Well, you're in school" you're in mommy school: all your life, you have mom; so that's mommy school. Everything they learn from me is a part of mommy school. We had formal sessions, because the girls were home in the daytime and the boys were in school. So the girls had mommy school that they could call "Well, we do go to school!"

---

[13] Mrs. G2.

During the first ecological inventory, Mrs. G explained with reference to word games that they occur "quite often, because I make them look everything up in the dictionary. Yeah, everything that, well, 'do you know what that means?' And they can't trip the other one up: 'you don't know what that means – Mom's going to make you get the dictionary!' So I make her get the dictionary, and we look it up." With reference to refrigerator displays, she recounted the following anecdote:

Well, now that John is reading and he's reading everything to Peter and everyone else, he looks on the refrigerator last week and said, "Wow mommy, I like that, that's looks cute". I said, "What is it?" "'Life isn't passing me by, it's running me over.'" [everyone laughs]. I said, "Yeah I've had that a while," and he says, "Yeah but now I know what it says." So it, you know he can read it now, we started out with words, you know a word a week. And one word a week we used the magnetic alphabet letters. And we put them on there and any time during the day I might say spell egg or whatever. And they have to remember they saw it on the refrigerator, what is it, and they spell it. So if I get them, I get to razz them and they hate that, they are like you couldn't even spell it so don't even, so we do that.

The family has a large collection of books for children of all ages. Mrs. G elaborates:

They have that Early World of Learning from, who makes that Childcraft? Rare Book Encyclopedia? We have that set, so we have the Childcraft, Early World and the World Book Encyclopedias. And that has all kinds of activities in it, books and coloring and all sorts of things. . . . We've got ABCs, we've got the laminated ones, we've got everything from the very first book you can have fabric, all the way up. Anybody of any age can come and there is something there for you. Even something if you just want something old we've got them from the 1940s.

In a way, the whole structure of Mrs. G's home constitutes an intervention strategy, a carefully designed context replete with literacy appropriation opportunities, or what James Gibson (1979) termed *affordances*. The classic examples of affordance refer to properties of the physical world that afford certain possibilities of locomotion and manipulation. However, as Eleanor Gibson (1982) noted, "man-made symbols like writing have affordances" (p. 62). Parents who design the home life of their child along the lines presented by Mrs. G are like an architect or an engineer, designing an environment whose inherent properties continuously invite the child to appropriate literacy.

FAMILY ROUTINES: MEANING AND PREDICTABILITY

The parents whose ethnotheories and practices we have considered in this chapter interact with their developing child within a system comprising not only dyads such as mother – child and sibling pairs, but also larger configurations known as families. The members of a family who live together share a history of joint participation in a distinctive set of activities, some of which are recurrent, and they co-construct over time a shared system of meanings for interpreting events and behavior within the framework of family life.

Sameroff and Fiese (1992) proposed the expression "family code" to designate a set of factors "intermediate between the cultural influences (on child development) and individual interaction patterns. This code is not a set of stable enduring characteristics, but is an evolving regulatory system" (pp. 357–358). Three facets of the family code are rituals, routines, and stories. Together they characterize a co-constructed representation of reality – a framework within which individuals situate themselves and are situated by others in relationship to other members of the family. To link this formulation with the theoretical perspective of our study, we may note that children's engagement with such a microsystem (Bronfenbrenner, 1979) involves not only social interaction, but also participatory appropriation (Rogoff, 1993). Research by Fiese and her colleagues suggests that rituals are the most consciously accessible facet of this organizing framework, and that they not only serve to give meaning to the shared life of participants, but may also serve a protective function by sustaining an individual's sense of continuity in the face of unpredictable behavior by other individuals, and preserving relationships that otherwise might collapse under stress. Furthermore they may be considered a reflection of family identity. These authors have therefore focused on the degree of ritualization as a general characteristic of a family's life.

Inspired by this analysis, we set out to explore a set of complementary questions regarding the influence of various characteristics of family life on the socialization of cognitive development, with particular attention to the appropriation of literacy. As we noted earlier, the activities, meanings, and technology that constitute the cultural practice of literacy are encountered by children early on in contexts mediated by the family through a filter that we have termed the *intimate culture* of the family. One dimension of that intimate culture may be characterized by the family's level of investment in various interactional routines that have a strong literacy-socialization potential, such as the "mommy school" described by Mrs. G. We took advantage of an early round of interviews with part of our sample to inquire about what recurrent activities might lend themselves to such an analysis. Several families agreed that one such activity was reading storybooks at bedtime. Other routine social activities that families said were characteristic of their family life were getting ready to go to school, going shopping/to the store, and saying prayers or grace at mealtimes. In addition to parents' responses to our exploratory inquiries, we reflected from a theoretical stance on what types of opportunities for advancing the appropriation of literacy were likely to occur in the homes of children enrolled in the first and second grade, and which of these might lend themselves to an inoffensive inquiry addressed to a wide range of families. In light of these various considerations, we decided to investigate the degree of ritualization of two easily explained and potentially routine types of activity: reading aloud and doing homework.

Several researchers suggested that, in middle-class literate families, another such routine occasion may be dinnertime conversation (Dickinson & Tabors, 2001; Heath, 1983; Schieffelin & Eisenberg, 1986). As a benchmark for comparison with Fiese's samples, we therefore replicated her Dinner Time scale, as well as devised two new scales in parallel format for the activities of reading aloud and doing homework. Fiese and her colleagues (Fiese & Kline, 1993; Fiese et al., 1993) examined the reliability with which different members of a family describe the characteristics of recurrent, routine activities that make up their family's rituals, and they standardized their assessment in terms of eight dimensions across each of seven different settings, one of which is "Dinnertime." The Dinner Time scale was administered as part of our fourth parental interview, when the focal children were in kindergarten or first grade, whereas the other two scales were administered in the fifth interview, when the children were in first grade. (See Serpell, Sonnenschein, Baker, & Ganapathy, 2002, for Fiese's scale and our two new scales, as well as further details about this investigation of family routines.)

Investment Scores

In our analysis of how ratings on these family routine scales are related to other variables, we emulated Fiese's strategy of creating subscales derived from factor analysis to represent different types of investment by the family in each activity. These are referred to, respectively, as investment in (1) Dinnertime as a regular, inclusive tradition; (2) Reading Aloud as a regular, valued tradition; and (3) Doing Homework as a role-specific, valued tradition. We examined the relations among a family's scores on these three investment subscales and found a moderate correlation between Reading Aloud and Doing Homework.[14]

We did not embark on this set of analyses with strong hypotheses about the exact impact on literacy development of particular dimensions of family culture or about their distribution across social groups. Nevertheless, the relations that we found lend themselves to some *ex post facto* interpretation. The finding that middle-income parents attributed on average more meaning to Dinnertime as a family ritual than lower-income parents is consistent with other reports in the literature that dinnertime conversation constitutes a valued practice of middle-class American culture (Dickinson & Tabors, 2001; Heath, 1983; Schieffelin & Eisenberg, 1986). An additional finding that maternal education was associated with a higher level of investment in doing homework as a family routine may be a reflection of the greater incorporation of mainstream cultural values within family life by families with more advanced degrees of parental education, which are overrepresented in the higher socioeconomic strata.

The family ritual scales were only moderately successful in capturing significant variation across families in their socialization of literacy. Nevertheless, the approach of seeking to identify family routines

[14] $r(64) = .28, p < .05$.

as a form of social organization of behavior above the level of dyads appears to us worth pursuing further in research on the sociocultural context of child development. The notion that parents may vary in the type of meaning they invest in such recurrent activities with their children is further elaborated in the next two sections of this chapter.

CULTURAL THEMES ABOUT THE MEANING OF
LITERACY DEVELOPMENT

The Skills Perspective on Literacy Socialization

Common sense points to the crucial significance of skill acquisition in the process of becoming literate. Obviously, the child must master a new skill, one that differs from her pre-existing skills of perception and speech in being less "natural" and less directly related to survival. Even in the highly literate world of contemporary American society, there are situations in which an able-bodied individual with intact senses and oral fluency in the natural language of the community could survive quite satisfactorily without any knowledge of a writing system, for instance, eating a meal at home, planting vegetables in the garden, or building a sand castle on the beach. Children, before they become literate, are routinely included in such activities and generally show themselves to be highly competent in such contexts. Yet, we regard them as much less competent to purchase food in the store, to find out where a movie is showing, or to plan a trip to the beach. These tasks depend on the ability to read texts, whose content – if it is read aloud to the child – is quite easy for her to understand.

The critical hurdle for becoming literate, it seems, is learning the code in which written texts are secreted. Moreover, the early steps of instruction are well known: the child must know her alphabet and her numerals. From this perspective, it seems evident that the central challenge of becoming literate consists of mastering codes. Once these are mastered, the child will be able to perform for herself the decoding process through which we explain to her what to do next as we guide her through those literate tasks of choosing an affordable item and paying for it in the store, searching in the newspaper or on the Internet for show times, and looking up a route to the beach with a map and a train timetable.

Yet there is something missing in this analysis. To be functionally literate, the child needs to know more than how to decode texts. She also needs to understand and appreciate the point of doing so – to appropriate the sense of purpose that infuses literate activity. An excessive focus on mastery of the techniques of reading and writing may in some cases actually interfere with the child's development on the plane of this broader appreciation of the functions and potential of literacy. Some professional educators became aware of this early in the 20th century, and advocated an early emphasis on helping children to grasp the meaning of texts before they have fully mastered the letter-sound correspondence rules that inform basic decoding. The resistance encountered by this idea, and the ensuing debate that raged throughout most of the century, is discussed in Chapter 6, as part of the context of curriculum guidelines in Baltimore public schools at the time of our project.

Our first intimation of variations in the degree to which families emphasize certain cultural themes about the socialization of literacy came from a qualitative examination of the content of the parent diaries (Baker et al., 1994). The following excerpt from the diary of Amina kept by her mother, Mrs. A, introduced earlier, illustrates the focus on explicit cultivation of literacy skills:

After the movie go off between 2:45 and 3:35, Amina and I sit down to do her homework. We goes over her homework. She has to learn ABC's. She already knows her ABC's, but she have to renew them everyday. She have to count from 0–30. She have 3 words, she have to name cat, dog and ball. Everyday she gets a different word.

Another mother with a similar emphasis was Mrs. C,[15] a low-income European American mother of three. During the first eco-logical inventory interview, Mrs. C indicated that educational activities were important to her, that she read to her children every night and that they would sometimes "make up homework" and that she "works with them" on their numbers. Forty-five percent of the diaries kept by parents of children in prekindergarten and 58% of those kept by parents of children entering first grade made spontaneous mention of one or more recurrent activities in the home that were explicitly

---

[15] Mrs. C6.

designed to afford the child an opportunity to practice literacy skills (Baker et al., 1994; Baker, Fernandez-Fein, Scher, & Williams, 1998).

Other studies of parental ideas and beliefs have reported similar findings in low-income American communities. McLane and McNamee (1990), for instance, wrote that the low-income African American mothers of the children they worked with in a Head Start program in Chicago "organize reading and writing activities for their children [that] resemble school lessons" (p. 107). Goldenberg, Reese, and Gallimore (1992) interpreted their extensive interactions with low-income Hispanic families in Los Angeles as showing that the parents believe that "learning to read (not necessarily the act of reading itself) is a process of learning decoding and other skills, not a process driven by children's interest in making meaning from texts . . . " (p. 504). As we discuss here, our findings in the Early Childhood Project confirm the pattern reported by Fitzgerald, Spiegel, and Cunningham (1991), that parents with low levels of education in low-income neighborhoods endorsed the use of explicitly skills-focused workbooks and flash cards more strongly than more highly educated parents in higher-income neighborhoods.

Several indices were used to determine whether parents had a skills perspective on children's literacy development. The content of each diary was coded for print-related activities that reflected each of three broad cultural themes informing the kinds of print-related experiences parents make available to their children: (1) literacy as a set of skills that should be deliberately cultivated, (2) literacy as an ingredient of everyday life, and (3) literacy as a source of entertainment (which we discuss in the next section of this chapter). The categories of activity coded as informed by the skills theme were homework and other school-related activities, and practice of literacy skills. We also rated responses to the question in the second parental interview about the most effective way of helping a young child to learn to read and write. Each parent's response to this question received two codes, one for the degree to which it reflected the theme of literacy as a set of skills to be cultivated, the other for the degree to which it was informed by the theme of literacy as a source of entertainment. The coded interview responses about preferred methods of fostering a child's literacy development were then combined with the diary codings to generate two composite indices that we labeled, respectively, skills orientation and entertainment orientation.

To further validate and refine our interpretation of this dimension of variation in the family's intimate culture, we revisited this topic in the sixth round of parent interviews, conducted when the focal child was in second grade. We asked the parent to think back to when her child was in prekindergarten and kindergarten, and to consider: when children learn to read, which things do you think are important for a child to become a good reader? They were then asked to rate each of the following items on a 5-point scale from "not important" through "very important":

Skills theme
1. Encourage children to recognize letters
2. Encourage children to recite the alphabet
3. Encourage children to practice reading words from lists or cards
4. Encourage children to learn letter-sound correspondences

Everyday life theme
1. Show children how reading is useful in going to the store
2. Show children reading can be used for getting places
3. Show children reading is necessary for understanding bills and letters
4. Show children reading is useful for preparing packaged foods

Entertainment theme
1. Show children that reading books is fun
2. Encourage children to pick out books about things the child has interest in
3. Encourage children to read/look at books in their spare time
4. Encourage children to pick out books about fictional characters the child likes

These items were presented to parents in a sequence that alternated across the three categories. Ratings of the four items pertaining to each theme were summed as a theme endorsement score. The correlation between parents' skills endorsement scores and the earlier composite index (based on the diary and interview responses) was low and not statistically significant, perhaps because of differences in measurement approaches. As already noted with respect to socialization goals, expressions of belief may generally depend on a variety of situational factors.

The Entertainment Perspective on Literacy Socialization

In one sense, the acquisition of the skills of extracting meaning from print may appear to be a logical prerequisite for enjoying reading as a form of entertainment. However, an important alternative to the skills perspective described previously takes the view that the enjoyment of reading can and should be nurtured from the beginning of a child's induction into the community of literate practice. Parents in the Early Childhood Project with this perspective reported that they sought actively in their interactions with their child in the preschool period to cultivate a playful attitude toward the domain of literacy. A striking example of this orientation was cited previously in the words of Anna's mother, Mrs. D, "why make reading boring?!" The following passage from the diary of Mrs. GG,[16] a middle-income European American mother, reflects a similar orientation less explicitly. She describes her 4 $^{1}/_{2}$-year-old son Peter's opportunistic learning from everyday life, during a trip to the grocery store:

> Unload groceries
> Has a good time spelling every cereal box
> Draws on chalk board with cereal box to copy letters

Our coding of the diaries to generate a quantitative index of the entertainment theme focused on the following features: joint book reading, independent or self-initiated reading, play involving print, incidental exposure to print while being entertained, and visits to libraries and book stores. Each of these features of the child's everyday home experience reflects a unifying theme of the home's intimate culture: that becoming literate is a process centered around the discovery that literacy is a source of entertainment. Significantly more

---

[16] Mrs. G4. We use double Gs to indicate that we are referencing a second mother whose child attends School G.

middle-income parents than low-income ones reported their children independently interacted with print (Wave 1: 78% middle income, 34% low income; Wave 2: 62% middle income, 10% low income).

As part of a master's thesis conducted by Deborah Scher (1996), parents in the Early Childhood Project were interviewed about whether their child liked being read to, what it was about reading that the child liked, and what let parents know that the child liked being read to. Respondents were Wave 1 parents whose children at the time were just beginning first grade as well as a sample of middle-income parents of first-grade children attending private schools in Baltimore. Almost all the parents reported that their children did like being read to. Responses abut what the child liked fell into three broad categories: interaction or involvement with the family, the routine of being read to, and the content of the story or the pictures. Middle-income parents were significantly more likely to mention that their child liked the routine of reading than were low-income parents (Baker, Scher, & Mackler, 1997). In Chapter 4, we present data linking the affective atmosphere during book reading with children's subsequent reading motivation. These correlates of an entertainment-oriented introduction to literacy have implications for the child's later development of literacy in the early years of elementary school, which we present in Chapter 5.

The entertainment theme was more often emphasized by middle-income families in our sample than by lower-income families, whereas the latter often placed relatively greater emphasis on the theme that literacy constitutes a set of skills to be learned. A number of individuals have reacted to our previous reports of these findings (Baker, et al., 1994; Sonnenschein, Baker, et al., 1996) by suggesting that maybe the middle class can afford to be more playful and laid back about the activities of literacy because they are secure in the confidence that their children will in due course become literate and find a place in the higher echelons of society. The broad cultural theme that childhood should be a period of fun grew in Western societies during the 20th century, and it contrasts significantly with 19th century views that emphasized the need for discipline (Lightfoot & Valsiner, 1992). Although the consumerism of capitalist societies has successfully exploited this theme for marketing toys to all social classes, it may be that families with limited experience of scholastic success tend to construe the agenda of cultivating their children's literacy as too important or too difficult to trivialize with play. McLane and McNamee (1990), for instance, wrote that their sample of African American mothers of children attending Head Start "do not seem particularly interested in or comfortable with their children's playful approaches to writing and reading" (p. 107).

However, this characterization of the entertainment orientation as a middle-class luxury is arguably only a half-truth because it tends mistakenly to equate play and leisure in contrast with seriousness and work. Many psychologists and biologists have noted that play represents a pattern of activity that is highly motivated and sustained over long periods of time. It is this intense commitment that some families manage to mobilize in their child's early engagement with literacy activities by presenting the domain as a source of entertainment. Just as in earlier phases of development children become skilled walkers and talkers primarily through the experience afforded by play, children who discover the potential of the literate world for play acquire the skills of literacy more efficiently than those who only read and write when required to do so as a duty.

Play is not adequately defined by contrasting it with work or with seriousness because it is closely connected to the highly valued cultural domain of aesthetics. Indeed, "play itself contains its own, even sacred, seriousness. . . . Play fulfills its purpose only if the player loses himself in his play" (Gadamer, 1975, pp. 91–92). At a recent international conference on the theme of "creating a world of engaged readers" (Verhoeven & Snow, 2001), much emphasis was placed on the prototypical experience of getting lost in a book, referring to an exclusive concentration of the reader's attention on a self-contained domain defined by the text – typically, but not necessarily, the domain of a fictional world. This subjective dimension of reading for pleasure appears to be symbolically important for many contemporary Western literate communities.

More speculatively, Serpell (1997) suggested that the comfort around literacy activities that a child derives from learning their potential as a source of entertainment may be one of the ways in which Western middle-class families offer their children inherited membership of a dominant class. However, some children find themselves at home confronted by anxiety from adults whose own mastery of the medium is incomplete and lacks legitimacy both in their own eyes and in the eyes of the establishment (represented by the teacher and the school). Eager that their child should fare better than themselves, such parents often emphasize the importance of avoiding mistakes; of aiming for correctness, an externally defined standard; and of learning the skills and knowledge on offer from the experts. Yet, as Bourdieu (1974) explained, requests for explicit guidance will quite early on be seen as grounds for suspicion that the aspirant does not truly "belong." A literal mindedness and constant attention to detail will soon be characterized as pedestrian, whereas "the inheritors" (Bourdieu & Passeron, 1964) will be excused their spelling errors and solecisms as slips of the tongue. Thus, the social recognition as an interpretive "authority" that constitutes part of the achievement of personal literacy may in fact be denied to those who acquire it only through a painstaking mastery of technique without concomitantly appropriating a sense of its potential as a source of intrinsic pleasure.

When Delpit (1988) called for greater explicitness in the educational practices of schools for children of low-income, inner-city communities, she was partly reacting to the unfairness of this double standard and the insider camaraderie that excludes children and would-be participants from true membership of the community of literate practice. We need to recognize, however, that the middle-class discourse strategy of understatement, which Delpit attacked, not only masks the basis of membership, but also connotes a substantive dimension of ownership. The child or adult who genuinely enjoys reading and playing with language manifests her ownership of literacy precisely through her lack of self-consciousness. The very act of focusing attention on the mechanisms of such intuitive understanding is liable to undermine it, distancing the expert from her craft and depriving her of spontaneity.

The findings of the Early Childhood Project reviewed in this chapter illustrate several complementary ways in which the intimate culture of a child's home structures his or her opportunities to become literate. The pattern of everyday activities in which the child participates reflects the socialization goals of the parents. Those goals in turn are embedded in the parents' implicit theories of what literacy means, of how children develop, and of how best to promote the child's developmental appropriation of literacy. Although we acknowledge instances of strong correlations between family address and some features of the intimate culture, we contend that it is important to look beyond appearances to the underlying mechanisms or processes through which some families succeed in cultivating early literacy development, while others seemingly do not. In Chapter 4, we consider some processes through which families facilitate their children's literacy development.

4

Processes of Literacy Enculturation in the Home

In this chapter, we focus on co-constructive processes during children's participation in literacy-relevant activities with others. As discussed in Chapter 1, our views are influenced by Vygotsky's (1978) theory of the importance of sociocultural context and by Barbara Rogoff's (1990) notion of the importance of guided participation for enculturation. According to Rogoff, a key influence on a child's successful appropriation of a skill is working with a more competent partner, one who can serve as a model by demonstrating necessary competencies and who can also help regulate the difficulty level of the task so it falls within a manageable range for the child. We favor the term *co-construction* because it acknowledges the importance of collaborative processes between participants, such as sharing different perspectives and reaching consensus. The evidence we present in this chapter supports the view that the most effective form of social interaction for fostering a child's literacy development is one that affords the child opportunities to play an active role in initiating events and generates positive affect.

We consider here both the cognitive and social-affective nature of children's interactions by documenting co-constructive processes in children's interactions with adults and peers in different literacy activities. Children growing up in industrialized societies have many opportunities to engage with printed material even before entering school. The breadth of the Early Childhood Project enabled us to observe children's interactions with others during several literacy activities. A large portion of the chapter focuses on cognitive and affective characteristics of storybook reading interactions at two points in time. We show how specific aspects of what is said about the books being read, as well as the affective nature of the interactions, impact later reading development. We also consider co-constructive processes in domains other than storybook reading through our observations of siblings playing oral word games and writing a greeting card. The final section of this chapter examines parent–child interactions on a writing task.

STORYBOOK READING INTERACTIONS

Shared storybook reading has been one of the most heavily studied of the various literacy-related activities engaged in by young children and their parents, perhaps because of its assumed relevance for fostering language development, emergent literacy skills, interest in reading, and reading development (Baker et al., 1997; Bus, 2001; Bus, van IJzendoorn, & Pellegrini, 1995; Purcell-Gates, 2000; Scarborough & Dobrich, 1994; Whitehurst & Lonigan, 1998). Two independent reviews of research on adult–child storybook reading interactions attempted to quantify the impact of such activities on children's literacy development (Bus et al., 1995; Scarborough & Dobrich, 1994). Both sets of reviewers concluded that (1) the frequency of storybook reading accounts for about 8% of the variance in preschoolers' literacy development, and (2) the type of talk during the reading interaction may be less important for young children than how frequently such interactions occur.

Most of the research on storybook reading interactions has considered the frequency of such interactions, what is discussed, and children's subsequent cognitive outcomes. Research investigating what children learn by reading with others has shown that reading can increase one's knowledge of the world and foster vocabulary acquisition (e.g., Senechal, LeFevre, Hudson, & Lawson, 1996), which in turn can positively impact literacy development. Reading certain forms of text can increase phonological awareness and word recognition, as we discuss in Chapter 5. Until recently, however, much of the research on storybook reading interactions focused on the cognitive aspects of the interactions without considering the relevant social components. Shared storybook reading is by definition a social activity and characteristics of the social interaction may affect children's interest in reading, which in turn affects the growth of reading skills.

As we noted in Chapter 1, shared storybook reading is just one of various recurrent activities in which a child may routinely encounter opportunities at home to interact with adults about literacy. Heath's (1983) landmark study compared it with other types of literacy events across three different communities in the United States (Maintown, with middle-income African American and European American residents; Roadville, with working-class European American residents; and Trackton, with low-income African American residents). Heath's study documented stylistic differences in how parents from these communities interacted with their children in activities involving oral language and literacy. Roadville parents, when they did read with their children, seldom attempted to relate the text to their children's lives, whereas this was the normal practice among Maintown parents when reading with their children. Trackton parents did not read much to their children. Unlike many middle-income parents, Trackton parents also did not engage in known-answer question routines with their children. Another difference between Trackton parents and the other two groups of parents was in their oral narratives practices. Roadville parents told their children stories about actual events. These stories followed a chronological storyline. In contrast, parents in Trackton encouraged creativity in narratives more than veridical content or chronological storylines.

Other researchers have found relations between type of text, familiarity of text, and nature of talk during reading interactions. For example, Pellegrini, Perlmutter, Galda, and Brody (1990) showed that low-income African American mothers in Georgia interacted differently with their preschoolers when reading expository versus narrative text. Mothers were more likely to elicit their children's participation and ask cognitively demanding questions when reading expository text. This type of interaction is widely advocated by educators for promoting children's understanding of all texts, but was apparently more readily triggered for these parents by the communicative load of expository text.

The longitudinal design of the Early Childhood Project enabled us to collect a wider range of information than is typically available in one study. Our analysis of shared storybook reading in children's homes: (1) examines both cognitive and social affective aspects of reading interactions, (2) uses quantitative and qualitative analytic approaches, (3) considers how the nature of the material impacts the process by comparing reading of familiar and unfamiliar text, (4) considers similarities and differences in the nature of the interaction between sibling and adult readers, (5) examines how the pattern of interactions changes over the course of development, (6) documents similarities and differences between the ways an adult reads to a child and the ways children read aloud, and (7) explores similarities and differences among sociocultural groups.

Describing Storybook Reading Interactions
With Preschool-Age Children

Type of Talk

According to Snow (1994), the talk that occurs during reading interactions is at least as important as the actual reading of the story: "Talk is the site of the learning; book reading is important because it is the site of the talk" (p. 271). Talk about nonimmediate content is the type of talk that Snow considered particularly relevant for literacy development, especially reading comprehension. Such talk can "convey novel information to audiences who may share only limited background knowledge with a speaker or who may be physically removed from the things or events described" (Whitehurst & Lonigan, 1998, p. 851). Engaging in talk about nonimmediate content, such as asking the child to predict or evaluate outcomes, encourages the development of the child's higher-level reasoning and comprehension skills. Snow called this type of talk *decontextualized language*, but we consider this term misleading because using this type of language still requires tailoring communications to a specific context.

Snow (1991, 1994) argued that the literate genre is different from a conversational one (see Olson, 1994). It is experience with the literate genre, with its focus on extended discourse for audiences of diverse backgrounds, that allows a child to develop certain language skills, including abilities to reflect on language, to discuss abstract issues, and to tailor communications to different audiences that, in turn, fosters comprehension skills when reading. Rereading and discussing already familiar stories is particularly effective in fostering these skills because the type of talk engaged in when discussing familiar text differs from that used when the text is unfamiliar (Pellegrini et al., 1990; Phillips & McNaughton, 1990). Because the child is presumably familiar with the storyline of a previously read book, discussion can more readily focus on topics conducive to the development of more abstract or higher-level reasoning skills, such as the motivation of characters.

Kim Munsterman (1996; Sonnenschein & Munsterman, 2002) examined shared reading interactions as part of her master's thesis, conducted within the Early Childhood Project. Participants were 30 dyads recruited during the first wave of enrollment into our study. The sample was predominantly low income (13 low-income African Americans, 12 low-income European Americans, 3 middle-income African Americans, and 2 middle-income European Americans). Sociocultural differences were not explored due to the small and unbalanced sample size. Children were entering kindergarten at the time we observed their reading interactions. These children were selected because their parents had indicated on the ecological inventory that their child engaged in reading interactions with others at home at least once a month.

A few days before the scheduled home visit, a research assistant telephoned the parents to determine who usually read with the focal child. In most of the cases, the identified person was an adult. In seven cases, it was an older sibling between the ages of 8 and 12 years. Parents were asked if we could videotape their child reading two books, a familiar one, available in the home, and an unfamiliar one, to be provided by us. The unfamiliar book was *The Wolf's Chicken Stew* (Kasza, 1987). In the few cases where the family had no available favorite book, we also provided *Where's That Bus?* (Browne, 1991).

Upon arriving at the child's home, the research assistant asked the parent to choose a place in which the dyad usually read and the video equipment was set up there. Dyads were told, "We would like the two of you to read a story like you normally would. Try if possible to pretend we are not here and act as natural as possible." The camera was then turned on, and the research assistant left the room or pretended to be busy, remaining as unobtrusive as possible. Dyads first read the familiar book, followed by the unfamiliar one. In three cases, only one book was read due to either the reader's request to discontinue or the child's inattentiveness or misbehavior.

We adapted Morrow's (1988) method of classifying utterances, which were defined as complete thoughts, typically a phrase or sentence in length. Utterances were coded as focused on content (immediate or nonimmediate), organizational/story structure, and print/skills. Immediate content talk was conversation about facts or ideas explicitly presented in the text (e.g., "Is the chicken getting fat?"). Nonimmediate content talk was speech that requires one to go beyond what is explicitly stated in the text, calling for inferences, prediction, or relating to previous experiences (e.g., "Do you think he's gonna get his chicken stew?"). Organizational/story structure talk was speech about the structure of the story, such as reference to characters or setting (e.g., "All this took place on a rainy day."); it also included reference to previous readings of the text (e.g., "Remember when we read this before?"). Print/skills speech was any comment about print that would make children more aware of grapheme-phoneme associations or increase their graphemic knowledge (e.g., "What's that word? . . . Spell it.").

As shown in Table 4.1, the most common type of remark made about the books focused on the immediate content. Approximately 45% of remarks were so classified. The other three types of remarks were rarely made. The overall number of utterances and their distribution across types were comparable for the familiar and unfamiliar text. The amount of talk about story content, whether immediate or nonimmediate, was related to children's later reading motivation, assessed in first grade (see Chapter 5 for more details).[1] First graders displayed higher reading motivation when their earlier reading interactions included more talk about content.

Multiple regression analyses further explored how characteristics of the storybook reading interactions were related to children's early literacy development assessed at the end of kindergarten

---

[1] Immediate content and reading motivation r (27) = .37, p = .05, nonimmediate content and reading motivation r (27) = .40, p = .05.

TABLE 4.1. *Mean Frequency of Types of Talk During Storybook Reading Interactions and Total Affective Quality Ratings When Children Were Entering Kindergarten*

	Reader	
	Parents	**Siblings**
Familiar book	$N = 13$	$N = 7$
Immediate content	6.46	3.38
Nonimmediate content	2.38	2.75
Organizational/story structure	1.69	4.00
Print/skills	2.00	.63
Total utterances overall	12.54	10.75
Total affective score	11.69	8.71
Unfamiliar book	$N = 20$	$N = 7$
Immediate content	7.05	1.86
Nonimmediate content	1.50	.43
Organizational/story structure	3.2	2.00
Print/skills	.65	.00
Total utterances overall	12.40	4.29
Total affective score	11.11	8.57

Note: Mean frequency of types of talk refers to the number of times a certain type of talk occurred during the reading interaction.
Source: Adapted from Sonnenschein, S., & Munsterman, K. (2002). The influence of home-based reading interactions on 5-year-olds' reading motivations and early literacy development. *Early Childhood Research Quarterly, 17*, 318–337, with permission from Elsevier.

(see Sonnenschein & Munsterman, 2002). Only reading frequency significantly predicted children's early knowledge about the meanings and uses of print.[2] The more children read, the higher they scored on measures tapping their knowledge about print. The impact of the affective quality of the interactions on children's reading motivation is addressed in the next section.

Affective Quality of Reading Interactions
The affective quality of a reading interaction is important because a positive social interaction should be more likely than a neutral or negative one to foster a positive attitude toward reading in the young

[2] R^2 change .27, F (R^2 change) = 10.19 ($p = .004$), B .53, Beta .52.

child. Bus and van IJzendoorn (1988) found that the atmosphere during reading interactions was more positive when children's attachment to their parents was secure. Such children appeared less distractible and their mothers engaged in less discipline during reading • interactions. More recently, Bus (2001) suggested that when the attachment patterns are less secure, parents might be less successful in "creating engaging and enjoyable contexts for reading" (p. 181).

Leseman and de Jong (1998) investigated both cognitive and social aspects of reading interactions in a longitudinal study conducted in the Netherlands with low- and middle-income Dutch, Surinamese-Dutch, and Turkish-Dutch, families. The children in the study, 4 years old at the outset, were observed reading a book with their parents once a year for a 3-year period. Even after accounting for children's early language skills and their socioeconomic status, instructional quality of the reading interactions and cooperation between participants were significant predictors of children's reading achievement when they were 7 years old. Better instructional quality meant that parents used comments or questions that required the child to use abstract thinking and language to go beyond the immediate content of the text. Leseman and de Jong speculated that the impact of social-emotional quality on reading achievement may be indirect, such that it influences either the opportunity for engaging in reading activities or the quality of discussion, which in turn could affect later reading achievement.

Within the Early Childhood Project, we examined the relation between the affective quality of shared storybook reading and children's subsequent motivation for reading. Our measure of affective quality was a composite based on ratings of observable behaviors that reflected an enjoyable, engaging interaction. The reader's behavior was coded for reading expression, physical and visual contact with the child, appearance of engagement in the activity, and sensitivity to the child's engagement (see Sonnenschein & Munsterman, 2002, for further details). The better the affective environment during the reading interaction, the stronger the children's subsequent motivation for reading. Affective quality of the reading interactions in kindergarten accounted for 18% of the variance in children's motivation at the start of first grade. Affective quality accounted for 23% of the variance when motivation for reading was again assessed at the end of second grade.

Quality of Reading Aloud: Parents Compared With Older Siblings

Most studies of storybook reading have used an adult reader, either a family member (typically the child's mother) or the researcher. Such an approach is valid in families where the child is normally read to by a parent. However, what is accepted as a cultural practice in middle-income European American families may be less common in low-income families or families from different ethnic backgrounds.

Older siblings may contribute more to the socialization of younger siblings' cognitive development in low-income families or in families of non-European heritage. For example, Heath (1983) discussed how school-age siblings played a larger role in language socialization of younger siblings in her low-income African American community (Trackton) than in her working-class European American community (Roadville). Weisner (1989) found that Hawaiian children engaged in literacy activities with siblings rather than adults. As reported in Chapter 3, our ecological inventory data indicated a similar pattern of income-based differences in the tendency to engage in literacy activities with adults or older adolescents.

Recall that we observed reading interactions involving the focal child and the person who most commonly reads to him or her. In seven families, the reading partner was an older, preadolescent sibling. This enabled us to compare whether the reading interactions differed depending on whether the reader was a parent or sibling. Such a comparison is of interest in view of theoretical speculation about the differential impact of working with experts and nonexperts on tasks. For example, Rogoff (1990) suggested that adults may be better than children in establishing intersubjectivity or shared understanding between themselves and their partner even when the children are proficient at a task. Her review of research on dyadic interactions across a variety of tasks that involved different cognitive skills yielded the following conclusions: adults were effective as teachers when they made their internal thought processes explicit, tailored their instruction to the child's changing level, encouraged the child to think about longer-term and more immediate goals, focused the child's attention on key elements, and made their comments contingent upon what the child was discussing or gazing at. Rogoff acknowledged that her conclusions might not generalize to societies or cultures where peers play a larger, caregiving role with their younger siblings than is the practice in middle-class European American families. Furthermore, the results might not apply to tasks where peers view themselves as expert in a domain.

We turn now to our own analyses, with the caveat that conclusions must be tentative given the small number of siblings who served as readers. We found no significant differences in the type of talk used by adult and sibling readers when reading familiar books, but with unfamiliar books, adult readers made significantly more remarks, particularly about the content (Table 4.1). Regardless of whether the text being read was familiar or unfamiliar, the affective quality of the interactions was significantly higher with adult readers than with sibling readers. To understand these differences in affective ratings, we compared how the adult and sibling readers interacted with their partners along several dimensions.

The sibling readers were less fluent readers than the adults, reading in a more halting manner and making more errors. Ninety-two percent of the adults were rated as fluent readers when reading familiar text and 85% of them were rated as fluent when reading unfamiliar text. In contrast, only 50% of the siblings were considered fluent readers with familiar text and 33% were so rated with unfamiliar text. Even when the sibling readers were considered to be fluent readers, their reading style was less expressive than that of the adults.

The difference in reading fluency may account, at least in part, for why siblings were less likely than adults to hold the attention of their listeners, as judged by whether the listener appeared to be "on-task" for most of the story reading. With the unfamiliar book, 14% of the listeners appeared to attend to the book when the reader was a sibling compared with 55% when the reader was an adult. With the familiar book, 25% of listeners attended to sibling readers and 83% to adults.

When the listener's attention wandered off-task, siblings were more likely than adult readers to ignore their listener's inattention (unfamiliar text: sibling 71%, adult 17%; familiar text: sibling 67%, adult 0%). When siblings did attempt to re-engage their listener's interest, they tended not to use particularly effective techniques. For example, one sibling elbowed the listener as a means of re-engaging him. In contrast, adults either told the child to pay attention or stopped reading. However, in only one case did the adult use the text to refocus the child's attention. Readers rarely asked a question about the text or modulated their voice to recapture a listener's wandering attention.

Sibling readers seldom interacted with their child listeners beyond just reading the words of the text. Because reading fluency was higher for familiar text, difficulties in reading should have been less of an impediment to interaction. However, there was little or no interaction in 63% of the cases when the siblings read a familiar book. What interaction occurred was more commonly initiated by the listener. There was even less interaction between participants when the text was unfamiliar: 71% of the sibling reader dyads displayed little or no interaction.

When the reader was an adult, there was some interaction in almost all cases, although the interaction was, at times, quite limited. Only one adult reader routinely ignored questions by the listener; in contrast, ignoring questions was fairly common when the reader was a sibling. Familiarity of the text also influenced the performance of the adult readers, in that only one-half of the observed sessions were characterized by interaction when the text was unfamiliar.

Who initiated interactions within a dyad when they occurred? Adult readers were more likely than sibling readers to direct or control the interaction when the text was unfamiliar (33% of adult readers, 14% of sibling readers). A similar pattern occurred with familiar text, with adult readers (41%) more likely to initiate interactions than sibling readers (25%). The listeners initiated more of the interactions when listening to familiar text than unfamiliar text.

Let us now return to the differences between adult and sibling readers in the affective quality of the reading interactions. As previously suggested, at least some of the differences in affective quality may have been attributable to differences in reading fluency between sibling and adult readers. If all one's effort goes into decoding, less effort is available for other things such as modulating one's expression to make the text more interesting or monitoring a listener's engagement with the task. Moreover, it is likely that the effort required of a limited proficiency reader to read aloud was itself a negative affective dimension of the activity for many of the older siblings. It is undoubtedly difficult to inspire pleasure in an activity if one experiences no pleasure with it oneself.

Relations Between Storybook Reading Interactions in Kindergarten and Reading Competencies in Third Grade

Were there any long-term outcomes associated with these storybook interactions? To address this question, we examined the correlation of key interactional variables with children's basic reading skills and reading comprehension composite scores on the Woodcock-Johnson. The ability to detect significant patterns was limited by the fact that only 19 of the original 30 children who were observed during storybook reading also took the reading tests in third grade. The type of talk that took place during the shared storybook readings did not relate to subsequent reading competence, regardless of whether the text read was familiar or unfamiliar. Similarly, affective quality was not significantly related to reading competence. However, with unfamiliar text, one aspect of affective quality was related to subsequent reading scores. Children who listened to readers who modulated their voices more scored higher on basic reading skills and reading comprehension in third grade.[3] Modulation, or expressiveness, may be important because it enhances the interest level of the listener, and it provides a model of an important component of fluent reading.

The Nature of Storybook Reading Interactions Between First Graders and Their Parents

By the end of first grade a child has received almost a full year of formal instruction in reading. Because most of the research on parent–child reading interactions has been conducted with preschool children, our knowledge of reading interactions once children begin formal instruction is limited. The design of the Early Childhood Project allowed us to address this gap. We examined the nature of the reading interactions, relations between interactions and children's subsequent reading development, and changes in interactional styles over

---

[3] $r\,(16) = .51, .58; p = .03, .01$, respectively for basic skills and reading comprehension.

time. We videotaped mother–child reading interactions in the children's homes when they were in the spring semester of first grade. We brought with us two storybooks, *Don't Wake Up Momma!* (Christelow, 1992) and *Tucking Mommy In* (Loh, 1988), chosen to be unfamiliar to the children. These books had reading levels appropriate for children between 4 and 8 years of age. Mothers were told that they and their child should choose which of the two books they wanted to read. We emphasized that mothers and children should behave as naturally as possible, doing what they normally would when reading together (see Baker, Mackler, Sonnenschein, & Serpell, 2001, for a full report of this study). Implicit in our instructions was that children could read to their mothers or mothers could read to the children.

We used a coding scheme similar to the one we had used for the kindergarten storybook readings, with the addition of several categories to better capture developmental changes in reading styles. One new category was picture talk, which referred to comments about pictures found in the text. Another was talk related to word recognition, defined as assistance the parent provides to help the child read the printed text (using references to pictures or context clues, stating the word, helping with the sounds or letters of words). As before, in addition to coding the type of talk, we coded the affective quality of reading interactions.

Sixty-one dyads participated in the reading interaction. Thirty-four of the dyads had the parent as a reader and the remaining 27 had either the child as a reader, or both the child and parent took turns as readers. Usually, in 73% of the cases, the mother allowed the child to select the book that the dyad would read by asking the child which one he or she wanted, by telling the child to pick a book without giving any guidance, or by telling the child to look through both books and then choose one. In about 9% of the cases, the mother selected the book to read without any consultation with her child. In the remaining 18% of the cases, the dyad, led by the mother, either discussed the titles of the two books or discussed what the books were about. This latter pattern is illustrated in the following interchange between a a middle-income mother (G9) and her child. The mother said, "There are two books here, *Tucking Mommy In* and *Don't Wake Up Momma!*." She held up both books for the child to see. The child said, "I don't like that (points to *Tucking Mommy In*). The mother replied,

TABLE 4.2. *Mean Number of Different Types of Comments During Storybook Reading Interactions When Children Were in First Grade*

	Reader	
	Child	Adult
Type of Talk	$N = 27$	$N = 34$
Organizational/story structure	.48	.44
Immediate content	2.00	1.44
Nonimmediate content	3.56	3.09
Comments about pictures	4.11	4.71
Talk about print	37.81	2.24
Word recognition strategies	3.11	0.15
Word provided	30.15	1.41

Note: For all but two categories, word recognition strategies and word provided, either the mother or child could have uttered the comment. Word recognition strategies and word provided were coded only when the mother uttered the comment. Mothers either told children strategies for decoding words (word recognition strategies) or stated the word (word provided). The column marked "Child" reader included dyads in which the child did all or almost all the reading and dyads where the child and parent alternated reading.

"You don't like that? You like monkeys, don't you?" (referring to characters in *Don't Wake Up Momma!*).

The distribution of various types of comments on this task is presented in Table 4.2. Relatively little talk about the text being read took place, either during the actual reading or afterward. Most comments were about the content of the story, either immediate or nonimmediate, with mothers making on average about nine comments. Twelve mothers (about 20%) never made any comments about the text to their children. There were no significant differences due to whether the child or the mother was the primary reader in the number of comments across categories, with the exception of talk about word recognition. As shown in Table 4.2, there was more discussion about ways to recognize words when the reader was a child rather than an adult. In fact, there was almost no talk focusing on word recognition when the parent read to the child. When such talk occurred it was in response to errors made in decoding by the child reader. This lack of discussion about print by parents when reading stories to their children parallels what we found when children were a year and a half younger.

This finding is also consistent with reports from other researchers that storybook reading does not appear to be a preferred venue for explicitly teaching children word recognition skills (see Baker, Fernandez-Fein, et al., 1998; Philips & McNaughton, 1990). Instead, it may be conceived as a venue for engaging in an enjoyable interaction with a child, which in turn may foster an interest in learning to read. Our use of the term *venue* here is similar to James Gibson's (1979) notion of affordances or Leont'ev's (1981) notion of activity settings. These terms highlight the importance of the context in which activities occur, as it is the interaction between a person and the environment that fosters development. One feature of an activity setting that constrains the range of interactive opportunities it affords is the implicit purpose for which the co-participants have agreed to engage in joint activity. With respect to the recurrent activity of shared storybook reading, the social convention that emerges in most families is that the purpose of getting together has more to do with entertainment than with cultivating skills (a distinction that we discussed in Chapter 3).

Comments about print occurred when the reader made an error or could not decode a word. In assisting the child to recognize words, mothers typically told the child the word or mentioned picture clues as opposed to commenting on the sounds or letters. For example, Mrs. G, a middle-income parent we introduced in Chapter 3, helped her daughter Amina decode the word "tucking" by pointing to a picture in the book of two children tucking their mother into bed: "What are they doing with her?" Mrs. G then answered her own question by stating, "They're tucking her in. That says tucking." In another instance, Mrs. G explicitly told Amina to use the picture to figure out a word. Assisting a child to read a word by pointing to a relevant picture will help the child with that particular word in that particular context. It will also minimize time spent away from discussing the content of the story that, as we discuss later, maintains a more positive affective atmosphere. However, it does not seem to be a useful strategy to foster skills in decoding because the child has not learned a viable technique that can be applied when there are no pictures.

A fairly common occurrence was for the mother to ask the child a question requiring rote recall of some aspect of the story. Sometimes these questions addressed facts central to the main theme of the story, but others were about less pertinent details. For example, one low-income mother (A6) read a statement about participants frosting a cake and then immediately asked her child, "Are they frosting the cake?"

Why would parents engage in discussion about material not centrally relevant to the storyline? According to Bus (2001), "To bridge the gap between the book and the child, the parent has to become both 'reader' (of the original written text), and 'creator' (of the story as actually told)" (p. 183). She noted that being a "creator" may require deviating from the actual storyline. Thus, parents might focus on details, even less central ones, that they think would be of interest to their children or ask questions that they know their children can answer. Bus's explanation aligns well with our own emphasis on co-constructive processes in literacy appropriation. That is, the parent may reconstruct the storyline to bring it within the range of interests or competencies of the child. Alternatively, it may be the child's questions or comments that cause such reconstruction to occur.

Comments that were coded as nonimmediate content frequently related the story to aspects of the participants' lives. For example, in reading a story about children who "surprised" their mother by bringing her breakfast in bed, a middle-income mother (G8) stated, "This reminds me of you and your brothers and sisters." As teachers of reading are routinely reminded, relating stories to children's own lives engages a child's interest. Other nonimmediate remarks required the child to make predictions or helped the child make inferences about why actions had taken place. For example, one of the books told about children making a "surprise" birthday cake for their mother. In the story, the mother seemed to have slept through a din that would awaken most people. A middle-income African American mother (J6) pointed to a picture showing the mother in the story wearing earmuffs and said, "What's she got on her ears? That's why she couldn't hear anything."

After reading the book, many mothers commented to the research assistant that the book was funny or cute. Such comments are sometimes deployed as a coda by teachers at school after reading a storybook aloud to the class, and are used to summarize, clarify, or draw children's attention to aspects of the story. However, such discussions may be less typical between parents and children. In our study, children usually did not take part in any post-text discussion that the mothers had with the research assistant.

We were interested in determining the extent of open-ended questions posed about the text, because it is this type of question that is most likely to require the child to go beyond the text when formulating a response, and it is therefore most likely to foster higher-level comprehension skills (Whitehurst et al., 1998). We found, however, that our participants asked very few open-ended questions; the majority of questions were of the closed type, calling for a simple yes/no response or a known short answer. When the mothers did ask such questions, the focus was more likely to be on content that goes beyond the text (nonimmediate content), consistent with the premise noted previously.

We turn now to the affective quality of the shared storybook reading interactions. We first consider the stability of affective quality ratings over time for a subset of the families, those with children who in both kindergarten and first grade had read an unfamiliar book with a parent. The ratings of affective quality in kindergarten and first grade were significantly and strongly correlated.[4] This suggests that individual differences across families in the affective quality of shared storybook reading may get established quite early and thereafter be maintained.

Overall, affective quality of the first-grade reading interactions did not vary according to who the reader was. Affective quality was greater when there was more talk about pictures and about nonimmediate content.[5] One would not necessarily expect all dimensions of the affective quality composite to be related to the type of talk occurring during discussion of the text. Of most interest was whether children's engagement in the task was related to what was said because this could have implications for children's reading development. Children's engagement was significantly and positively related

---

[4] As the data for the type of speech were significantly skewed, all analyses were based on log(10) transformations of the proportion of different types of remarks during the first-grade reading interactions. However, the untransformed proportions or frequencies are presented in the text and tables. Correlations between affective quality ratings and types of talk: talk about pictures r (55) = .45, p = .000; talk about nonimmediate content r (55) = .42, p = .001.

[5] r (12) = .58, p = .023.

to talk about immediate content, talk about nonimmediate content, and talk about pictures. However, children's engagement was negatively related to the amount of talk about print.[6] Thus, children appeared more engaged when talk focused on content or pictures and less engaged when talk was about print. Mothers' sensitivity to their children's engagement followed a similar pattern. Mothers themselves showed greater engagement when talk was about nonimmediate content or pictures.

Our discussion thus far has not addressed the possibility of differences in interactional patterns among the four sociocultural groups. Heath (1983) noted differences between middle-income and working-class families in their storybook reading styles, with working-class families less likely to discuss and relate text to children's lives. She perceived these differences to be part of the mismatch between home and school experienced by children of certain social addresses. Bus, Leseman, and Keultjes (2000) observed cultural differences in storybook reading interactions among Dutch, Surinamese-Dutch, and Turkish-Dutch families in the Netherlands. Although all the parents had low income levels, their reading habits and enjoyment of reading differed, with Dutch parents reportedly reading more books and journals for pleasure than parents in the other two groups. Dutch parents were more likely to simplify text for their children when the vocabulary was too difficult and to initiate discussion relating the story to their children's lives. As discussed previously, the negotiation of meaning and discussion that goes beyond immediate content of stories is considered important for children's literacy development. Bus et al. (1995) attributed the differences in interactions to the parents' literacy levels and their personal enjoyment of reading, but also acknowledged the possible role of cultural mores about child-rearing.

Analysis of sociocultural differences in the reading interactions we observed during first grade partially supported Heath's findings. Middle-income European American families made more nonimmediate content remarks ($M = 5.87$) than did low-income European American families ($M = .88$). However, the two African

---

[6] Correlations between children's engagement and types of talk: talk about immediate content r (55) = .30, $p = .026$; talk about nonimmediate content $r = .39$, $p = .003$; talk about print r (55) $= -.35$, $p = .008$.

American groups did not differ from one another (low-income African American $M = 3.25$; middle-income African American $M = 3.67$), nor did they differ from the European American families. The four groups were similar with respect to the frequency of other types of remarks and the affective quality of their interactions.

Relations Between Parent Beliefs About How Children Learn To Read and Storybook Reading Interactions in First Grade

In Chapter 3 we discussed the importance of an entertainment orientation toward literacy, that is, an emphasis on making literacy-relevant interactions enjoyable and engaging for a child. Would parents who more strongly hold an entertainment perspective for early literacy development interact differently with their children than those who more strongly hold a skills perspective?

The preference expressed by parents for how to facilitate their children's reading development was indeed reflected in the nature of their dyadic storybook reading interactions. The degree to which a parent emphasized entertainment or engaging a child's interest was positively related to the overall affective quality of the first-grade reading interactions.[7] At a more specific level of analysis, parents who more strongly endorsed an entertainment approach were more sensitive to their children's engagement in the reading task and modulated their reading expression more.[8] In addition, parents who more strongly favored an entertainment orientation talked less about print, whereas those who more strongly favored a skills orientation talked more about print.[9] Our interpretation of this set of relations is that the higher sensitivity of these entertainment-oriented parents enabled them to detect that their children became less engaged when discussions about print occurred and therefore avoided such discussions.

Relations Between Storybook Reading Interactions in First Grade and Later Reading Skills

Do certain types of talk during reading interactions predict children's subsequent reading development? Similarly, does the affective

[7] $r (40) = .38, p = .01.$
[8] $r (40) = .38, p = .01.$
[9] $r (25) = -.50, .42; p = .016, .048.$

quality of a reading interaction predict subsequent reading development? In contrast to expectations based on the "decontextualized" speech hypothesis of Snow and others, talk about nonimmediate content during reading interactions when children were in first grade did not relate to their third-grade reading comprehension. In addition, affective quality of the first-grade reading interactions was not related to children's third-grade decoding skills or reading comprehension.

There was, however, evidence of an indirect link between talk about the content of the book and children's subsequent reading ability. The affective quality of reading interactions was higher when there was more talk about the content of the book being read. Children subsequently read more when earlier reading interactions were rated higher in positive affect.[10] Children who read more in third-grade had higher reading scores.[11] The relation between frequency of reading chapter books and third-grade basic reading skills and comprehension was maintained even after we statistically controlled for differences in the children's first-grade basic reading skills.[12] In other words, the frequency of chapter book reading was predictive of *improvement* in basic reading skills between first and third grades.

We speculated that the importance of talk about nonimmediate content may vary depending on the child's level of engagement in the reading interaction. We therefore divided the sample into children who were rated as highly engaged and those who were less engaged. For children who were highly engaged, the more talk about nonimmediate content that occurred, the better their later reading comprehension.[13] For children who were less engaged, talk about nonimmediate content was not related to subsequent reading abilities. These findings suggest that, in combination, engagement and cognitively stimulating talk are important shared storybook reading ingredients that play a role in literacy development.

---

[10] $r\,(55) = .45, .31; p = .000, .04$, respectively.

[11] $r\,(55) = .59, .59; p = .000$, respectively.

[12] $r\,(54) = .32, .40; p = .049, .012$, basic reading skills, comprehension skills, respectively.

[13] Talk about pictures and basic reading skills, comprehension: $r\,(27) = -.50, -.41; p = .01, .04$, respectively. Talk about nonimmediate content and reading comprehension: $r\,(27) = .44, p = .03$.

INTERACTIONS WITH SIBLINGS ENGAGING IN OTHER TYPES OF LITERACY ACTIVITIES

Shared storybook reading is a commonly occurring form of engagement with print for many preschoolers in American society. However, such interactions are not the only opportunity children have for engaging in literacy activities with others. Reading a book when one member of the dyad is a preschooler almost always guarantees a certain asymmetry in roles, because the young child is usually not able to independently decode the words in the text. What would happen in situations where the roles are more symmetric? What does collaboration look like when tasks require different forms of cognitive competence? Would activities that do not entail the challenge of reading allow for more productive interaction between siblings than we observed during storybook reading?

As part of our visit to children's homes at the start of kindergarten, we observed children and their siblings playing several oral language games requiring the utilization of phonological skills pertinent for literacy. We also observed these child dyads composing a written message on a greeting card. Although phonological and writing skills are often called for in school settings, we designed these tasks to demand the skills in ecologically valid out-of-school contexts. Rhyming and alliteration activities often occur in the context of games, such as jump rope or hopscotch. And writing is a fairly routine daily living activity.

We focus here on the 21 dyads for whom we have usable video-taped interactions of both storybook reading and engagement in other literacy activities. Six of the children interacted with the same person across all activities, but 15 of the children were read to by someone else. The focal children were about 5 years old at this time and their older siblings were typically 2 years older ($M = 7.73$ years, ranging from 6.00 to 12.08 years). The focal children and their older siblings were asked to do the task together, but we did not specifically tell the older child to instruct the younger one.

On the same day that the storybook reading interactions were observed, the focal child and his or her older sibling were told by the research assistant that she was going to videotape them doing some things together, starting with rhyming games. The two children and the research assistant then played "One potato, two potato" followed by "Miss Mary Mack." (Pilot testing showed that both of these rhyming games were familiar to prekindergarten and kindergarten children in Baltimore.) After completing these two games, the research assistant told the children, "That was great. There are lots of games like this, aren't there? . . . Why don't you two think of one that you like to do and show it to me?" After responding with a game example or, failing that, listening to the research assistant demonstrate another one, children were asked to complete the phrase "There once was a boy named Dan . . . " with a rhyme. If necessary, the research assistant added the phrase "who lived in a . . . " Children were then asked to work together to make up their own rhyme. A similar procedure was followed afterward for tongue twisters. After these activities, the two children were asked to write a message on a postcard for a "sick" puppet familiar to all the focal child from a prior competency testing session at their schools.

Almost all the children appeared to enjoy playing the rhyming games when the research assistant participated, and 12 of the 21 pairs talked with each other during this part of the task. The number of sibling pairs interacting and the cooperation between pair members declined when it was time for the research assistant to decrease her involvement. It is difficult to tease apart whether the more limited interaction between the siblings was due to their now having slightly harder tasks to do or to their having to work without the help of the research assistant. Both factors seemed to play a part. Although the tasks were selected to reflect a range of difficulties, they all appeared to be difficult. We were surprised at the difficulty many of the children had producing rhymes because these were activities they reportedly engaged in at home.

Thirty-eight percent of the dyads never produced their own rhyme. Nine percent produced something, but it was not a rhyme. For example, one pair of siblings produced the following response after much whispering to each other, "There once was a boy named Dan who lived in a house with a dog." When rhymes were produced, they were usually produced by the older siblings. In general, there was little co-construction or interaction between the older and younger siblings on this task. Such interaction as did occur did not necessarily result in what would conventionally be considered a rhyme.

Sylvia Fernandez-Fein (1995) investigated children's rhyming and alliteration skills with 39 children from the first wave of the Early Childhood Project, as well as 20 additional children recruited from several private preschools in the city. These additional children came from middle-income families; approximately one-half were African American and one-half were European American. Children's scores on the language play tasks were compared for differences across social address, but no differences were significant. Children's production of original rhymes during the language play tasks was significantly and moderately related to their scores on individually administered measures of rhyme detection and production (described more fully in Chapter 5, see also Fernandez-Fein & Baker, 1997), suggesting that the language skills used and cultivated during informal play activities may relate to the phonological analysis skills necessary for reading.

Observations of children's interactions with each other while completing the writing task illustrated the different means that dyads used to work "together" on a task. We selected the writing task because almost all the families reported that their children made or sent cards to others. We told the children that it was the younger child's job to complete the card however he or she wanted, and that the older child should assist as necessary. A set of crayons and a card were provided, and the entire session was videotaped.

For her master's thesis, Hibist Astatke (1996) coded and analyzed the transcripts of 25 dyads on this task and examined the relations between the frequency of various types of interactive processes (instructional and engaging behaviors, and type of information exchanged) and characteristics of the card produced, as well as long-term literacy outcomes. Based on the theoretical account of African American socialization proposed by Hale (1982), Astatke hypothesized that African American children would be exposed to relatively more extensive mentoring by their older siblings so the quality of their interaction on a card writing task with a sibling would be more predictive of their literacy development than for European American children. However, she found no reliable differences in patterns of correlations across the four social addresses sampled in the Early Childhood Project.

Astatke scored the card produced by each dyad with a scheme derived from Sulzby, Teale, and Kamberelis (1989). Each card product was assigned a score reflecting the degree to which it conformed to the conventions of adult literacy. Two significant relations were found between the number of directives and corrections made by the older children and the conventionality of cards produced by the dyad. The most conventional card products emerged from interactions in which the more mature participant played a highly directive role, but they were associated with less rather than more corrections by the older child. We attribute this to the complex relations between interactive processes and immediate outcomes. Several of the older children appear to have calibrated the intensity of the guidance they offered to match their perception of the younger child's competence. No significant relations were found between the interactive processes we coded and the long-term literacy outcomes.

Reflecting on our failure to find many statistically significant relations between our measures of interactive processes and either the family's social address or developmental outcomes, we conclude that a qualitative, narrative interpretation of interactions is probably necessary for understanding the processes of co-construction. The following sample observations illustrate various ways that dyads applied their emergent understanding of literacy to writing the get well card.

Children in 23% of the dyads completed the task independently, working side by side but not together. The children chatted about what each was doing but seemed to be engaged in two separate tasks. Interaction between the two children, when there was interaction, focused on how to share or divide supplies. For example, one low-income African American dyad (E7) bickered over who would work on which side of the paper. The older child said, "You do that side and I'll do this side." The younger child said, "This is my side." The older child responded, "It's all my side." The children continued arguing until the older child changed the topic by saying, "I'm going to make a star."

For another 23% of the dyads, the older sibling completed the task with little or no consultation or discussion with the younger sibling, even when the younger sibling asked to be included. In other dyads, the pattern was reversed, with the younger child not including the older one, even when the younger child did not have the necessary skills to perform the task independently. For example, one low-income African American boy (A4) informed the research assistant that the older sibling did not know how to write but he (the younger one) did. After watching his younger brother struggle to write the letter R, the older sibling said, "This is how you make your R." The younger child maintained his independence by responding, "I make my Rs different way."

The remaining dyads displayed some form of co-construction, although its exact nature differed across dyads. In one case, the older child guided the younger child's hand. In several cases, the younger child told the older one what he wanted done and the older child did it. Sometimes the collaborative nature of the interaction was quite subtle. For example, an African American low-income dyad (B6) began the task with the older one telling the younger one, "You gonna tell me what to write." However, the older child often seemed to ignore his younger brother and wrote what he himself wanted. The older child began, "Dear Lily how are you?" The younger child said, "Write my name." The older child did not respond to the younger one but continued stating while writing, "I am sending this letter. . . . " The younger child then suggested, "I hope you feel better," but the older one responded, "No, I heard you got sick and I really hope you get well." In this case the older child may have been giving feedback about a better way to express the younger child's sentiments. A little while later the younger child repeated his request for the older one to put his name on the card. The older child responded, "I already got your name on it. . . . You can't read it because it is in cursive." Thus, the older child acknowledged the younger one's twice-voiced request and explained why the name did not seem evident to the younger child.

Regardless of the type of interaction between the focal child and older sibling, in most of the cases the younger children appeared to be enjoying themselves. However, if one views the writing task as an opportunity for the younger children to appropriate literacy skills by receiving assistance from someone more competent, then about one-half of the children did not have such opportunities. Given the nature of the interactions, it is unclear how much the remaining children would have benefited from their interactions. For example, when the older sibling in dyad E7 (quoted earlier) stated that she was going to make a star, the younger one asked how one makes a star. The older one responded, "I make it like a star." Either this older child could not be more informative or she did not understand the nature of the younger child's question.

Looking at the learning opportunities across the tasks, we were struck by how hard it was for many of the siblings to work together in a manner that would foster the younger child's appropriation of literacy. This was most apparent on the writing task, where in 50% of the cases the children did not work together. Were the tasks so difficult that the demands on the older sibling were too great to allow for collaboration? These tasks were indeed more difficult for the children than we had expected. As we stated with respect to sibling reading interactions, if the task is too hard for the older sibling, it is not reasonable to expect that sibling to serve as a coach or tutor to the younger one. However, one of the tasks simply required the completion of a line to a poem. Even on that task there was little explicitly co-constructive interaction between the children. In contrast, task difficulty did seem to play a role. When we looked at the videos of the interactions, we saw that children interacted more on the games than on the reading tasks.

Children's working together also may have been affected by additional factors. Although we told the older siblings to assist the younger ones as necessary, it was not clear that the children understood or accepted our instructions. Some of the older siblings were more intent on demonstrating their own competence than on assisting their siblings. In other cases, the younger siblings maintained that they needed no assistance and, in fact, refused offers of help. In addition, some of the dyads may have interpreted the writing task differently than we intended by turning it into a drawing task, which could more readily be completed independently. By focusing their efforts on drawing, these young, semiliterate children appropriated the task in a way that afforded them the opportunity to perform at their own level. This may well reflect one important difference between the pattern of co-construction that emerges most easily between partners without a large gap between them in relevant competencies (as was the case for the children who completed the rhyming and card writing activities) and the pedagogically oriented model of guided participation emphasized by Rogoff (1990) and others in their accounts of how a more mature partner can help a less mature one to grow within her zone of proximal development.

INTERACTIONS BETWEEN PARENTS AND THIRD GRADERS ON A CO-CONSTRUCTED WRITING TASK

During a home visit when the focal children in the Early Childhood Project were in the middle of third grade, we asked the child and his or her parent(s) to write about an enjoyable activity, engaged in together, that had taken place during the past year. We requested that the parents help their child write about the activity. We were interested in what assistance, if any, parents would provide for their children. In contrast to the reading tasks where the parents might have viewed themselves as being on display, we expected that they would view the writing task as more of a measure of the child's skill level. Accordingly, parents might be more comfortable interacting with their children or guiding their efforts. Furthermore, discussing and reminiscing about an enjoyable activity, which was an integral aspect of selecting a topic to write about, might make the writing task less threatening than the traditional storybook reading for parents whose own literacy levels are low.

As with the storybook reading interactions, we coded both the cognitive and affective aspects of the interaction from videotapes and transcripts. For the cognitive aspects, we considered three forms of parental assistance: topic selection, writing assistance, and editing. Assistance with choosing a topic was coded as minimal, medium (helps structure the task by suggesting a general topic; e.g., writing about a vacation) or high (tells the child what to write about; e.g., writing about the family's trip to Disney World). Similarly, writing assistance was coded as minimal (help with a word or two), medium (helping with more than a word or two, up to a sentence or so), or high (tells the child what to write or writes for the child). For both aspects, we coded whether the mother offered assistance in response to a request of the child or initiated such assistance independent of the child's needs. For editing, we coded whether it occurred and if so, when and what type of editing was done (e.g., checking spelling or grammar). We also looked at who seemed to control the dynamics of the entire interaction (the parent and child played equal roles, mainly the child, mainly the mother). For the affective aspects, we coded whether each participant was engaged in the task and the quality of the interaction (pleasant, neutral, or not pleasant).

We had useable videotapes and accompanying written transcripts for 42 dyads (12 low-income African American, 13 low-income European American, 5 middle-income African American, and 12 middle-income European American). In most cases, the mother was the parent who participated in this task. In one case, it was the father; in another case, both parents participated. Given that few middle-income African American families completed this task, we did not test for differences among the four social addresses. However, we did test for differences related to income and found none.

We begin with discussion of the affective ratings. In most of the cases, both the parent and the child were engaged in the task. The atmosphere was rated as pleasant in 64% of the cases ($n = 27$); in only two cases was the atmosphere considered to be unpleasant. What made the interactions so pleasant was that the participants seemed to enjoy talking about what had been a fun activity for them. Both mother and child were rated as engaged in the task in 86% of the cases ($n = 36$). Affective quality (whether engagement in the task or the atmosphere) did not relate to other aspects of the interaction.

We consider now the cognitive aspects of the interactions. How did a parent and her child decide on a topic to write about? In most cases (72%), the parents offered their children a fair amount of assistance in selecting a topic by either attempting to structure the task for them (e.g., "It is often easy to write about vacations"; 44% of the cases) or by just telling the child what to write about (28% of the cases). In slightly more than one-half of the cases, parents provided assistance selecting a topic before the child had made any response or requested assistance. In one instance, a parent rejected several ideas voiced by the child and instead insisted the child write about what the parent wanted. In several other cases, parents tried to influence their children's selections through negotiations. For example, a middle-income African American mother (J7) suggested writing about a bus trip to another state to attend a family reunion. Her child rejected the topic by saying, "No, I was bored with the bus trip." The mother responded, "But that was fun being with family." The child disagreed until his mother reminded him of an incident involving swimming and shopping. The child then acknowledged, "Yeah we were jumping in the pool and stuff," and smiled as he talked a bit more about the event. His mother laughed at his recollections. After a little more discussion, the child voiced a desire to write about that incident.

After the selection of a topic, attention turned to the actual writing. Twenty-one percent of the parents gave minimal assistance, whereas 50% gave a high level of assistance, including dictating or even writing the passage for their child. Two-thirds of the parents who gave a high amount of assistance initiated such aid before it seemed necessary. However, the amount of writing assistance given was negatively related to the child's reading skills, suggesting that parents may have been reacting to what they knew about their children's literacy skills in general beyond this one context.[14] How much assistance parents gave was also associated with their views of how to foster their children's literacy development.[15] Parents who more strongly favored a skills orientation gave more assistance with writing, independent of their child's basic reading skills.[16] In addition, parents who provided more assistance were more likely to initiate the assistance without waiting for their children to request it.[17]

Sixty-seven percent of the dyads edited the document. In almost all these cases, editing was done by the parent, who usually read over the document while the child wrote it. Parents who gave writing assistance were more likely to edit the document.[18] Editing was typically limited to checking spelling and, at times, grammar/punctuation. Discussion about actual content usually had taken place during topic selection, if it occurred at all.

Also of interest was whether there were any similarities in participants' behaviors on the shared reading and writing tasks. We did not find any significant relations. However, given the differences in the nature of the tasks and the 2 or more years that elapsed between the tasks, it might have been unrealistic to expect such relations to emerge. We did notice one interesting difference in parental behavior:

---

[14] $r(34) = -.34, -.38; p = .05, .02$ (basic reading skills, comprehension skills, respectively).

[15] $r(30) = .43, p = .015$.

[16] $r(29) = .42, p = .02$.

[17] $r(34) = -.45, -.31; p = .006, .02$ (topic selection, assistance with writing, respectively).

[18] $r(34) = .43, p = .004$.

many of the parents who had looked ill at ease when engaged in reading tasks seemed more comfortable when engaged in the writing task.
As suggested earlier, this change may have been due to their enjoying
reminiscing about a pleasurable experience or their feeling that they
were not the main focus of our attention on this task.

SUMMARY

In this chapter, we considered some of the processes involved when
young children interact with others on various literacy tasks. Our
analyses of shared storybook reading interactions suggest that the
social/affective elements are at least as important as the type of talk
for young children. Affective elements of kindergarten children's
reading interactions predicted their subsequent reading motivation
and the frequency with which they read age-appropriate text that, in
turn, predicted their reading competencies in Grade 3. In addition,
we found a significant relation between parents' approaches toward
facilitating their children's reading development and affective quality of the interaction. Parents who stressed the importance of getting
children interested in reading interacted with their children in a more
engaging manner. Affective quality was also related to the type of talk
that occurred. Higher affective ratings were associated with more talk
about immediate and nonimmediate content as well as talk about pictures. Lower affective ratings were associated with more talk about
print.

How one interacts with others during literacy activities should
be a function of several factors, including the task and one's partner. Adults appeared to be more effective partners when engaging in
storybook reading. Siblings, perhaps because of their more limited
reading fluency, did best with familiar text and tasks that were not
challenging. Not surprisingly, there appeared to be more interaction
between siblings on literacy tasks that were simpler, such as completing predictable rhymes. Nevertheless, in many cases, even when
siblings appeared competent at a task, many of them did not interact with their younger siblings in a manner that would be likely to
facilitate literacy development.

The breadth of the Early Childhood Project allowed us to observe
children interacting with others in a variety of literacy activities.

Such direct observations provide informative detail over and above parental reports of engagement in literacy activities, and throw additional light on the nature of the literacy learning opportunities available to young children. There appeared to be consistency across the different interactions. Thus, the affective ratings of storybook reading interactions were stable over time. Moreover, parents' beliefs about how to facilitate their children's literacy development were systematically related to observed interactions during storybook reading and to the type of assistance offered during the writing task.

5

The Development of Literacy Competencies and Orientations

In this chapter, we focus on literacy-related competencies and their growth. A vast amount of research has been conducted on cognitive competencies of early reading. Because it is beyond the scope of our book to provide an extensive review of this literature, we refer the reader to such sources as Kamil, Mosenthal, Pearson, and Barr (2000); National Reading Panel (2000); Neuman and Dickinson (2001); Pressley (2002); and Snow, Burns, & Griffin (1998). We examine here the course of development in cognitive skills that are necessary but not sufficient for proficiency in reading, such as phonological awareness, knowledge of the alphabet, word attack skills, and word identification (Baker, 2000). We also examine the course of development of oral narrative production, knowledge about print, story comprehension, and reading motivation. We analyze these component competencies and orientations with respect to their relations to various dimensions of intimate family culture considered in Chapter 3. We also examine how early competencies relate to measures of literacy in Grade 3, including standardized tests of word recognition, vocabulary knowledge, and passage comprehension.

In an ideal world, all the children in the Early Childhood Project would appropriate literacy in such a way that as adults they exhibit the characteristics of the expert readers studied by Pressley and Afflerbach (1995). These expert readers engaged in "constructively responsive reading" that includes (1) active processing that begins before, continues during, and persists after reading; (2) purposeful focus; (3) varying speed; (4) predictive, flexible interpretation; (5) inference and integration; (6) personalized interpretation (an important facet of appropriation); (7) review, note-taking, and reflection after reading; (8) metacognitive monitoring of their own comprehension; and (9) affective engagement with and response to the text. As the data presented in this chapter show, however, many of the children left third grade without the prerequisite skills necessary for attainment of expert status. Research shows that, too often, children who do not learn to read well by the age of 9 will struggle to become fully literate throughout the remaining years of their basic schooling and beyond (Snow et al., 1998, for the National Research Council).

In the first section of the chapter, we examine the literacy-related competencies of the children prior to formal schooling. In the second section, we examine those competencies in the primary grades. The third section focuses on the nature of the children's motivation for reading and their perceptions of reading. The fourth section of the chapter examines the developmental consequences of particular characteristics of the intimate culture, especially with respect to the different cultural themes about literacy. The concluding section of the chapter examines the developmental journeys of particular children as they make the transition from emergent to conventional readers.

CHILDREN'S COMPETENCIES PRIOR TO FORMAL SCHOOLING

When the Early Childhood Project was first conceptualized in the early 1990s, the term *emergent literacy* was just coming into common usage (e.g., Sulzby & Teale, 1991). Researchers and educators alike recognized that many of the behaviors engaged in by young children during the course of their daily lives contributed in important ways to literacy development. No longer was there a clear demarcation between nonreader and reader; rather, it was understood that children gradually appropriate the skills and orientations of a reader. Guided by this perspective on literacy, we designed tasks assessing competencies across three different strands of development: orientation to print, narrative competence, and phonological awareness. Several of the tasks were individually tailored to the unique intimate culture of each child's home; others were identical for all children.

The Development of an Orientation to Print

Long before children are conventional readers, they attend to print in their environment. They discover that the signs and labels all around them signify different products and opportunities. They notice features of the books that are being read aloud to them. They see printed materials being used around the house to accomplish different goals. They begin to recognize letters of the alphabet. All these experiences foster an orientation to print that facilitates their appropriation of literacy.

Our interest in assessing orientation to print in the Early Childhood Project arose from seminal work by Lomax and McGee (1987), who provided evidence that an orientation to print serves as a foundation for later literacy development. These researchers proposed that early reading skills are clustered into five components: (1) concepts about print – children are aware that print and reading are meaningful and that print represents objects or speech; (2) graphic awareness – children attend to the graphic details of printed letters or words; (3) phonemic awareness – children are aware that spoken words can be analyzed into their component sounds; (4) grapheme-phoneme correspondence knowledge – children know the letters of the alphabet and their associated sounds; and (5) word reading – children are able to read isolated words. Lomax and McGee studied children between 3 and 6 years of age and found that concepts about print and graphic awareness were among children's earliest developing skills, but even the oldest children continued to improve in concepts about print.

Four tasks tapping children's orientation to print were administered to the Wave 1 children in the spring of their prekindergarten and kindergarten years. (The same tasks were also administered to the Wave 2 children when they entered the project at the beginning of first grade.) Empirical evidence of the validity of the orientation-to-print strand, as well as the other two strands, is provided in Sonnenschein, Baker, et al. (1996).

Word Recognition in Environmental Context
(Environmental Print)
As discussed in Chapter 2, a distinctive feature of our methodology was the inclusion of measures that assess children's competencies

within authentic, motivating, and ecologically valid contexts. These measures have the potential to reveal strengths that might not manifest themselves in more traditional literacy assessments that more closely resemble those children experience at school. The environmental print task, inspired by Harste, Burke, and Woodward (1982), was carefully developed and pilot tested to meet these criteria.

To make the task more similar to an authentic everyday activity, we placed the task of recognizing objects within the context of unpacking grocery items, a widespread recurrent activity in Baltimore homes, as elsewhere. The items selected for inclusion were individually tailored to each child's home experiences. Parents were presented ahead of time with a list of common cereals, soft drinks, toothpastes, cookies, and canned goods, such as soups and pastas, which pilot testing had revealed were commonly used by children in neighborhoods similar to those in this study. They were asked to indicate which items they used at home on a regular basis and their child thus would be likely to recognize. These items were selected as target items for the focal child in a series of component tasks, presented in the sequence shown in Table 5.1. First, the child was asked to identify then name a product by the actual container in which it is marketed, next to identify and name it by its logo (cut out from the packaging and pasted on a card), next to identify and name it in response to its printed name, and finally to match its logo to its printed name.

These component tasks were analyzed separately (Table 5.1). Children's scores improved significantly from prekindergarten to kindergarten on all but two component tasks: Identification and Naming of Printed Word. The children performed better on the identification than on the naming versions of the Environmental Print tasks. They also performed relatively better on product and logo identification than with print identification. The prekindergarten children did best on the Environmental Print tasks where they were asked to identify products or logos from those products available in their home. In fact, the majority of children succeeded on this task, which attests to their competence in recognizing print in their environment. However, they were less often successful in using their knowledge of print to match a logo with its printed name. By kindergarten, the majority of children had become much more strategic and were able to perform this matching task, even though they were no better than in prekindergarten at the word identification task when words were

TABLE 5.1. *Developmental Changes in Children's Competencies Prior to Formal Schooling in Three Strands of Literacy Development*

	Prekindergarten	Kindergarten
Orientation to print		
Environmental print (% correct)		
Product identification	77	88
Product naming	30	51
Logo identification	65	81
Logo naming	28	51
Printed word identification[a]	43	40
Printed word naming[a]	5	11
Matching logo and printed word	46	78
Concepts about print (% correct)	32	61
Functions of print (% correct identification)	45	59
Letter knowledge (% correct)		
Uppercase letters – full alphabet	25	78
Lowercase letters – full alphabet	20	72
Uppercase letters – child's name	40	85
Lowercase letters – child's name	27	84
Narrative competence		
Narrative production (% explicit referents)	90	NA
Story comprehension (% correct)	NA	76
Storybook reading (score on 0–3 scale)	1.50	2.03
Phonological awareness		
Rhyme detection (% correct)	56	88
Alliteration detection (% correct)	47	67
Rhyme production (% correct)	28	63
Alliteration production (% correct)[a]	9	13
Nursery rhyme knowledge (score on 0–3 scale)	1.43	2.14

Note: Data are from Wave 1 children only, $N = 39$.
[a] The difference between prekindergarten and kindergarten means on these tasks was not statistically significant. All other means differed significantly.

presented without the context of the logo or product. Informal observation suggested that the children attempted to analyze the logos into the relevant letters, and then match logo and printed card from the letters. This increased skill is likely related to the fact that the children's ability to recognize letters also increased significantly during the year.

The responses children gave that did not earn full credit shed additional light on how much information about print is acquired by the time children are in prekindergarten. These alternative responses included the following categories: naming the generic product (e.g., soup instead of Campbell's chicken soup), naming some other item from the task, describing the package (e.g., describing the picture on the package – "brown bear" for Teddy Graham cookies), and producing a word that had some phonetic similarity to the product (e.g., "Kick Fruit" for Kix cereal). Naming the generic product was the most common such response (42%), occurring not only when the full packaging was available, but also when only the product logo was available. Clearly the children had already appropriated some meaning from the print on the logo or product, even when they did not exactly identify its displayed printed name.

Concepts About Print

This task, adapted from Clay (1979), explored the child's emerging concepts about print. The child was shown the storybook *Where's That Bus?* (Browne, 1991) and asked 12 questions tapping knowledge about particular letter names (two letters), word boundaries, punctuation, where on the page the story is contained (e.g., print vs. pictures), and directionality of reading (left to right, top to bottom).

Table 5.1 shows the scores of the children when tested in prekindergarten and kindergarten. Analyses revealed significant growth across the 2 years, with prekindergartners responding correctly on less than one-third of the items and kindergartners responding correctly on almost two-thirds. This growth may be attributed in part to the fact that children who did not have frequent opportunities to learn about books at home gained increasing familiarity with books at school.

Knowledge of the Functions of Print Materials

This task, adapted from Lomax and McGee (1987), assessed children's knowledge of the functions and uses of various kinds of printed materials. The nine items included in this task were a newspaper, a television guide, a telephone book, a coupon for a rebate on the purchase price of a well-known cereal (Cheerios), a calendar, a children's storybook, a handwritten grocery list, a business letter in an envelope, and a road map. The child was shown each item one at a time and asked what it was. If the child did not know the name of the item, the name was provided. The child was then asked how people use the item.

Table 5.1 shows the scores on the task. Children improved significantly in identifying the items and describing the functions from prekindergarten to kindergarten. Prekindergarten children's familiarity with functional print is evidenced by more than one-half of them being able to correctly identify a storybook, a newspaper, and a business letter. However, there was variability in children's ability to label different types of print materials and to explain how these items were used.

Because our intention in administering this task was to assess children's knowledge of print materials that were actually available in their homes, we verified that the children were in fact exposed to these items. Parents were given a list of the items used on the Functions of Print task, and asked to rate whether their child knew and had experience with each item. Almost all the parents (89%) stated that the items were familiar to their children. The remaining parents reported that their child had no familiarity with the item, but in fact most of their children demonstrated knowledge of the item's function, indicating that the parents had underestimated their children's print-related knowledge.

When children did not identify an item using the conventional labels, their responses often provided evidence of emerging knowledge. How they responded to the television guide, telephone book, coupon, and grocery list, in particular, suggested that many children who did not know exactly what these items were called nevertheless knew something about these materials. For example, both the television guide and the telephone book were usually called books or magazines. Other items were identified in terms of a general description of how they are used. For example, a price rebate coupon for Cheerios was called a ticket or something you take to the market or Cheerios store. In fact, there was only one response where the child's answer did not obviously indicate an awareness that he or she was looking at printed material. That child reported that a newspaper was something you use to eat crabs with (not the response we were looking for but an understandable one in Baltimore, where it is customary to serve steamed crabs on tables covered with newspaper!).

Letter Knowledge
This is the only one of the orientation to print tasks that is traditionally included in prereading or early reading assessment batteries.

However, even this task had some individual tailoring to the child's own experiences. Children were asked to identify the letters of the alphabet, first in uppercase and then in lowercase letters. These letters were presented one at a time on note cards. Before the uppercase task was administered, the letters comprising the child's name were removed from a randomly ordered deck of note cards. The child was shown the initial letter of his or her first name and asked to identify it. Then the remaining letters of the child's name were shown in a scrambled order for identification. Subsequently, the child was shown the rest of the letter cards and asked to identify each letter. This order (except for the letters of a particular child's name) was the same for all children. If the child made five consecutive errors, the remaining cards were spread in front of the child and he or she was asked to identify any additional letters. The same procedure was followed for lowercase letters, with the exception that the child was not asked to identify the letters of his name first. A different random order of letters was used. As shown in Table 5.1, over the course of the year children gained significantly in letter knowledge. Whereas they identified only about one-fourth of the letters correctly in prekindergarten, by late kindergarten they identified about three-fourths. Again, it is likely that explicit instruction children received at school contributed greatly to this growth.

We also examined children's knowledge of the specific letters in their names in order to determine whether knowledge of personally significant letters is greater than knowledge of letters in general. These figures, too, are shown in Table 5.1. When the children were in prekindergarten, they identified 40% of the letters in their names when tested with uppercase letters, 15% more than the identification rate for all letters. By the time children were finishing kindergarten, they identified 85% of the letters in their names, as compared with 78% overall. When the children were in prekindergarten, only 55% of them correctly identified the first letter of their name, but this figure jumped to 95% by the end of kindergarten. Although the differences were not substantial, it is clear that children were indeed more familiar with letters that connected with their personal lives.

In sum, the four tasks indicative of an orientation to print all revealed substantial growth over the course of the year between late prekindergarten and late kindergarten. This growth reflects in part the contribution of schooling, as children begin to receive explicit instruction in letter knowledge, but it also likely reflects increasing attention to the print available to them in their everyday lives. Children who performed well on one of the tasks in this cluster tended also to perform well on the other tasks. Given these correlations and the underlying logic of this set of tasks, we created a composite measure, Orientation to Print, that was used in a number of our longitudinal analyses to be discussed subsequently.

The Development of Narrative Competence

When children learn to read and write, an important task they face is learning the symbol system and other conventions of their written language. However, they bring with them knowledge of the oral language, much of which transfers from the oral modality to the written (Olson, 1977; Snow, 1991). A focus on these commonalities highlights the significance of children's oral language competence for the development of print literacy. Because children's communicative competence begins to develop very early in their lives, without explicit instruction from parents, we expected that narrative production and comprehension would be one domain of emergent literacy in which children exhibit strengths during the preschool years. Representation of experience in the form of narratives is a fundamental cognitive activity that links the members of a community, displaying cultural norms and highlighting deviations from them, and affording individuals an opportunity to define their personal identity with reference to the group. As children learn to interpret the stories they hear others tell and to express their own point of view in narrative, they are also introduced to a cultural system of meanings (Bruner, 1986; Miller & Sperry, 1988). Children in middle-class Western home settings are frequently asked to tell about their day or experiences they have had, and they also listen to others do the same (Snow & Dickinson, 1990). Although all children likely have such experiences, sociocultural differences may characterize the narratives themselves. For example, Heath (1983) suggested that low-income African American parents are more likely than others to emphasize the entertainment value of narratives for their children. Such differences could have implications for how well different groups of children fare in school if there is a mismatch between their home and school narrative styles (Michaels, 1981).

Children's experiences with narrative contribute to their early literacy development in at least two ways. One is that aspects of oral language that are important for reading comprehension appear in narrative productions, such as specifying referents clearly to avoid ambiguity and recounting events using a logical or temporal ordering (Watson, 2001). The second is that the type of reading material most commonly used in elementary school reading instruction conforms to the narrative genre (Duke, 2000); familiarity with narrative structure will facilitate comprehension.

Given the importance of narrative competence, we included several tasks in the Early Childhood Project designed to characterize this domain of development across the years. As with the orientation to print domain, some of the tasks were individually tailored to the children's personal experiences whereas others were standardized across children. Children were asked to produce a narrative account of an experience they had had with their families, and they were asked to recount an event experienced in the company of the research assistant. Children's understanding of the conventions of storybooks was assessed using a book that was familiar to them. Children's comprehension of narrative was examined by reading an unfamiliar standard story to the children and asking them a series of questions about the story.

Narrative Production

Children were asked to produce narratives about what had ostensibly been memorable events for them. Prior to seeing the children at their schools for competency testing, we asked their parents to describe to us over the telephone six recent events in the child's life that were especially fun, exciting, unusual, or otherwise memorable. These descriptions were used as prompts to elicit narratives from the child. The prompts were systematically interspersed between other competency tasks and were presented as a means of engaging the child in casual conversation. So, for example, if one of the events reported by the parent was that the child went to the beach to play and saw a friend she hadn't seen in a long time, the research assistant began, "I heard you went to the beach the other day. What was it like? What did you do there?" On each occasion, the research assistant attempted to elicit as detailed a narrative as possible by expressing interest and probing with nonleading questions.

The narrative productions were tape recorded and subsequently transcribed. A coding scheme was devised, consisting of seven categories. The first step in coding the narratives was to identify the longest narrative, defined as that which had the greatest number of clauses without intervening questions from the interviewer or substantive topic changes by the child. In an analysis reported in more detail in Sonnenschein, Schmidt, Pringle, Baker, and Scher (1996), each child's longest narrative was then coded on a scale from 0 to 2 for each of the following categories: informativeness, digressions, ambiguities, logical or temporal ordering, entertainment (i.e., how engaging it is for the listener), and evaluation (i.e., expresses a point of view about the recounted incident).

Children's narratives were most often about outings they had taken or places they had visited. About 50% of the narratives produced when the children were in prekindergarten and in kindergarten fell into this category. The remaining narratives dealt with children's interactions with friends or family, experiences the children had had, or objects they owned. Overall, the narratives children produced were informative, but did not include much detail. The narratives had few digressions and few ambiguous remarks. They tended to have a logical ordering and were reasonably entertaining.

The following narrative was produced by a low-income European American girl when she was in prekindergarten. The interviewer prompted, "So how are those fish you have doing? You still got those fish, yeah?" The child received scores of 2 on all categories except digressions (0).

But that other hamster died. But my dad's gonna get a little teeny one. He's going to get a little, teeny, baby one. About that big. But a sniffly one. Call him Sniffies. Cause he's going to sniff you. The Chinese and the American one. But, but the Chinese I like cause he sniffs me. He sniffs me a lot. And know why? Cause he smell that food! Hamster food, that's it.

The global ratings of children's narratives were fairly constant from prekindergarten to kindergarten. Analysis of the narratives of the low-income portion of the sample revealed a developmental trend in clarity of reference, such that children's narratives had fewer ambiguities when they were in kindergarten. An income-related difference was apparent in the extent to which prekindergarten children inserted a point of view into their narratives, with higher scores among the low-income children.

A complementary analysis of the children's narratives was undertaken in a master's thesis by Susan Hill (1994), who contrasted these narrative accounts of an event to those elicited in a different manner. During prekindergarten competency testing, children were asked to retell a short event in which they had participated earlier in the testing session with the researcher who requested the retelling. This event, which was staged in the same way for each child, involved a special box covered with a picture of the TV character, Barney; an excursion to carry the box from one part of the school to another; an accident in which the researcher dropped several items in the corridor and the child assisted her to gather them up; and a search for another special box in which the child discovered a colorful sticker that he or she was allowed to keep. Of interest was the children's command of different genres of narrative, depending on the context of the request for them to talk. It was predicted that the narrative accounts of an event experienced independently of the audience (elicited by prompts based on information supplied by the parents) would contain significantly more frequent use of evaluative devices to express the narrator's point of view than retellings by the same children to the same interviewer of an event in which the two had jointly participated earlier in the testing session (the Barney box). Results supported these predictions. When the researcher asked the child to describe the Barney Box episode, the child's reply was generally quite brief and flat. However, when the researcher requested the child to tell her about an exciting recent event in his or her own life, the narratives children produced were often quite elaborate, providing not only a description of what happened, but also a strong indication of the child's point of view – what he or she liked about the event, the characters, and their actions.

The two different elicitation contexts differed in the authenticity of the tasks. The children's accounts of personal, out-of-school experience were addressed to an audience (the researcher) who was naive as to the details of what had transpired, whereas the retellings were addressed to an audience who was already informed. Thus, although the first method could be regarded as an authentic request for descriptive information, the second was more likely to be interpreted by the child as a request for a display of her/his competence. Some children readily agree to such requests for display, whereas others evade or resist them as inauthentic. Consistent with the principles of discourse described by Grice (1975), the children were more likely to include an expression of their point of view when providing authentic accounts than when merely displaying competence.

To what extent do children's narratives relate to other aspects of their language competence? To address this question, we created a composite measure of narrative quality by selecting those dimensions judged as most important to a good narrative by a group of college students: informativeness, entertainment, and evaluation. The quality of the narratives children produced in prekindergarten was positively related to their level of comprehension of a story they listened to 2 years later [*The Monkey and the Crocodile* (Galdone, 1969); discussed later in this chapter].[1]

How might the experiences children have within the intimate cultures of their own home contribute to their narrative competence? In an analysis involving the ecological inventory data of the Early Childhood Project, Schmidt (1998) found that the more often the child engaged in activities at home with a storyline (i.e., oral storytelling, reading storybooks, watching situation comedies on television, watching movies on television), the more likely the child's narratives reflected an evaluative point of view, and the greater the entertainment rating they received.[2]

Story Comprehension

We assessed children's comprehension of a story that was read aloud to them in kindergarten. The child was told, "Let's read the book *Where's That Bus?* together now." The book presented a story about a rabbit and a mole who were waiting for a bus to take them to their friend Squirrel's house for lunch, and for a variety of reasons they kept failing to see the buses that went by. Comprehension of the

---

[1] $r(28) = .39, p < .05.$
[2] $r(33) = .33, p = .05; r(25) = .40, p = .01,$ respectively.

story required both listening to the story and looking at the pictures. After completing the book, the child was asked five comprehension questions. The majority of children did quite well, with 76% correct responding. In fact, on three of the five questions, the percentage correct was greater than 90%. These results provide clear evidence that children attended to the story as it was read and understood the narrative. Later in this chapter we consider the pattern of comprehension of another story read to the children in Grade 2.

Storybook Reading Conventions

This task, adapted from Sulzby (1985), provided information about the child's knowledge about the conventions of stories as well as the books themselves. Children were asked to read or tell about a familiar book. In most cases, the child's teacher selected the book as one that had been read in class. About 10% of the children chose their own book from among a shelf of books used in class. The books generally were between 20 and 30 pages, and had a simple storyline.

The book selected for reading was presented to the child with the following instructions: "Your teacher showed me this book that you have heard her read. I've never read this one and I would love to hear this story. Will you read or tell me about it?" If the child protested that she/he could not read, the research assistant said, "Well, let's go through the book together and you show me the pictures." Of particular interest were the accompaniments to reading that were revealed in the child's behavior, rather than the accuracy of the reading itself. A composite score was derived from the orientation in which the child held the book, how she turned the pages, whether she looked at the words on the page while reading, and if so, the direction she scanned the words. Also coded was the degree to which the child's "reading" conformed to the actual story.

Performance improved significantly across the 2 years, increasing from a mean rating on a 0–3 scale of 1.50 in prekindergarten to 2.03 in kindergarten (Table 5.1). Of particular interest in the context of children's growing awareness of narrative structure is the "reading" of the story. In their prekindergarten phase of development, children made more use of the pictures than of the print to construct the narrative, whereas in the kindergarten phase they paid more attention to the print and less to the pictures. When children were in prekindergarten, 26% of them described the pictures but did not attempt to tell a story, whereas 62% used the pictures to tell a story. None of the children attempted to read the words of the story, and 13% of the children essentially did not attempt the task at all. In contrast, by kindergarten, 30% of the children attempted to decode the print, and no children were unwilling to respond. The percentage of children describing the pictures remained stable at 24%, but the percentage telling a story from pictures declined to 46%.

The Development of Phonological Awareness

Considerable evidence has accumulated demonstrating the powerful connection between phonological awareness and learning to read (Baker, 2000; Bus & van IJzendoorn, 1999; National Reading Panel, 2000; Snow et al., 1998; Stahl & Murray, 1998). The term *phonological awareness* refers to awareness of any of the phonological units of the spoken language, including syllables, intrasyllabic units (rimes and onsets), and phonemes. The more sensitive children are to the component sounds in words they hear spoken, the more easily they are able to understand the phoneme-grapheme connections in an alphabetic writing system. Children who score well on measures of phonological awareness in prekindergarten and kindergarten are more successful in learning to decode words in first grade.

Goswami and Bryant (1992) suggested that sensitivity to rhyme and alliteration is the first kind of phonological awareness to arrive and the easiest to demonstrate in young children. Accordingly, we restricted our competency assessments in the first 2 years of the Early Childhood Project to rhyme and alliteration tasks. Once children began first grade, we added a more challenging assessment of phonemic awareness.

The tasks comprising the phonological awareness strand of literacy development include four phonological awareness tasks, adapted from MacLean, Bryant, and Bradley (1987). Because we were also interested in the origins of preschoolers' rhyme and alliteration sensitivity, we added an additional task used by MacLean et al. to serve as a proxy of children's home experiences with rhyme. These authors proposed that young children may learn about rhyme and alliteration with the help of linguistic routines because such games often include awareness of the component sounds in words. Treiman (1991) similarly speculated that an informal but useful kind of phonological awareness training may take place when children learn nursery rhymes at home or at preschool. MacLean and her colleagues (1987) found a strong relation between knowledge of nursery rhymes and the detection and production of rhyme and alliteration in a sample of English children from low- and middle-class backgrounds.

Children's Performance on Measures of Phonological Awareness

Tasks used to assess rhyme and alliteration detection within the Early Childhood Project consisted of 10 forced-choice test items. In the rhyme detection task, the children were presented orally with a word and asked if it rhymes with or sounds like either of two other words, only one of which rhymes. The form of the question asked was, for example, "Does car rhyme with far, or does car rhyme with hen?" Similarly, in the alliteration detection task, the children were orally presented with a word and asked if it starts with the same sound as either of two other words. The experimenter asked, for example, "Does pin start with the same sound as pig, or does pin start with the same sound as tree?"

Tasks used to assess rhyme and alliteration production consisted of eight test items. In the rhyme production task, the child was asked to tell the experimenter a word that rhymes with a word provided by the experimenter. Similarly, in the alliteration production task, the child was asked to tell the experimenter a word that starts with the same sound as a word provided by the experimenter.

In the nursery rhyme knowledge task, the child was asked to recite five nursery rhymes: Twinkle, Twinkle Little Star; Humpty Dumpty; Jack and Jill; Baa Baa Black Sheep; and Hickory Dickory Dock. These rhymes were selected by MacLean et al. (1987) because they were familiar to children in England, and our informal pilot testing revealed that they were familiar to children in Baltimore as well. The nursery rhyme knowledge task consisted of telling children the name of each of the five rhymes and asking them to say it to the experimenter. The experimenter provided carefully structured prompts to assist the child in producing as much of the nursery rhyme as possible (see Fernandez-Fein & Baker, 1997, for details).

Table 5.1 presents children's scores on the rhyme detection and production tasks, the alliteration detection and production tasks, and the nursery rhyme task. Children improved significantly between prekindergarten and kindergarten on each task except for the alliteration production task, where performance was very low in both years.

Experiential Origins of Phonological Awareness

To what extent do home experiences contribute to the development of phonological awareness? Research suggests that many preschoolers are exposed to linguistic games involving rhyme and alliteration, as revealed through parental reports that children regularly engage in activities involving songs, rhymes, and rhyming games (Chaney, 1994; Raz & Bryant, 1990). It is possible that language play helps children develop their rhyme and alliteration skills. Several of the recurrent activities included in our ecological inventory (see Chapter 3) had the potential to foster phonological awareness, such as playing word games, playing hand clap games, singing, and reading storybooks (many of which contain rhyme and/or alliteration). Children were also observed interacting with their siblings in language play where they generated tongue twisters and "poems" with rhymes (see Chapter 4). We examined the relations between these home experiences, children's knowledge of nursery rhymes, and their emerging phonological awareness. This analysis was undertaken when the children were in prekindergarten. Because we had a small number of middle-income families during the first year of the Early Childhood Project, Sylvia Fernandez-Fein (1995), as part of her master's thesis, supplemented the sample with middle-income families attending private preschools in the city. The additional children were tested for their competencies in the same manner as those in the Early Childhood Project; the mothers were interviewed by phone.

With the larger sample, we were able to examine whether performance on these tasks was related to social address. This question was of interest given previous reports of differences related to family income in phonological awareness (Chaney, 1994; Raz & Bryant, 1990), such that middle-income children score higher. Statistical analyses revealed a similar pattern in this study, with middle-income children having higher scores than the low-income children on rhyme detection, rhyme production, and alliteration detection (scores were so low for all children on the alliteration production task that no group differences were apparent). Nursery rhyme knowledge also differed across groups: the African American low-income children's performance in recitation of rhymes was significantly lower than that of the European American low-income children, whose scores were comparable to both groups of middle-income children (see Fernandez-Fein & Baker, 1997, for statistical details).

As expected based on the work of Bryant and his colleagues (Bryant, Bradley, MacLean, & Crossland, 1989; MacLean et al., 1987), nursery rhyme knowledge was highly correlated with sensitivity to rhyme. Children may gain sensitivity to rhyme when they learn to recite nursery rhymes; alternatively, correct recitation of nursery rhymes may depend on rhyme sensitivity. The Fernandez-Fein and Baker (1997) analysis extended these findings to show that a number of home experiences are also correlates of both rhyme sensitivity and nursery rhyme knowledge. Children's production of original rhymes during the language play observation was significantly correlated with their performance on the rhyme detection and production tasks. Children who were reported on the ecological inventory to participate in word games more often also performed better on these measures of rhyme sensitivity, as well as on the nursery rhyme recitation task. Rhyming word games most commonly involved making up words that rhyme with other words. Children who engaged with books more often were generally more sensitive to rhyme and showed a better knowledge of nursery rhymes. Children who sang more often also showed better knowledge of nursery rhymes.

The extent to which children's knowledge of nursery rhymes, their relevant home experiences, and their social addresses jointly contributed to their rhyme sensitivity was explored in a regression analysis. Nursery rhyme knowledge accounted for 35% of the variance in sensitivity to rhyme. Frequency of participation in word games accounted for an additional 6% of the variance supporting the hypothesis that engagement in activities that involve rhyme fosters sensitivity to rhyme. Once these variables were controlled, interactions with books did not account for a significant amount of variance. Maternal education accounted for 13% of the variance and ethnicity accounted for 5% of the variance, suggesting that these demographic variables relate to children's rhyme sensitivity in a manner independent of their nursery rhyme knowledge and experiences with word games and books.

What might be responsible for the relation between ethnicity and rhyme sensitivity? One possibility is that, although African American and European American children may engage in relevant activities with the same frequency, other aspects of these interactions may differ. For example, the ecological inventory data indicated that African American children participated in such activities with children, whereas European American children more often engaged in these activities with adults. Among mothers who reported that their child engaged in word games and book interactions at least once a week with either adults or children, more European American mothers than African American mothers reported that the most common co-participant was an adult. When children engage in such activities with more knowledgeable adults, the experience may be more conducive to fostering rhyme sensitivity, just as interactions with adults rather than peers facilitate learning in other cognitive domains (Rogoff, 1990).

Thus, there are indications that the home variables related to the development of rhyme sensitivity are different for children from different sociocultural backgrounds. In designing our study, we sought through pilot work to identify linguistic routines that might be differentially familiar to children from different sociocultural groups to include among the competency measures. Our elicitation attempts were unsuccessful, suggesting that these preschoolers may have not yet learned a repertoire of street rhymes. The fact that low-income African American children in the sample were less knowledgeable of the nursery rhymes suggests that these rhymes were not as salient a feature of their early literacy experiences as they were for children from the other social addresses. Because the rhymes children are most likely to be interested in learning will be those that are common and valued in their community, characterizing such routines would be an important first step in designing an intervention program for promoting phonological awareness that is grounded in everyday cultural practices.

CHILDREN'S COMPETENCIES IN THE PRIMARY GRADES

Once children in the Early Childhood Project entered first grade, our focus shifted from documenting the emergent literacy competencies of the children to documenting their early literacy. In other words, we recognized that the children were on the verge of becoming conventional readers, and so we administered tasks that more closely resembled the reading and writing activities children might encounter in school. These included standardized assessments of word recognition, comprehension, and vocabulary. However, at the same time, we sought to assess competencies that are relevant to children's lives beyond the traditional domain of schooling, such as looking up information on a calendar and filling out a coupon for an award. The three strands of emergent literacy competency assessed in the preschool years, phonological awareness, narrative competence, and orientation to print, were also represented in tasks administered during the primary grades.

Growth in Phonological Awareness During the Primary Grades

We continued to assess children's phonological awareness in Grade 1 using the rhyme production, rhyme detection, alliteration production, and alliteration detection tasks. We dropped the nursery rhyme knowledge task because it was meant to serve as an indicator of preschool children's exposure to rhyme and was no longer of theoretical interest once children began formal schooling. Several new measures were introduced in Grade 1 to reflect children's changing competencies, including a more complex measure of phonological awareness, phoneme elision. This task had not been used earlier because it is known to be difficult for preschool children in that it requires explicit manipulation of phonemes. It was selected on the basis of Yopp's (1988) analysis showing it to be a strong predictor of word recognition skills.

The phoneme elision task, modified from Bruce's (1964) phoneme deletion task, consisted of 15 items, with equal numbers of items requiring elision of a phoneme from the beginning, middle, and end of the word. For example: What word is left if you take away "J" from the

TABLE 5.2. *Developmental Change in Children's Phonemic Awareness and Word Recognition Across the Primary Grades in Relation to Social Address*

	Low Income		Middle Income	
	African American	European American	African American	European American
Phonemic awareness				
Grade 1	3.00	5.00	5.57	9.53
Grade 2	7.17	7.39	7.37	11.50
Grade 3	9.17	8.93	10.60	13.21
Word recognition				
Grade 1	12.22	9.13	13.50	25.93
Grade 2	24.43	18.67	28.70	40.00
Grade 3	29.74	26.87	37.20	47.43

Note: The phonemic awareness scores are based on the phoneme elision task, with a maximum score of 15. The word recognition scores are the Basic Reading Composite created by summing the scores on the Word Attack and Word Identification subtests of the Woodcock-Johnson tests.

beginning of JAM? What word is left if you take away "T" from the middle of STAND? What word is left if you take away "T" from the end of TENT?

By Grade 1, children's performance on the rhyme detection and alliteration detection tasks was nearly errorless. Even on the production tasks, although some children were still weak, 41% had perfect scores on the rhyme task and 44% had perfect scores on the alliteration task. The production tasks were the only two of the original tasks that were administered in Grade 2. Analyses of change across the 2 years revealed a significant improvement in both tasks, with no effect of sociocultural group. All children performed at very similar high levels by Grade 2. These primary-grade analyses, unlike those reported previously in this chapter, were based on the full sample of Early Childhood Project participants, not just those recruited in prekindergarten.

The phoneme elision task was administered across all 3 years and is therefore selected for presentation in Table 5.2. There was a strong improvement over time for children in all four sociocultural groups. However, the middle-income European American children showed a pronounced advantage relative to the other three groups of children at each phase of development.

Growth in Word Recognition During the Primary Grades

When children were completing first grade, we administered for the first time a standardized test of children's word recognition skills from the Woodcock-Johnson – Revised Tests of Achievement (1989/1990). As discussed in Chapter 2, the Word Identification test calls for the child to identify common words, and the Word Attack test calls for the child to apply phonic and structural analysis skills to decode pseudowords. A Basic Reading Skills composite score was constructed by combining scores on the two tests.

The word recognition tests of the Woodcock-Johnson were administered in all three grades. Table 5.2 shows the mean scores on the Basic Reading Skills composite across each year for children from each social address. Children's scores improved over time, but the growth in scores from first grade to second grade was greater than the growth from second to third. The European American middle-income children performed significantly better than children in the two low-income groups; the middle-income African American children occupied an intermediary position.

Multiple Precursors of Word Recognition

What aspects of the intimate culture of children's homes might foster the development of word recognition, a critical component of early reading? Evidence is strong that phonological awareness and orthographic knowledge (e.g., knowledge of letter names) are important prerequisites to word recognition (Ehri, 1998; Scarborough, 1998), but the contributions of home experiences are not yet well understood (Baker, Fernandez-Fein, et al., 1998). Within the Early Childhood Project, we examined how children's home experiences with print and their emergent literacy competencies when they were in prekindergarten and kindergarten related to their word recognition skills in the primary grades (Baker, Mackler, Sonnenschein, Serpell, & Fernandez-Fein, 1998).

We hypothesized that experience with books that focus on basic skills (i.e., preschool books, such as alphabet books) might be more beneficial for the development of word recognition skills than experience with storybooks. During storybook reading, the focus is on meaning and attention to print tends to be minimal (see Chapter 4; Baker et al., 2001). Bus and van IJzendoorn (1988) found that mothers of 3- and 5-year-old children in the Netherlands engaged in more talk about print when sharing ABC books than storybooks. Moreover, the children engaged in more "protoreading" behaviors with the ABC book; for example, they tried to spell words and identify letters. These findings suggest that different genres of books may have differential impact on the development of word recognition abilities, and that it may be misleading to look only at book reading in general or storybook reading in particular. We also hypothesized that children's knowledge of nursery rhymes would predict subsequent word recognition skills, consistent with longitudinal data collected by Bryant, MacLean, Bradley, and Crossland (1990).

Participants in these analyses were those for whom we had competency data and ecological inventory data during prekindergarten and kindergarten (Wave 1). A series of regression analyses revealed that, consistent with our expectation, frequency of engagement with ABC-type books during the prekindergarten year was a significant predictor of word recognition in all three grades. It accounted for 11% of the variance in Grade 1, 29% in Grade 2, and 39% in Grade 3. Frequency of visits to the library during the prekindergarten year also uniquely predicted subsequent word recognition scores, accounting for 19% of the variance in Grade 1, 9% in Grade 2, and 7% in Grade 3.

How do we interpret these relations? ABC book reading likely contributes to subsequent word recognition skills because these kinds of books provide children with explicit opportunities to learn to recognize letters, words, and letter-sound correspondences. The limited predictive power of storybook reading once other relevant literacy experiences were taken into account is consistent with observational data showing that very little attention is directed to spelling-sound correspondences and word identification during storybook reading (see Chapter 4; Baker et al., 2001). Visits to the library were also strongly predictive of word recognition. Of course, it is not going to the library that in itself accounts for this relation, but rather all that going to the library entails. First, it reflects parental valuing of books and reading. Second, it exposes children to a place that exists almost entirely for the purpose of making large numbers of books widely accessible, demonstrating the importance of books and reading in the larger society. Third, it gives children an opportunity to make choices about what they would like to read or have read to them; intrinsic interest is critical to self-initiated interactions with print. These three factors converge to generate an inviting cultural context for the child to appropriate the activity of reading in a spirit of positive appreciation. Over and above these factors, frequent visits to the library make it likely that a breadth of print materials will be available in the home. This is a particularly important consideration given that the Wave 1 sample consisted primarily of low-income families whose resources for purchasing books of their own were limited.

We also examined the relations between the phonological and orthographic measures collected in the preschool years and subsequent word recognition. Nursery rhyme knowledge and letter knowledge measured both in prekindergarten and kindergarten were significantly and moderately correlated with word recognition in all three grades.[3] Rhyme sensitivity and alliteration detection were not as uniformly correlated, although 9 of the 12 correlations were statistically significant.[4] These results replicate the growing body of longitudinal research demonstrating that early phonological and orthographic competencies contribute to subsequent word reading skills (Evans, Shaw, & Bell, 2000; Hecht, Burgess, Torgesen, Wagner, & Rashotte, 2000; Lonigan, Burgess, & Anthony, 2000; Olofson & Niedersoe, 1999).

Multiple regression analyses were conducted to examine which competencies accounted for unique variance in word recognition performance. Nursery rhyme knowledge in prekindergarten accounted for significant amounts of variance in all three grades (19% in Grade 1, 13% in Grades 2 and 3). These data are noteworthy in demonstrating the continued predictive power of nursery rhyme knowledge, extending the findings of Bryant et al. (1990) to older children. Which other competencies accounted for additional variance differed across grade level. For Grade 1 word recognition, nursery rhyme knowledge in kindergarten was also a significant predictor (13%). For Grades 2 and 3 word recognition, letter knowledge in kindergarten was also a significant predictor (24%).

---

[3] $r(24)$ with ranges from .45 to .74, p with ranges from .05 to .000.
[4] $r(24)$ with ranges from .41 to .51, $p < .05$.

That the nursery rhyme task accounted for significant variance in performance but the purer phonological awareness measures did not suggests that the significance of nursery rhyme knowledge for literacy development goes beyond phonological knowledge. It also depends on the kinds of experiences children have had at home, as well as their verbal abilities and memory skills. As Olofson and Niedersoe (1999) commented,

> knowledge of nursery rhymes acts as an indicator of the child's basic language development. A child with enough talent for appreciating phonological structure will find it interesting and amusing to engage in nursery rhymes and language play and thus learn more rhymes. . . . The child is choosing and creating an environment that will include nursery rhymes. Parents with children who are interested in rhymes will probably be more encouraged to engage in language play with their children than parents whose children do not show any interest in such activities. (Olofson & Niedersoe, 1999, p. 471)

That letter knowledge in prekindergarten did not account for unique variance in word recognition, whereas letter knowledge in kindergarten did, indicates that children who start preschool with good letter knowledge are not any more likely to be successful readers than children who acquire this knowledge a little later, perhaps through the combined influences of home and school. Indeed, four of the children who had high letter knowledge in prekindergarten ended up with average or low average word recognition in third grade. Their parents reportedly provided extensive opportunities for their children to learn the letters, but this early knowledge did not "protect" them from later difficulties. Indeed, one child who had among the highest scores on letter knowledge, rhyme sensitivity, nursery rhyme knowledge, and alliteration detection in prekindergarten was described by her second-grade teacher as having real difficulties with reading.

Children's Knowledge and Use of Functional Print in the Primary Grades

At the end of first grade, all children were given five tasks designed to tap their knowledge and awareness of how print is used, as well as their ability to use it in functional contexts. Two tasks had been used in the previous rounds of competency testing and assessed children's knowledge (Concepts About Print and Functions of Print). The other three were developed for use for the first time in Grade 1 and assessed children's usage of print in functional contexts. These tasks, like the environmental print task used in the earlier years, were designed to be motivating, authentic, and ecologically valid.

Mail Sorting

On the mail sorting task, the child was presented with four sealed envelopes individually tailored with different names and addresses. On one was his own name and home address, on another was his mother's name and home address, a third had his teacher's name and school address, and the last, constant for all children, contained the name of a fictional person with an address in Baltimore. The child was asked to say who each letter was for. Each letter was subsequently used for an authentic purpose (e.g., the envelope with the teacher's name contained a letter describing the day's competency testing, which was subsequently delivered to the teacher). Responses were scored on a 3-point scale, with 0 for incorrect, 1 for partial understanding, and 2 for independent performance.

Calendar Use

The child was shown a calendar from 5 years past and was asked to find out what day his or her birthday was on that year. He/she received points for finding the correct month, date, and day. Prompts were given as needed, including the research assistant modeling how she would find her own birthday (or a fictitious birthday if it was the same month as the child's). Responses for each component of the date were scored on a 3-point scale, with 0 for incorrect, 1 for assisted performance, and 2 for independent performance.

Coupon Completion

The child was given a form (a coupon) that provided him or her the opportunity to have a sticker sent home as thanks for participation in the study. Completing the coupon served as a measure of competency on a functional print task yielding a meaningful goal. Children needed to read the information telling them about the opportunity, they needed to complete the form by writing in their name, address,

TABLE 5.3. *Children's Performance on Tasks Assessing Knowledge and Use of Print in Grade 1 in Relation to Social Address*

	Low Income		Middle Income	
	African American	European American	African American	European American
Knowledge tasks				
Concepts of print	15.04	15.52	15.27	17.07
Functional print				
Identification	5.92	6.43	7.14	7.40
Functions	12.68	14.61	14.33	16.47
Usage tasks				
Mail sorting	4.81	4.48	5.93	6.67
Calendar use	3.46	3.87	4.53	5.40
Coupon use				
Writing	10.00	9.00	9.67	9.47
Reading	3.61	2.78	5.53	6.27

Note: Maximum scores on concepts of print = 18; functional print identification = 9; functional print functions = 18; mail sorting = 8; calendar use = 6; coupon use writing = 27, coupon use reading = 10.

age, and grade, and they needed to select which sticker they wanted to receive. Performance was scored in terms of the child's ability to read different sections of the coupon independently or with assistance, and to fill in the blanks appropriately, independently or with assistance. These reading and writing components were examined separately and also summed for a total score.

Table 5.3 shows children's performance on the tasks assessing knowledge and use of functional print when they were in first grade. Analyses revealed sociocultural differences in performance on all these tasks. The middle-income European American sample generally scored higher than the other three groups, and the two low-income samples generally scored lower than the middle-income groups.[5] (Those group differences that reached conventional levels of statistical reliability are indicated in Table 5.3.)

[5] On the Concepts of Print task, middle-income European American children scored significantly higher than African American children of both income levels. On the Functions of Print task, middle-income European American children scored significantly higher than low-income African American on the functions component; there were no sociocultural differences on the identification part. On both the Mail

As already noted, one of the unique features of the Early Childhood Project is the use of measures linked more directly to the children's own experiences and backgrounds. The three functional print
tasks introduced in Grade 1 all entail the use of personally meaningful print. Completing coupons to send away for prizes, going
through family mail to identify recipients, and looking up dates on
a calendar are literacy activities that many children experience at
home. Children's performance on these tasks was strongly related
to their performance on the formal assessment of word recognition
skills (Woodcock-Johnson), accounting for 51% of unique variance.

Children's Narrative Competence: Listening Comprehension and Story Retelling

One of the strands of competency we assessed when children were in
prekindergarten and kindergarten was narrative competence. As reported earlier in the chapter, children in the Early Childhood Project
displayed strengths in their oral narrative descriptions of personally
experienced events, and they showed good comprehension of a storybook that was read aloud to them. Narrative competence continues
to be an important aspect of literacy development in the early years
of schooling. Accordingly, as part of the Grade 2 competency assessments, we included tasks within this domain. Children were read the
story *The Monkey and the Crocodile* (Galdone, 1969). This is an engaging
story with multiple episodes and a compelling storyline about how
a young monkey tricks a crocodile that wants to eat it. After listening to the story, children were first asked a series of comprehension
questions, and then they were asked to retell the story.

The comprehension assessment consisted of a mix of literal and
inferential questions tapping seven key features of the story. Some
questions received up to 1 point, others up to 3 points, with a maximum score of 17. Children performed quite well on this task, with

Sorting and Calendar Use tasks, middle-income European American children scored
significantly higher than low-income African American children. On the coupon task,
there were no sociocultural differences on the writing component, but on the reading
part the middle-income children of both ethnicities had higher scores than the low-
income European American children, and the middle-income European American
children also scored higher than the low-income African American children.

TABLE 5.4. *Children's Narrative Competence and Script Production in Grade 2 and Reading Comprehension and Oral Reading Fluency in Grade 3 in Relation to Social Address*

	Low Income		Middle Income	
	African American	European American	African American	European American
Narrative competence				
Listening comprehension	12.56	12.31	11.80	12.79
Length of story retellings	237	179	153	176
Story retelling quality	5.73	4.71	3.43	5.42
Script production				
Length of scripts	40	38	42	39
Number of script elements	3.04	3.76	4.38	3.35
Spelling accuracy	88%	77%	91%	90%
Reading comprehension	23.91	23.20	33.00	45.21
Oral reading fluency	55	66	75	92

Note: The narrative competence measures are based on comprehension and retelling of *The Monkey and the Crocodile* (Galdone, 1969). The script production measures are based on children's writing about a typical visit to a McDonald's fast food restaurant. The reading comprehension score is a composite created by summing the scores on the Vocabulary and Passage Comprehension subtests of the Woodcock-Johnson. The fluency data are based on oral reading of an expository passage on dolphins, the number of words read accurately divided by the total time in minutes to read the passage.

a mean score of 12.4 (73%). Unlike many of the other competency tasks, performance did not differ significantly as a function of social address. The mean scores displayed in Table 5.4 are remarkably similar for the four groups of children.

We also assessed productive language skills more directly through a story retelling task. As Morrow (1988) noted, the task of retelling a story can serve as an index both of a child's narrative comprehension, requiring the child to assimilate and reconstruct textual information, and of her expressive mastery of narrative genre, affording the child an opportunity to respond to a story from a personal perspective. Both of these dimensions of cognition are highly relevant to the literacy competencies of reading and writing. However, in the context of retelling a story that has been read aloud by someone else, a child can deploy these skills without actually reading or writing. We were interested, therefore, to find out whether children's performance on this task would be closely related to their performance on our more explicitly literate tasks, or whether some of the children whose reading skills were relatively weak would nevertheless display high levels of story retelling competence in the oral medium.

After asking the child the comprehension questions, the research assistant asked him/her to retell the story into a tape recorder. She meanwhile busied herself with other tasks. The full text of the child's retelling was transcribed verbatim, preserving the child's lexical and grammatical forms. The retellings varied considerably in their length, ranging from 5 to 471 words, with a mean of 192. Descriptively, the low-income African American children produced the longest retellings and the middle-income African American children produced the shortest (Table 5.4; these group differences were not statistically reliable).

Working with the transcribed retellings, Brenda Haynes applied a scoring system designed by Morrow (1988), the Story Retelling Evaluation (SRE) guide (Haynes, Baker, Serpell, & Sonnenschein, 2003). The SRE gives credit for sense of story structure, including the setting, the theme, episodes, resolution, and sequence. Scores ranged from 0 to 11, with a mean of 5.0. When we analyzed the retelling quality scores for group differences, we found a strikingly different pattern from those obtained for most of the other competency measures (Table 5.4). In most of our analyses, the lower-income children of both ethnic groups obtained significantly lower scores than the middle-income children of both ethnic groups. In contrast, for retellings, the low-income African American children received significantly higher scores than the middle-income African American children. The two groups of European American children's scores fell in-between the extremes and were not significantly different from the low-income African American children's scores.

That the low-income African American children exhibited oral narrative skills on a par with the middle-income European American children is a striking finding. The home experiences of the low-income African American children likely afforded them an advantageous opportunity structure for developing storytelling skills. Heath (1983) described how in the rural, working-class African American community she called Trackton, young children learned effective rhetorical and narrative skills. In the first 2 years of their everyday home life, as she put it, they "must learn to give performances and to play roles to fit the context: to tease, defy, boss, baby and scold" (p. 83). In the later preschool years, Trackton children "must . . . be highly creative and entertaining to win a way into an ongoing conversation. They practice the skills which they must learn in order to do so through ritualized insults, playsongs, and . . . attempts at telling stories to their peers" (p. 187). The early narrative productions that Heath documented for the children of Trackton reflect the influence of a distinctive local storytelling tradition quite different from either the didactic, moral tales of the low-income, European American community she studied in the neighboring mill town of Roadville, or the bedtime storybook reading practices of middle-class families. "In Trackton, various types of language play, imitations of other community members or TV personalities, dramatic gestures and shifts of voice quality, and rhetorical questions and expressions of emotional evaluations add humor and draw out the interaction of story-teller and audience" (p. 186). When they enter elementary school, the children of Trackton continued to practice this tradition in the playground, by trading ritualized insults with their peers (see also Smitherman, 1977), incorporating play songs in games such as jump rope, and later in cheerleading for school sports teams. All these recurrent activities afforded children both incentives and opportunities for appropriation of an African American narrative tradition that places a premium on expression of a personal point of view, use of verbal tropes, such as metaphor and repetition, and imaginative creativity. It did not, however, connect well with the cultural preoccupations of the school teachers in Heath's study, and Trackton's children did not fare well in the school's curriculum.

Children from the inner-city, African American neighborhoods that we sampled in the Early Childhood Project may have brought with them from their home experience some aspects of the "ways with words" that Heath (1983) documented for Trackton. The pattern of scores displayed by our cohort over the 5 years of the study suggests that this section of our sample did not fare well in mastering the basic reading skills on which their teachers were focusing instruction, but continued to maintain a well-developed repertoire of cognitive and linguistic skills that, among our measures, were tapped only by those focusing on narrative production and story retelling. Within the eco-cultural niche of our Baltimore sample, some data consistent with this line of interpretation were reported by Morakinyo (1995; see Chapter 6 for discussion).

Children's Reading Comprehension and Its Relations
With Narrative Competence

As discussed in Chapter 2, two additional tests from the Woodcock-Johnson were administered only when the children in the Early Childhood Project reached third grade: Passage Comprehension and Reading Vocabulary. A Reading Comprehension composite score was constructed by combining scores on the two tests. Table 5.4 shows the reading comprehension scores of the children in Grade 3. The pattern is similar to that observed on a number of other competency measures: middle-income European American children had the highest scores, the two low-income samples had the lowest scores, and the middle-income African American children had scores midway between.

How did the children's oral narrative competencies assessed in Grade 2 relate to the formal reading comprehension assessment administered in Grade 3? We examined patterns of correlations for the full sample and then for each of the four sociocultural groups separately. For the full sample, scores on the listening comprehension task for *The Monkey and the Crocodile* were moderately correlated with the retelling scores, indicating that children who understood the story well enough to respond to the short answer comprehension questions effectively also could retell the story more completely.[6] The listening comprehension scores were moderately correlated with the Woodcock-Johnson Reading Comprehension composite, indicating some commonalities in listening comprehension and reading comprehension.[7] Scores on the story retelling measure were weakly correlated with the Woodcock-Johnson comprehension measure, but fell short of statistical significance. Only in the subgroup analyses for the middle-income European American sample did story comprehension and story retelling correlate significantly with Grade 3 reading comprehension.[8]

These findings suggest that the strengths brought to the story retelling task by the low-income African American children and the

---

[6] $r(54) = .47, p = .000.$
[7] $r(49) = .42, p = .002.$
[8] $r(13) = .57, p = .032.$

middle-income European American children may have different origins. The latter children likely performed well on this task by virtue of their sociocultural group's greater access to the shared storybook reading with adults that fosters familiarity with the narrative genre. These experiences would promote reading comprehension as well as listening comprehension, but to recognize printed words (prerequisite to comprehending them), the children also need ample experiences with letters and sounds. The low-income African American children likely performed well on the retelling task not because of their experiences with shared storybook reading but rather because of the greater emphasis placed by their sociocultural group on oral expression and rhetorical skills, a strength that would not give them an advantage in a print-based context.

Children's Production of Narrative Scripts in the Written Register

Although most of the measures of children's early literacy development administered during the course of the Early Childhood Project assessed reading and its precursors, we recognize the importance of writing as a dimension of literacy. We did not systematically assess writing development over the years, primarily because of the need to keep the competency testing sessions at a reasonable length. We required writing for the first time in Grade 1 on one of the functional print tasks, but this was at the basic level of filling in one's name, address, and grade on a coupon. We decided when the children were in Grade 2 to supplement our measures of expressive language skills in the oral domain (narrative production and story retelling) with an expressive task in the written domain.

Researchers whose primary concern is children's early reading development typically do not examine children's writing beyond the level of spelling. Because children's spelling is intimately connected with their knowledge of the alphabetic principle, it is a strong correlate of word recognition as well as phonemic awareness (Foorman & Francis, 1994; Treiman, 1998). To what extent does children's ability to express ideas in writing relate to their ability to extract ideas from text? To address this question, we included a measure in the Grade 2 competency testing that would enable us to examine reading-writing connections at both conceptual and orthographic levels. Because children often have difficulty deciding what to write in a free-writing task (Scardamalia & Bereiter, 1986), and because we wanted to minimize the possibility that children from different social addresses would differ in their background knowledge, we asked children to write about a typical visit to McDonald's, a fast food restaurant with many Baltimore-area locations. As early as preschool, children develop scripts of events they experience frequently in their lives, such as attending a birthday party or eating out at a fast food restaurant (Furman & Walden, 1990).

Children were provided with a sheet of lined paper with the title, "Eating at McDonald's," at the top. The first sentence, a statement of the first event in the prototypical script, was provided for them as a starter: I walked into McDonald's. Children were instructed to write what they typically did when they went to McDonald's. In a couple of instances children said they did not eat at McDonald's, in which case they were instructed to write about eating at another fast food restaurant. The written products were scored for content, using as a guide a list of events (script elements) highly associated with eating at McDonald's (based in part on Furman & Walden, 1990). For example, some highly likely script elements include getting in line, placing an order, and taking the food to a table. Script elements that were not part of the prototypical adult script, but which were highly salient for the children in the study, included playing with the toys that accompanied Happy Meals and playing in the room filled with balls (Baker, Garrett, & Morse, 2003).

Children from all four social addresses performed comparably on the conceptual aspects of the writing task. There were no group differences in the length of the scripts nor in the number of script elements, as shown in Table 5.4. Performance on this task, then, was consistent with that on the story retelling task: even though the low-income children in our sample did not perform as well as the middle-income children in mastering basic reading skills, their cognitive and linguistic skills served them well on a measure that drew more heavily on out-of-school experience. Furthermore, the data provided evidence that the ability to express ideas in writing was indeed associated with the ability to extract information from text. The number of appropriate script elements included in the writing samples was associated with Grade 3 reading comprehension, even after controlling for word recognition.[9]

We also took the opportunity to examine the writing specimens for spelling accuracy, given the close associations with word recognition and phonemic awareness. We calculated the number of different words that were misspelled (ignoring multiple occurrences of the same word) and, through analysis of variance, determined that the mean number of misspelled words did not differ significantly across sociocultural groups (overall mean = 4.18). Correlational analyses replicated previous research in showing strong correlations of spelling accuracy with word recognition and phonemic awareness measured in Grades 1, 2, and 3.[10]

Children's Oral Reading Fluency

One of the major hallmarks of skilled reading is the ability to read text with speed, accuracy, and, if reading aloud, proper expression (National Reading Panel, 2000). Children who are not able to read with fluency will have a difficult time constructing meaning from text. Slow and laborious decoding interferes with children's abilities to process the meaning of the printed words and to remember what had just been read because of the well-documented limitations in short-term memory capacity. Fluency is thus critical to comprehension, but a child also must have a certain degree of understanding of what is being read in order to read with proper expression or prosody (Gersten, Fuchs, Williams, & Baker, 2001). Reading fluency is a topic that is only now beginning to receive wide research attention. In fact, reading fluency was not included on the Woodcock-Johnson Tests of Achievement at the time data were collected for the Early Childhood Project. The 2001 edition is the first to include such an assessment. To assess reading fluency within the Early Childhood Project, we constructed our own measure, an expository passage about dolphins. This expository passage contained about 300 words and was written at an upper second-grade level of reading difficulty (as indicated by the Harris-Jacobson Readability formula; Harris & Sipay, 1980). A

[9] $r(61) = .33, p < .05$.
[10] $r(61)$ ranges from .34 to .57; p ranges from .01 to .000.

set of comprehension questions was constructed to test literal and inferential understanding of the passage.

The task was administered to the children in the Early Childhood Project during their competency testing in Grade 3. They were asked to read the passage aloud as well as they could. After the oral rendering, which was audiotaped, the researcher presented the comprehension questions to the child orally, and the child responded orally. The audiotapes were subsequently analyzed for the speed and accuracy of the reading. Fluency was operationally defined as the number of words read accurately per minute. Note that although prosody is often considered to be a dimension of fluency, we decided to use the more objective measure commonly used in the research literature.

The last row of Table 5.4 shows the fluency data. The middle-income European American children read the text with greatest fluency, and the low-income African American children read with the least fluency. (The means for children in the other groups did not differ significantly from these two groups.) The sociocultural differences revealed in phonemic awareness, word recognition, and reading comprehension previously discussed are thus reflected in fluency as well. All children were quite accurate in their reading, with a mean 91% accuracy rate. Where the groups differed was in reading speed. On average, children answered about two-thirds of the comprehension questions correctly, with no differences across social addresses. Children who read the passage with greater fluency had higher scores on the comprehension test,[11] indicating, consistent with other research, that children who read more slowly – even if they read the words accurately – will have more difficulty comprehending what they are reading.

We also examined how fluency measured with the Dolphin passage related to Woodcock-Johnson basic reading skills and to phonemic awareness assessed in the preceding 2 years and in third grade, as well as to Woodcock-Johnson reading comprehension, assessed concurrently. The correlations were consistently high, even with the measures administered 2 years earlier.[12] Multiple regression analysis was conducted to examine the relative contributions of the Grade 1

[11] $r(64) = .30, p < .05$.
[12] $r(64)$ ranges from .64 to .86, $p < .001$.

measures and the fluency measure in predicting reading comprehension in Grade 3. The measures of word recognition and phonemic awareness (phoneme elision) measures were entered first, stepwise, followed by the fluency measure. Phonemic awareness accounted for the most unique variance (59%). Word recognition accounted for an additional 5% of the variance (not significant). Fluency accounted for 11% of additional variance. Altogether, these three measures served as very strong predictors of reading comprehension.

These data showing the strong predictive power of Grade 1 measures on fluency and comprehension indicate just how important it is for children to get off to a strong start in reading. These findings are not unique to the Early Childhood Project, but rather replicate those now widely reported in the literature. One novel contribution from this study is the evidence that children's orientation to print and phonological awareness competencies assessed as early as kindergarten are also moderately associated with fluency in Grade 3.[13]

CHILDREN'S MOTIVATION FOR READING AND THEIR PERCEPTIONS OF READING

Much of the research on early literacy development has focused on the cognitive competencies believed to be prerequisites to reading, such as phonological awareness, letter knowledge, and concepts about print. Considerably less attention has been given to the motivational underpinnings, to critical questions such as how children's concepts of themselves as readers and their reasons for reading relate to subsequent achievement. Most children begin schooling with optimism and interest in learning to read, but those who experience difficulties quickly develop a concept of self as poor reader and their motivation for reading declines (Chapman & Tunmer, 1995). They read less, both in school and out, than children who are succeeding. Because the amount that children read contributes to further growth in reading (Baker, Dreher, & Guthrie, 2000; Stanovich, West, Cunningham,

---

[13] The orientation to print composite included emergent literacy skills such as concepts about print, functional print knowledge, and letter knowledge. The phonological awareness composite included rhyme detection and production, alliteration detection and production, and nursery rhyme knowledge. For orientation to print, $r(61) = .70$, $p = .000$; for phonological awareness, $r(61) = .43$, $p = .000$.

Cipielewski, & Siddiqui, 1996), it is important to understand the role that motivation plays in early literacy development.

Research on early motivation for reading is limited, in part because there are few instruments appropriate for children who are not yet conventional readers. As part of her master's thesis research within the Early Childhood Project, Deborah Scher (1996) developed a questionnaire that was sensitive to the multidimensional nature of motivation (Scher, 1996; see Baker & Scher, 2002, for further details). Children may be motivated to read because they perceive it as an enjoyable activity, they think it is valuable to them, it affords an opportunity for social interaction, or they will be praised by others for reading (Baker & Wigfield, 1999). The questionnaire was administered to the Wave 1 children in the fall of first grade, as well as to a sample of middle-income children who were not participating in the Early Childhood Project. The questionnaire was administered again in the spring of second grade to all participants in the Early Childhood Project.

Administration of the Motivations for Reading Scale required the child to choose which of two descriptions he or she more closely resembled. Response choices were presented to the children using two stuffed animals (e.g., "Regal likes to read but Cha Cha doesn't like to read. Who are you more like?"). Children were then asked to further differentiate their response by indicating if they were "a lot" or just "a little" like the animal in the statement ("Are you a lot like Regal/Cha-Cha, or just a little?"). The 16-item scale was designed to tap four separate components of reading motivation: enjoyment of reading, an indicator of intrinsic motivation (e.g., I like to be read to), perceived value of reading (e.g., I think I will need to know how to read to do well in school), perceived competence as a reader (e.g., I think I will do well in reading next year), and interest in library-related activities (e.g., I like to get books from the library).

The children who were assessed at the beginning of first grade had a mean score overall on the questionnaire of 3.16 out of 4 possible, indicating that most children were positively disposed toward reading. Motivation levels were comparable across social addresses. The second-grade administration, which included the full sample of children in the Early Childhood Project, revealed similar patterns. Children again reported generally positive motivation toward reading, with a mean overall rating of 3.21. Analysis using data from the 30 children who were given the Motivation for Reading Scale at the beginning of first grade and at the end of second grade revealed that the total scores at the two points in time were moderately correlated.

Contributions of Home Reading Experiences and Parental Beliefs to Motivation for Reading

To what extent do children's home experiences with print and the beliefs of their parents relate to their motivation for reading? Snow et al. (1998) identified enjoyment and engagement as critical mechanisms in the intergenerational transmission of literacy. DeBaryshe (1995) found that mothers who believed that book reading should be motivating and child centered, and that a focus on meaning is more important than emphasizing skills, engaged in more frequent storybook reading with their children and also had children who were more interested in reading. Along similar lines, we expected that children whose parents indicated that reading was important as a source of pleasure would exhibit higher motivation levels than children whose parents did not identify pleasure as a reason for reading.

Baker and Scher (2002) examined relations between children's motivation scores and their print-related experiences, as indexed by the ecological inventory, as well as relations with parents' responses to interview questions about reading. They used data collected from the Wave 1 first graders in the Early Childhood Project and the supplemental middle-income sample. Motivation scores were moderately correlated with parental endorsement of the view that reading served as a source of pleasure.[14] It was also expected that parental perceptions that children were actively interested in learning to read would be related to children's self-reported motivation, and this expectation too was upheld through a moderately strong correlation.[15]

Regression analyses were conducted to examine the joint contributions of social address, parental beliefs, and home reading activity on children's motivation for reading. Parental endorsement of pleasure as a reason for reading accounted for 14% of the variance, parental

---

[14] $r(64) = .38, p < .01.$
[15] $r(64) = .32, p < .01.$

reports of the child's active interest in learning to read accounted for 8% of additional variance, and the shared use of preschool skills books was a negative predictor, accounting for 7% more of the variance. Social address variables did not account for any variance, demonstrating once again the importance of examining the intimate culture of the home for its contribution to children's literacy orientations.

How might we account for the negative relation between motivation and shared preschool book reading? Consider the likely nature of the activity: most of the preschool books parents reported using were ABC-type books, emphasizing basic letter knowledge and letter-sound correspondences. These materials are probably inherently less interesting for children on the verge of conventional literacy than storybooks, although it is likely that these same children might have found the materials quite interesting a year or two earlier when they were just beginning to learn about print. If parents or older siblings treat these interactions as teaching opportunities characterized by drill and practice, they may have the undesirable effect of depressing children's motivation for reading. Moreover, we found that the more frequently children used skills books, the less often they experienced shared storybook reading with an adult (as opposed to another child), and the more likely the storybook co-participant was an adult, the more likely the parent endorsed pleasure as a reason for reading. These relations suggest that frequent users of preschool skills books did not have many opportunities at home for pleasurable interactions with adults around the reading of meaningful stories. Hence, they would not perceive the enjoyment potential of reading and would not be motivated to read for enjoyment. Another possible interpretation of the negative relation is that the children who interacted more often with skills books were in fact less advanced in their literacy skills than those who did not use them as often or at all. The feedback they received from their co-participants may have served to reinforce views of themselves as less competent in reading.

Children's Motivation in Relation to Their Reading Competencies

Children's motivation at the beginning of first grade (Wave 1) was not significantly related to their performance on the Woodcock-Johnson assessments at the end of first grade or at the end of third grade. However, scores on the subscale reflecting children's perceived competence in reading were moderately correlated with their word identification skills in Grade 2.[16]

Children's motivation at the end of second grade (full sample) was not significantly correlated with performance on the Woodcock-Johnson word recognition measures administered at the same time, but the total motivation score was associated with children's comprehension of a storybook (*The Monkey and the Crocodile*) that was read to them.[17] In addition, children who considered themselves better readers, as reflected by scores on the perceived competence subscale, performed better on word identification and passage comprehension a year later, in Grade 3.[18]

Children's Conceptions of Reading

Children's home experiences and the beliefs of their parents likely influence the beliefs children themselves hold about reading and learning to read. Because children's conceptions of reading are related to their early reading achievement (Padak, Vacca, & Stuart, 1993; Stewart, 1992), these beliefs are important areas of study. As part of the competency testing at the end of Grade 1, children in the Early Childhood Project were asked a series of questions tapping their conceptions of reading.

To understand children's conceptions of how they learn to read, we asked them how they would teach a small child how to read. The types of things the children talked about included teaching the child letter-sound correspondences, reading to the child, having the child read, helping the child with words or telling the child words they did not know, and encouraging the child's efforts. Following are some representative responses:

"I'd give her an easy book and read it to her and then tell her to try and remember it and then she would read the book over and over again to me

---

[16] $r(29) = .37, p = .046.$
[17] $r(61) = .25, p = .047.$
[18] $r(58) = .32, p = .015$ and $r(58) = .26, p = .045$, respectively.

and then when she finally got it without memorizing it she would be able to read the book."

"I would help her read the book. I would point out the words and sound 'em out and get her to guess 'em."

"Teach him how to read by saying the letters, sounding them out . . . help him say words and when he get it right I clap."

"I'd read him a lot of stories. . . . I would tell him to try to read."

These responses reveal that by the end of first grade many children have appropriated the cultural concept that shared storybook reading at home plays an important role in helping children learn to read, and they are able to articulate the instructional practices they experience, with an emphasis on letter-sound correspondences. Stewart (1992) obtained similar kinds of responses from kindergarten and first-grade children when they were asked questions about how they were beginning to learn to read at home and at school. The children in her study mentioned being taught letters and sounds at home and reading books at home about equally often.

Children were also asked why people read. Fifty percent of the children indicated that *learning* was an important reason (e.g., to learn about others, to get information). Thirty percent identified *entertainment* as a reason for reading (e.g., they like to, it's fun). Twenty percent of the children said people read in order to *learn about reading* (e.g., to learn how to read, to read better) This was the only response category that revealed a sociocultural difference: 32% of low-income children talked about reading to learn to read, whereas none of the middle income children did so. Fourteen percent of the children mentioned *social reasons* for reading (e.g., to read with their children, teach someone to read). Eight percent mentioned *features of books* (e.g., they like the characters, they like the author). Eight percent mentioned *school* as a reason (e.g., to get good grades, to pass). Five percent mentioned *daily living* (e.g., so they can read signs you need to know), and 5% mentioned *external incentives* (e.g., because they have to for reading group).

The children may not have fully appropriated their reasons for reading at this early phase of development, but their readiness to respond with multiple reasons indicates that a good deal of cultural transmission from parents, teachers, and the media was already underway. The fact that almost one-third of the low-income children indicated that people read in order to learn to read provides evidence of such transmission. As discussed in Chapter 3, many low-income parents endorsed the cultural theme that literacy is a set of skills to be deliberately cultivated.

DEVELOPMENTAL CONSEQUENCES OF THE INTIMATE CULTURE OF THE CHILD'S HOME

A central concern of the Early Childhood Project, reflected throughout this book, is how the intimate culture of the child's home contributes to the child's literacy development. In this section of the chapter, we offer several sources of evidence that the intimate culture does indeed have important developmental consequences.

In an early set of analyses with data from Wave 1 families, we examined the relations between parental perspectives on literacy development and children's emergent literacy (Sonnenschein, Baker, et al., 1996, 1997). We compared the developmental progress of children being brought up in homes predominantly oriented toward the view of literacy as a source of entertainment and of children in homes where literacy is more typically viewed as a set of skills to be acquired, along the three strands of competency discussed at the beginning of this chapter: phonological awareness, narrative competence, and orientation toward print. As discussed in Chapter 3, these two different perspectives on literacy socialization were inferred from parents' answers to questions about how to help foster reading, as well as our review of the children's home activities reported by the parents. Parents' taking the perspective that literacy is a source of entertainment was positively related to the child's development of an orientation toward print, as well as to aspects of narrative competence and phonological awareness. Taking the perspective that literacy is a set of skills to be learned was either negatively related or not significantly related to development on each of the three strands.

The data strongly support the notion that if the intimate culture is more consonant with the theme that literacy is a source of entertainment, children's literacy development is facilitated. An entertainment perspective was significantly and positively related to phonological awareness (prekindergarten), orientation toward print (prekindergarten and kindergarten), and narrative competence (kindergarten).[19] In all cases (even when the correlation failed to reach significance), the correlation between an entertainment orientation and the literacy-related strands was positive. In all cases (except for narrative competence, prekindergarten), the correlation between a skills orientation and the literacy-related strand was either near zero or negative.

We replicated the analysis of connections between parents' perspectives and children's competencies with the sample of families recruited in Wave 2 (see Sonnenschein, Baker, Serpell, & Schmidt, 2000, for details). The orientations were determined as they were for the original sample, based on an analysis of the kinds of activities parents reported in their diaries and their responses to a question asking the best ways to help children learn to read, collected at the beginning of the first-grade year. The children's emergent competencies were assessed at the beginning of first grade using the same set of tasks that had been administered to the Wave 1 children at the end of kindergarten. In addition, as for all children in the study, scores on the Woodcock-Johnson tests were available to index literacy competencies at the end of Grades 1, 2, and 3. Significant positive correlations were found between parental endorsement of an entertainment perspective for helping their children learn to read and the following competencies: children's orientation toward print and phonological awareness measured roughly concurrently; word identification at the end of Grades 1, 2, and 3; and reading comprehension at the end of Grade 3. Significant negative correlations were found between parents endorsing a skills perspective and children's orientation toward print, phonological awareness, and word recognition in both first and second grade.

Multiple regression analyses were undertaken with the full sample of children to examine combined influences of parental perspectives and emergent literacy competencies on primary grade outcomes (Sonnenschein, Williams, & Schmidt, 1997). The more strongly parents endorsed the perspective that literacy is a source

---

[19] $r(34) = .36$, $p < .05$, $r(34) = .51$, $p < .01$, $r(30) = .46$, $p < .05$, $r(30) = .45$, $p < .01$, respectively.

of entertainment, the better were children's scores on the Woodcock-Johnson word identification tests in Grades 1, 2, and 3 and the better the children's scores on the Woodcock-Johnson passage comprehension test in Grade 3. In no analysis did a skills perspective predict outcomes. In addition, in most of these analyses, children's scores on either or both of the literacy strand composites, phonological awareness, and orientation to print predicted significant additional variance, indicating a combined influence of parental beliefs and emergent literacy competencies on subsequent reading achievement.

Parental perspectives on literacy were examined in conjunction with children's engagement in literacy-related activities in an outcomes analysis reported in more detail in Sonnenschein et al. (2000). Participants were those recruited in Wave 2, and the source of home experience data was the ecological inventory conducted at the beginning of Grade 1. Recurrent activities were classified as to whether they were more consistent with an entertainment orientation toward literacy or a skills orientation.

The first step in the analysis was to examine the zero-order correlations between children's activities and the Woodcock-Johnson reading achievement outcome measures. Significant positive correlations were obtained between the following entertainment types of activities and children's word identification and reading comprehension: the frequency with which children reportedly played board games, looked at any printed material alone, told stories, engaged in writing activities, and played word games. Skills types of activities were either unrelated or negatively related to children's reading scores.

We next examined simultaneously the contributions of parent perspectives and children's activities on literacy development. To do so, we took the three activities that were most strongly associated with outcomes and entered these into regression equations with the outcome measures as the dependent variables. The general pattern was that parental endorsement of an entertainment perspective and children's engagement in activities consistent with such a perspective positively predicted literacy development, whereas a skills orientation did not. For example, children's word identification at the end of Grade 1 was jointly predicted by the frequency with which children played board games, engaged in oral storytelling, and looked at/read printed material on their own and by the extent to which parents rated entertainment types of activities as important in helping children learn to read. Children's reading comprehension at the end of Grade 3 was also jointly predicted by the frequency of looking at/reading printed material on their own and parents' ratings of the entertainment types of activities. These findings make clear the enduring importance of playful interactions around literacy in the intimate culture of the child's home.

DEVELOPMENTAL JOURNEYS OF SELECTED CHILDREN

To what extent do early literacy competencies predict later outcomes? As previously discussed, many studies, including the Early Childhood Project, have shown that children's early competencies in the preschool years, such as phonological awareness, are good predictors of their reading performance in the primary grades. However, just because certain variables are good predictors in general does not mean that all children follow the same pattern. In this section we report an analysis of a subgroup of children whose literacy competencies diverged over the course of the project.

Sonnenschein, Schmidt, and Mackler (1999) identified a group of 14 children whose scores on the phonological awareness and orientation toward print composites were low relative to the sample as a whole at the start of first grade. Eight of these children continued to have low scores at the end of third grade, as reflected by performance on the Woodcock-Johnson word recognition and passage comprehension tests. Six children had scores at or above the mean on these measures by third grade. Clearly, it was not the case that all low-scoring children were left behind. What factors might contribute to these differences in growth over the 3 years?

An analysis of the intimate culture of the children's homes proved informative. First, consider parental beliefs. Parents of all the children tended to endorse a skills perspective on literacy development, both in the open-ended questions asked shortly after project entry and in the rating scales administered when children were in Grade 1. However, about one-half of the parents in the group of children who showed substantial growth also endorsed an entertainment perspective, whereas only one-fourth of parents in the other group did. All parents wanted their children to succeed at school and all knew that the activities engaged in at home are important.

Ecological inventory data were examined over a 3-year period to determine whether the groups differed in relevant activities. During the first year, the groups were not significantly different, although there was a tendency for children in the greater growth group to have more frequent daily interactions with print. In Grade 2, children in the greater growth group had significantly more frequent engagement with printed material as well as more daily engagement. Differences were not significant in third grade. When children in the low-growth group had interactions with print, they were more likely to be with others, whereas children in the high-growth group were as likely to read printed materials on their own as with others. Children in the high-growth group engaged in a wider variety of relevant activities each year. In addition to more frequent print interactions, these children also had more interactions with educational toys, engaged in more storytelling, went to the library more often, and took more extracurricular classes than children in the low-growth group.

It is clear from these analyses that the experiences children have at home in the early years of schooling contribute in significant ways to their literacy growth. Home experiences and emergent literacy competencies prior to formal schooling are important foundations, but a child's developmental potential is not fixed at school entry. What children do at home in their spare time – and with whom they do it – make a difference in whether children will overcome a slow start on the pathway to literacy.

SUMMARY

In this chapter, we examined children's early literacy development over the 5 years of the Early Childhood Project. We began by describing children's competencies prior to formal schooling within three broad strands of literacy development: orientation to print, narrative competence, and phonological awareness. It was clear that children had already acquired considerable emergent literacy knowledge by the time we first tested them at age 4. Nevertheless, there was room to grow, and children did indeed show growth on the same measures when assessed in kindergarten.

We then considered how development within these strands proceeded over the primary grades, in conjunction with the development of basic skills in word recognition and reading comprehension. Consistent with much research since the mid-1990s, we found that children from poorer families did not perform as well as children from wealthier families on many of the indices of early literacy. However, when we used measures that were more closely tied to children's home lives, we often found children displaying greater strengths than they did when the measures were more formal in nature. We also found that home literacy experiences and parental beliefs about how literacy is acquired were associated with children's subsequent competencies and orientations toward reading.

Of course, it is not just the experiences children have at home that contribute to their developing literacy competencies. In contemporary America, schools and teachers are widely regarded as bearing primary responsibility for the socialization of literacy. We turn in the next chapter to an examination of schooling practices in Baltimore and the beliefs of the teachers of the children participating in the Early Childhood Project.

6

The Agenda and Practices of Schooling

The children we have described in earlier chapters were engaged in the process of becoming literate through interactions with their parents, siblings, and peers in their homes and communities. Why then is it seen as a matter of such importance for their literacy development that they be enrolled in school? School in contemporary Baltimore society, as elsewhere in America and in many other societies, is understood to be a place where children receive advance preparation for many of the challenges of adult life, and becoming literate is seen as an essential part of that preparation (Serpell & Hatano, 1997).

In this chapter, we explain how this responsibility for preparing children for the challenges of adulthood was interpreted by the public schools of Baltimore in the 1990s. We begin by discussing how the construct of public schooling has come to be interpreted in the United States. We next review the politicization of educational opportunity for children of African heritage. The first two sections provide a foundation for understanding the Baltimore City Public Schools System, the topic of the third section in this chapter. In the remainder of the chapter, we focus on the specific schools attended by the children in the Early Childhood Project and the teachers who taught these children. We describe the practices of the teachers, their account of the meaning and purposes informing those practices, and their impressions of the cohort of children in their classrooms.

THE RATIONALE OF ELEMENTARY SCHOOLING

Because of the evolutionary adaptation of our species, most children acquire their first language quite effortlessly. With the exception of a few rare congenital conditions, provided that a child encounters opportunities to interact with other humans who share a common language, she or he will master the basic structure of that language (its phonology, its grammar, and its lexicon) without any deliberate, systematic instruction. Within a few years, the child will display that mastery more fluently than most adult students learning the language for the first time through an intensive program of instruction. However, the cultural invention of writing systems is too recent for us to suppose that much evolutionary adaptation of the human species has fine-tuned our developmental propensities toward the kind of efficient mastery of literacy that we see in the case of spoken language.

Once societies decided that literacy should be regarded as a basic, universal competency, they devised specific arrangements for imparting it to children. Thus, within the context of basic schooling, we see a much more strategic approach to the cultivation of literacy. Knowledge of the properties of the script and the associated skills of reading and writing are explicitly defined as targets of instruction, alongside competencies in other specialized cultural domains such as mathematics and science. Learning opportunities are systematically prepared, instructional procedures are applied, and experts are trained in how to manage this process. In the case of contemporary American society, this package has come to be known as elementary education, and it is mainly delivered through the vehicle of schools.

The rationality of schooling as a system is grounded in its history. The Western tradition of formal education, whose general philosophical premises and organizational principles we cited in Chapter 1, evolved in Europe in the 17th and 18th centuries, and was exported to the United States during the colonial period, in the form of tutors for the children (typically only the sons) of wealthy families. This tradition of focused, explicit instruction was incorporated into the first public elementary schools established in Baltimore in the late 1820s. The emphasis was on advance preparation of children for future cognitive challenges, and learning outcomes were monitored with reference to predetermined instructional targets. The content of the curriculum comprised grammar, geography, history, and book-keeping, in addition to the "three Rs." Instruction relied heavily on textbooks, on memorization, and on lectures addressed to students in large groups (BCPSS, 1999, section 2).

The provision of basic education expanded gradually in the industrialized countries of the West over the course of the 19th and early 20th centuries, to include girls as well as boys, children of the poor as well as the rich, and children of politically oppressed and marginalized groups, such as the native American and African American populations of the United States (Resnick & Resnick, 1977). In Baltimore, the first public secondary school (for white, male students only) was opened in 1839. The second half of the 19th century saw the introduction of "the class system of instruction," that is, the separation of students into classes at various stages of proficiency. During that period, the first secondary schools for girls were opened, and teachers were for the first time offered professional training and certification. In the first decade of the 20th century, public kindergartens became available to the children of Baltimore.

THE POLITICS OF EDUCATIONAL OPPORTUNITY

We turn now to a closer examination of the process through which public schools in the United States were gradually opened to children of African heritage. One of the foremost objectives of the social movement for the abolition of slavery in the first half of the 19th century was for Americans of African heritage to gain access to education. Following the Emancipation Proclamation and the end of the Civil War, various initiatives were launched to implement this project, including the opening of public "colored schools" in Baltimore (BCPSS, 1999, section 4). Until what Fordham (1996) termed *the second emancipation* arising from the civil rights movement of the 1950s and 1960s, most school districts in the United States operated separate, segregated school systems for black and white students, with gross disparities in funding. In Maryland in 1920, for instance, the public schools' annual expenditure per student for white children was $36 as compared with $13.20 for black children (Olson, 1991). Some policy makers defended such disparities, arguing that the schools serving black families were predominantly located in relatively low-income residential areas that had a lower tax base. This unjust school finance formula continued to operate to the disadvantage of Baltimore's public schools relative to the public schools of the adjacent counties for many years, as it did for many other metropolitan school systems in the United States (Wilson, 1987). Steps were taken to correct this situation in Baltimore in the 1990s.

A more radical line of political justification for segregated schooling drew on the notion of different degrees of capacity to benefit from education, depending on the individual's endogenous intellectual endowment, which some social scientists and administrators held to be unevenly distributed across social groups identifiable by race, class, or gender (e.g., Jensen, 1969). Political opposition to this ideological linkage between endogenous characteristics and entitlement to high-quality education was a central theme of the civil rights movement. One of the landmark achievements of the movement was the 1954 ruling of the Supreme Court in the case of *Brown v. Board of Education*, that segregated access to public schooling was unconstitutional. The Baltimore City Public School System was the first urban public school system in the nation to comply with that ruling by desegregating its schools.

Two related historical changes occurred in Baltimore over the four decades between the landmark *Brown v. Board of Education* ruling and the period in which we conducted the Early Childhood Project, which are relevant for understanding current functioning of the Baltimore City Schools. First, the population of Baltimore and of the public schools went through a process of demographic change that was dramatic both in speed and in political symbolism. The middle-class white population of Baltimore departed in huge numbers, mainly relocating to the adjacent suburbs. In the 20 years between 1950 and 1970, the racial composition of the city's population changed from 24% black to 47% black (Orser, 1991). In the middle of that period, over just five years, the proportion of the school system's student population classified as white declined from 60% in 1955 to 48% in 1960 (BCPSS, 1999, section 7).

A second development was the growth of African American representation within the professional and administrative staffing of the city school system. With the growing preponderance of African

American children in the student population, concern began to grow among civil rights activists about both the disproportionate dominance of European Americans in the personnel staffing the schools and the segregated concentration of black teachers in schools populated by black students. In 1966, 75% of the city's elementary students and more than one-half of secondary students attended "virtually segregated schools, while 90 percent of black teachers were in schools that were 90-to-95 percent black" (BCPSS, 1999, section 7.2).

The first African American superintendent of schools, Roland Patterson, served from 1971 to 1975; the second, Alice Pinderhughes, served from 1982 to 1988. A third African American superintendent, Walter Amprey, ran the schools from 1994 to 1997, covering most of the period of the Early Childhood Project. The philosophies expressed by Pinderhughes and Amprey, that all children can learn and are capable of high achievement (BCPSS, 1999, sections 7.7 and 7.9), were echoed by many of the African American teachers interviewed in the Early Childhood Project, as we discuss later in the chapter. It was not until 1987 that the city elected its first African American mayor, Kurt Schmoke, who campaigned for the office on a ticket advocating education and literacy as instruments of progress for the oppressed and impoverished black population of Baltimore. Yet Schmoke's administration, also covering the period of the Early Childhood Project, was marked (for reasons we will not attempt to analyze in this volume) by an overall decline in the level of funding for the public school system.

BALTIMORE PUBLIC ELEMENTARY SCHOOLS IN THE 1990S

Baltimore's public school system represents a policy-driven attempt to provide unified, consistent schooling to all children resident in the city (109,000 students in 1997) through a network of 113 elementary schools, 23 middle schools, and 27 high schools, plus a number of special schools. The relative uniformity of these schools arose from a deliberate policy of centralized supervision introduced early in the 20th century (BCPSS, 1999, section 5). However, in the 1980s, a contrary theme gained considerable influence, grounded in the concept of professional autonomy, and supported by research showing that the most effective schools were those in which a distinctive philosophical orientation or vision was consensually shared among the personnel of the school under strong leadership by the principal (Cole-Henderson & Serpell, 1998; Silver, 1994). To foster such local unity of purpose, a policy of site-based management was introduced in Baltimore, according considerable authority to the principal. By 1997, however, at the time the Early Childhood Project drew to a close, site-based school management had come to be regarded as a failure (BCPSS, 2002), and policy swung strongly once again in favor of centralized curriculum development and regulation.

The schools in which the children of our study were enrolled shared important design features characteristic of the internationally contemporary model of institutionalized public basic schooling noted in Chapter 1. These design features included an emphasis on cultivating objectivity and rationality in children at a formative stage of their intellectual and moral development, and focused, explicit instruction to impart essential academic competencies, hierarchical organization of the curriculum, an emphasis on advance preparation of children for future cognitive challenges, standardized instructional targets, group instruction, regular scheduling of activities, and age-grading of classes. The schools also shared a number of characteristics that arose more directly from features of their ecocultural setting in urban America at the end of the 20th century. We return to this point when we discuss the schools attended by the children in our study.

Public and Administrative Pressure to Raise Academic Achievement

A crisis of credibility for public schooling in Baltimore that began to emerge in the 1970s was apparent at the time of the Early Childhood Project in the 1990s. The school system was widely recognized as the least effective in the state, with growing numbers of students dropping out of high school or graduating without achieving basic literacy. Following the recommendations of a commission on school performance appointed by the governor of Maryland, a system of statewide tests geared to the curriculum was introduced. These tests were both innovative in conception and very stringent. In 1994, only 9% of Grade 3 students in Baltimore attained satisfactory performance on the reading portion of the Maryland School Performance Assessment Program (MSPAP), 16% on writing, and 12% on mathematics. These figures compare unfavorably with the statewide satisfactory performance rates of 31%, 35%, and 34%, respectively (Westat, 2001). Even by more traditional, less stringent criteria, the Maryland Functional Reading Test (one of the requirements for high school graduation during this period) was passed by only 70% of the Baltimore City high school candidates who sat for it in 1996–1997, and the pass rate declined over the ensuing 4 years (BCPSS, 2001).

The governor's commission went on to stipulate that the schools themselves, and their principals, should be held accountable for measured improvements in student performance, conforming with a national pattern that emerged all across the United States in the 1990s and escalated with the federal passage of the No Child Left Behind Act in 2001. Schools that did not meet a specified criterion of percentage of students performing at a satisfactory level on the state tests were to be taken over by the state for reconstitution under a new administration. By 1997, in Baltimore "fifty of the system's 180 schools...had been designated for possible state takeover through the local reconstitution process" (BCPSS, 2002, p. 15).

SCHOOLING FOR THE CHILDREN PARTICIPATING IN THE EARLY CHILDHOOD PROJECT

We turn now from a more general discussion of issues facing the schools within the Baltimore City Public School System to a specific focus on the schools attended by the children participating in the Early Childhood Project and the teachers who taught the children. We report here the major findings concerning teachers' ideas and beliefs about child development, learning, and cognition, about literacy, and about their approach to the professional activity of teaching. We consider the degree to which variation among teacher beliefs reflected their ethnic heritage, their formal training, and the sociocultural characteristics of clientele to whom they were catering. In Chapter 7, we consider more explicitly the similarities and differences between teachers' perspectives on these matters and those of their students' parents.

A Concern With Discipline and Security in the Schools

Many of the practices of the schools that we studied were manifestly designed to maintain security or to instill discipline. Given schools' commitment to a set of standardized instructional targets, the grouping of students in classes of 20 or more children, and the adoption of a time-regulated schedule of activities, teachers are faced with the challenge of coordinating the behavior of a collection of individuals with diverse dispositions, interests, and aptitudes.

The 11 schools participating in the Early Childhood Project shared certain common features. All entrances to school buildings were kept locked. During school hours, children were only allowed to leave the building, and adults other than teachers to enter the building, in accordance with tightly enforced regulations. The rationale for this control was that the school was legally responsible for the safety of its students, and unauthorized adults entering the building might include persons liable to endanger the children. Combined with a heavy emphasis on disciplined movement within the building, the rigid control of access to the building for visitors, including students' parents, generated an unwelcoming atmosphere. The fact that a number of the schools were quite old and the hallways poorly lighted added to this impression.

Even a single student misbehaving can easily disrupt the performance of class routines. The teachers we observed were often obligated to control such disruptive behavior. In contrast with earlier periods of European and American history, all forms of corporal punishment were strictly prohibited. However, a great deal of verbal reprimand was used, backed with threats of reporting to the principal or to the child's parents, some of whom were known to favor the use of corporal punishment as an instrument of child discipline at home. Control over student behavior was especially noticeable when the schedule required a class to move from one location within the building to another, ensuring the quiet and orderly procession of students along corridors.

For many of the children in the Early Childhood Project, this regimented world was sharply segregated from their lives outside school. Other children, however, experienced comparable restrictions within their own neighborhoods; parents concerned with the children's safety in drug-infested and crime-ridden areas of the city would not allow them to play outdoors or venture outside without an adult.

Some of the teachers we interviewed construed the distinct school context as a valuable feature of the educational enterprise, an oasis of calm and safety in which vulnerable children could take refuge from the rigors of an unruly and dangerous world outside. For these teachers, the civilizing mission of schooling was integrally connected with a socioemotional and moral dimension of socialization. Other teachers perceived the compartmentalization of the school as more problematic, and sought ways to counteract it by fostering connections between the activities of their classes and the life of the surrounding community. We discuss this agenda of building connections further in Chapter 7.

The Early Childhood Project did not systematically assess school climate, but our cumulative impression was that the dominant climate of the overall institution was often somewhat oppressive, whereas the climate of particular classrooms was highly variable, ranging from conflictual or regimented to lively or peaceful and cooperative. Presumably, much of this variation was due to the exercise by teachers of their unique personal styles, guided by their philosophical convictions. Consistent with our impressions, the Baltimore City Public Schools System (2002) Master Plan II for reform of the schools noted succinctly that in the mid-1990s "the climate in far too many schools was not conducive to quality teaching and effective learning" (p. 15).

The Teachers of the Children in the Early Childhood Project

Much of the information included in this chapter comes from our interviews with teachers of the children enrolled in the Early Childhood Project. We interviewed almost all the teachers in whose classes children of our cohort were enrolled in the first 4 years, from prekindergarten through Grade 2. We interviewed a total of 64 teachers (7 prekindergarten, 8 kindergarten, 22 Grade 1, and 27 Grade 2). Four of the teachers were interviewed twice because the grade they taught changed during the study. For example, a prekindergarten teacher we interviewed began teaching kindergarten the following year.

Twenty-five of the teachers were African American, 31 were European American, and 8 were of unknown ethnicity. Almost all the teachers were female. The teachers had a mean of about 15 years' teaching experience, of which 6 were at the grade level they were presently teaching. African American teachers had been teaching significantly more years (mean = 20.14) than European American teachers (mean = 10.67). Most of the teachers had completed a college degree and earned some credits toward a master's degree. One of the teachers also had earned a law degree before moving to the Baltimore area. Those teaching prekindergarten had completed significantly fewer years of education than the others. Sixty-five percent of the teachers were educated locally; 35% were educated out of the state. Sixty-one percent of the African American teachers received their degrees from historically black institutions of higher learning in Baltimore; one of the European American teachers did so.

As part of our interview we asked teachers, "Why did you become a teacher?" and "What are your long-term goals?" Most of those we interviewed said they became teachers because they wanted to teach or work with children. Fifty-three percent of the teachers indicated that they wanted to remain classroom teachers. Most of the teachers who did not intend to continue in the classroom over the long term wanted to stay involved in some aspect of the educational system. Some of them intended to become a counselor or school psychologist (7%), others wanted to go into administration (5%), teach at the college level (8%), or become a curriculum specialist or support teacher (16%).

Teachers as Cultural Outsiders to the Community in Which Their Students Reside

Given the previously described middle-class exodus from the city of Baltimore, it was not surprising to find that most of the teachers (both European American and African American) in the Baltimore public schools attended by our study cohort in 1992–1997 regarded themselves as outsiders to the local community that the school served. Almost all the teachers we interviewed lived a considerable distance from the school and commuted to it daily by car, in many cases from a suburb outside the city limits. Their own children, if they had any, were enrolled in schools in the suburbs with a different climate and cultural style than that which prevailed in these urban schools. This pattern of cultural alienation was especially conspicuous for the schools in our sample that served low-income, inner-city neighborhoods, and has been noted with respect to other United States cities as well (Jordan, Bogat, & Smith, 2001).

A sense of cultural superiority also informed the attitudes of many teachers toward the families and communities in which their students lived. Condescension was sometimes expressed in their interviews with us in the form of disapproval of parental attitudes and practices, mixed with resentment for how difficult this alien parental culture made their task as educators. Other teachers were more sympathetic toward their students' parents, attributing the deficiencies of the homes they provided for their children to external influences such as material poverty and a history of inadequate educational opportunity for the previous generation. These teachers' understanding of their own responsibility thus included compensatory provision to their students of learning opportunities that the families were, through no fault of their own, unable to provide.

As Elliott, Bridges, Ebbutt, Gibson, and Nias (1981) observed with respect to a school system in England, feelings of negotiated accountability to parents for the kind of education offered in their classroom require an egalitarian stance, including a desire to learn from parents what their expectations are of their child's school, class, and teacher. We addressed the question of accountability directly in our interviews with the teachers, asking them whether they considered themselves accountable to anyone in their roles as teachers. About one-half of the teachers took a contractual stance in their response to the question, specifying that they were accountable to Baltimore City Public Schools (that is, to the principal, the administration, the curriculum, and/or their colleagues). The remaining teachers viewed themselves accountable to their students and the parents of the students. For example, a second-grade teacher at a low-income, predominantly European American school said, "Other than my students? . . . I'm accountable to the boys and girls I teach. But . . . parents are the ones paying me – so I'm accountable to them too." A first-grade teacher at a middle-income, predominantly

African American school responded, "Primarily accountable to? The children, because if I'm not doing my job they're the ones that lose."

Even teachers who stated that they were responsible to their principal or the administration often referenced the children in explaining their reasoning. "I have to be held accountable to make sure they (the children) are getting the best education" (a second-grade teacher at a middle-income, predominantly African American school). "I guess my principal would be the main person to whom I answer.... I don't believe in wasting children's time and I try to give to the children what I would want someone to give my children. You know, that's a full day of good solid teaching. First grade is so vital, so important, because it's a foundation" (a first-grade teacher at a low-income, predominantly African American school).

Philosophical Perspectives on Teaching

Quite close to the beginning of the interview with prekindergarten, kindergarten, and first-grade teachers, we asked, "Would you say you have a philosophy of teaching?" Our colleague, Dr. Abdeljalil Akkari, conducted a content analysis of the responses to this question (Akkari, Serpell, Baker, & Sonnenschein, 1998). Six major themes were identified in the responses of the 25 teachers to whom this question was put:

1. *Universal educability*: "Every child can learn." Every child is capable of being educated, a fundamental premise of teaching. For the teachers who invoked this theme, this principle constituted an essential point of departure for teaching.
2. *Child-centered education*: The most important thing is to be centered on the child. There are several ways of addressing this principle: focusing on the child's interests, cultivating a pleasure in learning, and seeking to motivate children.
3. *Individualized-differential teaching*: Every child has different abilities; teachers must stimulate various learning processes by using a diversity of instructional resources and techniques.
4. *Value of instruction*: These statements focused on the efficacy of actual instructional work by the teacher.

5. *Responsibilities of a teacher*: The teacher is responsible for promoting a student's learning process by providing good opportunities.
6. *Socialization goals*: The goal of schooling is to prepare children for an active and constructive role in society.

The theme of *universal educability* is illustrated by the following excerpt from an interview with an African American teacher who was based at a school that served a low-income, African American neighborhood:

My philosophy is that every child can learn, but you just have to take the time, and listen to the child. Because the child tells you every day how you can reach him, how you can instruct him, if you take the time, listen to me. And I believe that in order for us to have a society with good leaders educators should really put more time into children, put more time into children. So my philosophy is that if you take the time to listen to a child that child will learn. And all children are learners.

The following excerpt from an interview with an African American teacher at a school serving a low-income African American neighborhood illustrates the theme of *child-centered education*:

When I came into teaching my aim and ambition was that, as the children were learning, school would be a place where they would have enjoyment. It was not a place where, "Oh God, do I have to come into school again? Do I have to do this?" It would be as they entered school, it was almost a step towards working in our society as a job. School was one of their first indications of a workplace. This is where I'm going to learn how to get along with people. This is where I'm going to learn how to deal with life's processes. This is where I'm going to learn how to really make myself able to live in our society.

The theme of *individualized-differential teaching* is illustrated by the following excerpt from an interview with a European American teacher based at a school serving a low-income, mixed ethnicity neighborhood:

I try to remember . . . I guess I try to remember that every child is different, and I try to keep that in mind, to try to treat them each as individuals as much as possible. It's hard when you've got a whole class, and you've got groups to not think that because one's doing this, that one should be able to do it too. It's difficult, but I think I really try hardest to remember that each child is an individual.

Finally, an example of the theme *responsibilities of a teacher* is the following passage from an interview with a European American teacher who was based at a school serving a low-income, European American neighborhood:

The philosophy . . . is just, you take this child, you see where you need to meet them, like from A to Z. Some children come with a little bit of knowledge. Take that and grow. Some come with a lot of knowledge . . . growing. To be fair, to be firm, persistent, there's so many variables here, so many factors involved. Like someone said to me, "What did you do all day?" Well, ran off papers, made dittos, met with parents, talked with the children, took care of three little fights, the computer, you know, it's just, you know, at lunchtime called a parent. It's just so much going on. But my philosophy is basically I want to do my best, get it done. And when the kids leave the parents will know, wow, they had this teacher, she did her best and let's hope next year, too. I would hope even my own children, I would hope that they have good teachers, too.

Table 6.1 shows the distribution of the main themes endorsed by teachers across the two ethnic heritage groups. It is apparent that the principle of *universal educability* was expressed as a main theme by a higher proportion of the African American teachers than of the

TABLE 6.1. *Main Philosophy of Teaching Themes Expressed by First- and Second-Grade Teachers*

	Ethnicity of Teacher	
Theme	African American (%)	European American (%)
Universal educability	70	14
Child-centered education	10	20
Individualized-differential teaching	0	20
Value of instruction	10	6
Responsibilities of teacher	10	40
Socialization goals	0	0

Note: The percentages refer to the percentage of African American teachers or European American teachers expressing any of the six themes as a main theme. Socialization goals were not mentioned by anyone as a main theme, but were mentioned as secondary themes.

European American teachers, whereas the reverse is true of the theme of *responsibilities of a teacher*. *Child-centered education* was cited by 20% of the European American teachers as their main theme, and by a further 30% as a secondary theme, whereas the corresponding percentages for African American teachers were 10% and 0%, suggesting that this too was a less salient philosophical view for African American than for European American teachers in our sample. Likewise, the theme of *individualized-differential teaching* was cited by 20% of the European American teachers as their main theme, and by a further 27% as a secondary theme, whereas the corresponding percentages for African American teachers were 0% and 17%.

The greater emphasis on universal educability among teachers of African American heritage may reflect a greater concern with social justice in the wake of the civil rights struggle for equal educational opportunity. The educational philosophies of two of the earliest African American superintendents of the Baltimore public schools, Superintendents Pinderhughes and Amprey, also resonate strongly with the theme of *universal educability*. This difference in emphasis of African American and European American teachers may have arisen in part from differences in preservice education. Teachers who received their formal educational induction into the teaching profession at the historically black institutions in Baltimore, a substantial proportion of the African American teachers in our sample, may well have received greater systematic instruction in the political history of emancipation and its relation to the enduring inequities of access to educational opportunity than their colleagues who attended other colleges.

Akkari (1999) confirmed the salience of the universal educability theme for a larger sample of African American teachers not associated with the Early Childhood Project ($N = 56$). He presented the six themes for ranking in order of perceived importance in a questionnaire completed by students at a historically Black institution of higher learning in Baltimore. Fifty-two percent of this sample nominated the theme of *universal educability* as the most important. The questionnaire also asked respondents to rank a set of six possible sources of influence on their beliefs. Consistent with other studies on this topic, the factor most often ranked as the most influential was teaching experience, followed by previous experience with the school system as a student. If, as we speculated above for the Early Childhood Project teachers, their university courses had exercised a significant influence on their beliefs about education, it was not something of which these teachers were aware. Akkari found that more experienced African American teachers within his sample, who were attending the university with a view to moving out of classroom teaching into a higher level of educational administration, were significantly more favorably disposed toward *child-centered education* (25% ranking it highest) than preservice teachers in training (16%). Also, there was a negative correlation between the emphasis respondents placed on *universal educability* and the rating of teaching experience as an influence on their beliefs. It seems, therefore, that the strong importance attached by these African American teachers to the theme of universal educability is not generally attributed by them to any particular specifiable influence.

Coming back to the teachers interviewed in the Early Childhood Project, the European American teachers' greater attention to coping with the many responsibilities of a teacher may perhaps reflect a greater commitment to professionalism as a strategy of response to the public and administrative pressure on schools and teachers to raise academic achievement. These teachers as a group were considerably newer to the field of teaching than our sample of African American teachers. Their belief in professionalism may therefore have been less severely challenged by practical experience than was the case for the latter group. The greater frequency with which these European American teachers invoked the themes of *child-centered education* and *individualized-differential teaching* is more complex to interpret. Akkari (1999) argued that these philosophical themes may be less attractive to African American teachers because they perceive them as incompatible with a full commitment to their overriding concern with *universal educability*, resting his analysis on the radical critique of child-centered education advanced by Cannella (1997). We prefer at this juncture to retain an open mind about the grounds on which African American teachers, at least at the beginning of their careers, show limited enthusiasm for the principle of child-centered education. Whatever their origins, however, these variations in teachers' ideological formulations of "my philosophy of teaching" deserve attention because they likely operated as thematic principles for the organization of a teacher's ideas, for prioritizing her decision making, and so on.

As part of an exploratory, action-research initiative described fully in Chapter 7, we invited a small sample of the prekindergarten and kindergarten teachers through whose classes our study cohort passed to discuss their understanding of the challenges confronting them in their work. One theme that emerged strongly was that they perceived the climate of first-grade classrooms as generally less child centered than the climate they strove to create in their own prekindergarten and kindergarten classrooms. They expressed distress at what they perceived as a rude shock awaiting their students as they graduated from the nurturing climate of their classrooms into the more regimented, outcome-driven demands of the first grade and beyond (Serpell, Baker, Sonnenschein, Gorham, & Hill, 1996).

As we noted in Chapter 1, early childhood education has been the site of the most thorough application of the child-centered educational principles proposed by Rousseau. Some of the prekindergarten and kindergarten teachers we interviewed for the Early Childhood Project also expressed dismay at the contrast between their own child-centered approach and the much more didactic, skills-centered orientation of the first-grade classes into which their students were expected to proceed. To the extent that preschool education is conceived as a preparation for grade school (Vecchiotti, 2003), such a tension appears paradoxical. Indeed, some of the practices that we observed in kindergarten classes in Baltimore, and the rationale advanced for them by the teachers we interviewed, suggest that the early childhood education they offered was driven more by principles of direct instruction in cognitive skills than by principles of nurturance of the "whole child."

Nevertheless, other teachers we interviewed bemoaned the increasing emphasis in kindergarten on academic skills. For example, a first-grade teacher at a middle-income African American school noted, "I wish kindergarten was more social and they didn't require as many academic skills. Leave academics for first grade." Another first-grade teacher at the same school said, "They don't need to do all the academics that they're doing in kindergarten at this point. Concentrate on social skills." Similarly, a prekindergarten teacher at a middle-income, mixed ethnicity school remarked, "They don't need academic skills in kindergarten."

When prekindergarten and kindergarten teachers were asked as part of our interviews with them, "What skills does a child need to succeed in kindergarten?", 67% mentioned some form of social/emotional skills. Twenty percent mentioned skills such as paying attention or working independently. Only 13% mentioned academic skills such as knowing letters or numbers. However, as Vecchiotti (2003) noted, "some kindergarten programs no longer aim to foster all areas of children's development, but tend to focus only on academic skills once taught in the first grade" (p. 3). Current federal accountability demands in the United States are making today's kindergartens look like the first grades of decades past, with prekindergarten programs increasingly resembling yesterday's kindergartens.

Pedagogical Practices of the Teachers

What sorts of pedagogical practices might we see in the classrooms of teachers who are highly skilled at promoting children's literacy development? Pressley et al. (2001) observed first-grade teachers who had been nominated by their supervisors as exceptional or typical. The teachers judged most effective had classrooms characterized by the following: "high academic engagement, excellent classroom management, positive reinforcement and cooperation, explicit teaching of skills, an emphasis on literature, much reading and writing, matching of task demands to student competence, encouragement of student self-regulation, and strong cross-curricular connections" (Pressley et al., 2001; p. iv). In contrast, the classrooms of the least effective teachers fell short in all of these areas.

The observational studies conducted by Pressley and his colleagues (see also Pressley, 2002) show that students with outstanding teachers experience classroom environments that facilitate their literacy development and engagement. Unfortunately, such environments are all too rare in American schools (Baker et al., 2000), particularly those in underfunded urban areas such as Baltimore. Consider this trenchant critique jointly published by the National Association

for the Education of Young Children and the International Reading
Association (NAEYC, 1998):

Teaching practices associated with outdated views of literacy development
and/or learning theories are still prevalent in many classrooms. Such practices include extensive whole-group instruction and intensive drill and practice on isolated skills for groups or individuals. These practices, not particularly effective for primary-grade children, are even less suitable and effective
with preschool and kindergarten children. Young children especially need
to be engaged in experiences that make academic content meaningful and
build on prior learning. It is vital for all children to have literacy experiences
in schools and early childhood programs. Such access is even more critical
for children with limited home experiences in literacy. However, these school
experiences must teach the broad range of language and literacy knowledge
and skills to provide the solid foundation on which high levels of reading
and writing ultimately depend. (p. 31)

At the start of the interview with the teachers in our study, we asked
them to describe their daily routines. Most of the prekindergarten and
kindergarten teachers reported a set of routines that are now quite
traditional in American preschools: storybook reading aloud by the
teacher; sharing time (where selected children report orally to the
class on recent events in their personal lives); small-group activities
at various sites around the classroom, such as play at a sand box, artwork with crayons, paints, and clay, assembly of puzzles, construction with blocks, fantasy play in a play house equipped with various
domestic appliances and some clothing; singing, as well as a number
of explicitly literacy-oriented activities such as copying, matching or
forming letters, identifying written words, and number work, such
as counting aloud, forming sets, and matching digits. Such practices
are in keeping with recommendations from NAEYC (1998) and other
organizations whose interest is early childhood education. At our request, the teachers explained the purpose of these various activities,
indicating that they were intended to foster literacy-related skills,
notably reading and prereading skills (93% mentioned this), writing and vocabulary skills (36%), knowledge of the world (71%), and
independence and responsibility (57%).

The formal organization of space, time, and activity structures in
the first- and second-grade classrooms was more explicitly focused
on instruction, as one would expect, with greater emphasis placed

on the systematic cultivation of literacy skills. From Grade 1 upward, seating patterns in the classrooms conformed either to the classic pattern of institutionalized public basic schooling, with desks arranged in rows facing the teacher's desk or in a cluster pattern that facilitated small-group activities, with chairs facing inward around a shared table or a concentration of desks. The latter seating arrangement allows for more direct interaction among students, a characteristic of cooperative learning.

Collaborative or cooperative learning approaches to instruction are becoming increasingly common in American elementary schools. Such approaches involve groups of three to eight children working together on a task. Within these groups, peers co-construct solutions to problems and assist one another in complementary ways (Forman & McPhail, 1993; Rogoff, 1998). The educational potential of such collaborative learning arrangements is premised, at least in part, on the recognition that, in the "real world" outside the walls of the school, literacy tasks are often addressed through a process of "socially distributed cognition," in which no one individual has sufficient competence to achieve the desired outcome on his or her own (Salomon, 1993). School-based education in the Western tradition has often downplayed the value of such tasks in order to focus on the cultivation of individual competence. However, many teachers have come to realize that there are intrinsic benefits to creating classroom-based opportunities for children to interact co-constructively on projects that are rich in literacy-learning opportunities.

One of the consistent features of the classrooms of teachers in our study was the presence of displays of student work, a practice that is held to enhance the academic self-esteem of students by according recognition to their academic achievements. Such artwork was also found in the hallways between classrooms. A number of teachers, both in Grades 1 and 2, as well as in prekindergarten and kindergarten, made allusion to the importance of wall displays as a dimension of their educational program.

The Language Arts Curriculum

Before examining the details of the language arts curriculum experienced by the children participating in the Early Childhood Project, we present an analysis of the scientific grounding of introductory programs of reading instruction. The alphabetic script used by the English language achieves great cognitive economy through the adoption of a phonetic system that maps a small number of characters onto a very large number of words. In the languages for which these scripts were originally designed, this phonetic spelling system involves a direct correspondence between graphemes (e.g., letters of the alphabet) and particular phonemes (speech sounds). Thus, a competent speaker of the language (who has already mastered that set of phonemes) has only to learn the letter-sound correspondence rules of the spelling system in order to decode a written word into a spoken one, or to commit an oral word to writing. Unfortunately for beginning readers of English, the spelling system that has evolved over several centuries departs from this simple pattern in a number of ways, reflecting the complex etymology of the English language. Thus, for instance, the sequence of letters o-u-g-h corresponds to many different sounds depending on the word in which it occurs (through, though, plough, cough, rough, thought, etc.).

Because meaning is encoded in language at the level of words (or, more strictly, morphemes), some practitioners have suggested that the complex letter-sound correspondence rules of English could as well be skipped, by teaching children to recognize whole words. However, this approach overlooks the functional value of the economical alphabetic system, as well as other information about the structure of the language encoded within the spelling of a word, that together ultimately ensure that mastering the letter-sound correspondence rules of English, complex though they are, is an important prerequisite of mature reading fluency.

A great debate has raged throughout much of the 20th century in the English-speaking community of curriculum developers, instructional theorists, and developmental psychologists regarding the most effective way of teaching children to read. The whole language movement, pioneered by Goodman, Smith, and others in the 1970s, centered its position on the notion of written language as an extension of oral communication. Many of the activities promoted by this movement were designed to cultivate intrinsic motivation by building on children's existing knowledge of the world, enticing them to participate in literacy-based activities by embedding them in the framework of dramatic play, entertaining stories, and other simulations of everyday life. Although this approach greatly enriched the curriculum of the early grades in many schools, by underlining the value of narrative, drawing, and play for the promotion of literacy, it only enabled a certain number of children to become fully literate. Others did not fare so well, apparently never inducing the spelling rules of the script and gradually falling behind as the range of vocabulary in the texts they were expected to read increased beyond the scope of their initial memorized stock of recognizable "whole words."

Thus, a "back to basics" movement arose in the 1990s that placed greater emphasis on inculcating basic decoding skills as foundations for further learning. Unfortunately, the opposition to systematic phonics teaching by whole language advocates led during the 1980s in American education to a weakening of the preparation of teachers to offer effective initial reading instruction (Snow et al., 1998). Many teachers mandated to teach systematic phonics had little knowledge of how to do so effectively.

During the time period of the Early Childhood Project, individual schools were accorded a certain amount of autonomy in selecting curriculum materials, but were expected to conform with state and city standards. We interviewed the first- and second-grade teachers of the children participating in the project about their language arts curricula. Most mentioned drawing their curriculum from several different published programs, also making use of phonics skill development materials and trade books. Nine teachers stated they used Open Court, a program that gives explicit and systematic attention to the development of phonics skills. Five of the teachers said they used the Core Knowledge curriculum, based on E. D. Hirsh's work on what every child should know. Ten of the teachers did not specify the programs they used but simply said they used the BCPSS curriculum. Our sense from the interviews was that approaches for cultivating literacy were quite eclectic, as indeed they were throughout the city. Concerns about low reading scores led the school system to adopt a standardized curriculum in the late 1990s, with the majority of schools required to use Open Court through Grade 2.

Some teachers strongly endorsed the importance of using an approach that directly focused on phonics skill development, whereas others advocated a whole language approach. Several teachers

mentioned that they (or their students) found heavily scripted programs that emphasized phonics boring. Consider the views of two
teachers who worked at the same school serving low-income African
American students. One teacher believed that phonics development
was important for her students, whereas the other believed that her
students, a year older, had sufficient knowledge of phonics. The first-
grade teacher, who had 21 years' experience in the classroom, commented: "We're doing Project Read and Write to Read in Open Court
because last year we felt that the children . . . falling behind in reading . . . not recognizing sight words or doing any reading whatsoever.
So we decided to target . . . going for the phonetic." She further noted
that much of the morning was devoted to language arts with an emphasis on phonics; time in the afternoon was spent on reading for
meaning through the use of a read aloud program. The second-grade
teacher had just graduated from college and was in her first year
of teaching: " . . . don't spend a lot of time on phonics . . . my class,
their reading ability is impressive. I feel that teaching them phonics would more hold them back than help them. Because they are
such good readers I really don't think they need phonics. . . . " This
teacher noted that she stopped using Project Read because she and
her students found it boring, and unnecessary, given the students'
reading level. It is worth noting that 3 of the 4 children in the study
who were in this teacher's class scored significantly below grade level
on the Woodcock-Johnson tests tapping word attack skills and word
identification.

Reading Aloud Stories to the Class

Another shared theme across the grade levels was the cultivation of
intrinsic literacy motivation through storybook reading. In previous
chapters, we reported the findings of the Early Childhood Project
with respect to shared storybook reading at home, presenting evidence that the frequency of this activity, and the nature of the interactions surrounding it, are related to children's motivation for reading
and their reading competencies. Research has shown that storybook
reading in school can also have positive effects, such as enriching children's vocabulary (Elley, 1989) and story comprehension (Dickinson
& Smith, 1994). For many middle-class children, classroom storybook

reading connects with and extends positive experiences they have at home (Dickinson & Keebler, 1989). For those children who do not have frequent or positive home experiences with books, teacher read-alouds may perhaps afford comparable opportunities to experience the positive aspects of shared storybook reading at school to those experienced at home by children of middle-income families.

As part of her master's thesis within the Early Childhood Project, Helen Williams (1999; Williams & Baker, 1998) observed storybook reading interactions in first-grade classrooms and analyzed the areas of focus adopted by the teachers. Participants in this study were first-grade teachers of children in the Early Childhood Project. Twenty-seven teachers who reported reading storybooks to their classes at least occasionally were invited to participate, and 22 agreed to do so. Thirteen of the teachers taught in six schools serving low-income neighborhoods; included within their classes were 31 of the low-income children in our sample. Nine teachers taught in four schools serving middle-income neighborhoods, including 19 children in our middle-income sample. The research team selected a storybook written by a Canadian author that was not familiar to the teachers or students in the study, *Moira's Birthday*, by Robert Munsch (1987). Each teacher was provided with a copy of the book 1 week prior to video-taping so she could familiarize herself with the story and prepare for the reading. Teachers were videotaped as they read the book aloud to their class.

The videotapes of the teachers' storybook reading were transcribed. Each utterance and each action of the teacher was classified according to a coding scheme that included nine mutually exclusive categories:

1. Activation of prior knowledge, using the children's own experience to facilitate comprehension (e.g., Have you ever had a birthday party?)
2. Factual story comprehension, an utterance that aided the children's comprehension (e.g., How many kids was she supposed to invite?)
3. Beyond the story comprehension, an utterance that required the children to go beyond what was stated in the story (e.g., What do you think will happen next?)

4. Skills building, providing the children with tools for reading (e.g., pointing to the words on the page as the teacher read)
5. Knowledge about story, an utterance designed to improve children's knowledge about what is involved in a written story (e.g., Who was the main character?)
6. Factual picture comprehension, an utterance using a picture in the book to aid basic understanding of the story (e.g., How many kids are at the door?)
7. Higher-level picture comprehension, an utterance using a picture from the book to help increase comprehension of the story (e.g., looking at the front cover and asking what they think the book is about)
8. Interest enhancement, an utterance or gesture that provides entertainment or is an attempt to keep the children interested or involved in the story (e.g., using different voices for characters)
9. Enjoyment, an utterance that implied that books are to be enjoyed (e.g., Did you like that story?)

One question of interest was whether teachers differed in the approaches they took depending on the social addresses of the students they taught. No systematic differences were found in this regard. Descriptively, interest enhancement was the most common focus at both levels of income, observed on average 56 times during the activity. Teachers' comments were more likely to focus on comprehension, both factual (mean = 17) and beyond the story (mean = 22), than on skills building (mean = 10). These findings are consistent with those reported in Chapter 4 for the parents of the children participating in the Early Childhood Project. They, too, focused considerably more on story comprehension than on skills in their shared storybook reading interactions. The frequency of comments directly addressed to the topic of enjoyment was low (mean = 2), probably reflecting the fact that this focus is generally expressed in more indirect ways.

Williams also examined whether individual teachers could be characterized in terms of their particular patterns of emphasis in the shared reading interactions. A statistical approach known as cluster analysis revealed that teachers could be grouped reliably based on their patterns of emphasis. Five teachers had a dual focus on interest enhancement and beyond-the-story comprehension; three had this dual focus supplemented with knowledge about story, six had a primary focus on interest enhancement with a secondary focus on factual story comprehension, and three had a main focus on interest enhancement and a dual secondary focus on knowledge about story and skills building. Four other profiles included only one teacher each. The teachers of middle-income children and low-income children were quite evenly distributed across these groups. Clearly, teachers differed with respect to the nature of comments they made during a storybook reading activity, but it does not appear that there were systematic differences between teachers in low- and middle-income schools in how they presented a storybook reading.

Also of interest were data collected on teachers' reported frequency of read-alouds. The mean number of times teachers reported reading aloud to their classes each week was 5.9, with no differences related to the social addresses of the children attending the schools. The more often a teacher reported reading to her class, the fewer questions she asked and comments she made during the observed storybook reading.[1] It seems that teachers, whether consciously or not, make a trade-off between exposing children to many different books somewhat superficially or engaging in deeper discussion, but of fewer books. Evidence that the latter strategy is more beneficial comes from examination of the relations between these two variables and the reading scores obtained by children in the Early Childhood Project on the school-administered Comprehensive Test of Basic Skills in Grade 1. Frequency of teacher read-alouds was negatively related to a composite reading score (vocabulary and comprehension), whereas number of interactions during the observed session was positively related; both correlations were moderate in size.[2]

However, neither frequency of read-alouds nor number of interactions during the observed read-aloud were significantly related to children's scores on the Woodcock-Johnson word identification and word attack subtests administered that same year. This is consistent with the conclusion that we reached in Chapter 4 that shared storybook reading has benefits for children at the level of comprehension rather than basic reading skills. These data also help to explain a

[1] $r = -.39$.
[2] $r = -.36, .31$, respectively.

widely cited result that many advocates of teacher read-alouds have found troubling and perplexing: Meyer, Wardrop, Stahl, and Linn (1994) reported a negative relation between the amount of time teachers spent reading aloud and their students' reading achievement. However, that study did not include observations of storybook reading interactions; it may be that those teachers did little more than read the texts as printed. The data analyzed by Williams suggest that the amount of interpretation and guidance offered by the teacher to the class in the context of reading aloud stories is pedagogically more important than the sheer frequency of this activity.

We also examined teachers' approaches to storybook reading in relation to their responses to questions asked during the interview that took place later in the year. Would teachers who had a primary focus on interest enhancement and enjoyment during the observations also endorse an entertainment perspective on literacy and identify storybook reading as a means of conveying this perspective to their students? Eight of the 18 teachers who had interest enhancement as at least one of their areas of focus mentioned storybook reading as a way of conveying that literacy is a source of entertainment. For example, one of the teachers said, "I love to read and they know that. I love read-aloud time and I think that's contagious, because they love it. And if I don't reach them, it's like we had a program today and I didn't get to read to them. They want a story to be read. So they're really excited about the read-aloud time and they want to read aloud every day." Another pointed out that if she were to read the children a story she would "put the facial expressions in, the voice of the people, how they're going to act" so that the children could see the enjoyment she was getting out of it.

Also observed during the storybook interactions was a discourse format known as I-R-E (initiate-response-evaluate), in which the teacher initiates the cycle, typically with a question or command, the child responds, and the teacher then provides oral feedback evaluating the child's response in terms of its adequacy for her predetermined purpose (Mehan, 1979). This specialized mode of language use for instruction is quite unusual outside the context of schooling, and may be a source of particular difficulty for children whose home experience does not include the high prevalence of "known-answer" questions that is characteristic of parental discourse with preschool-age children in middle-class European American homes (Schieffelin & Eisenberg, 1986).

Literacy Activity Centers: An Ecologically Valid, Play-Based Educational Resource

We noted in earlier chapters the importance of ecological validity for ensuring children deploy their full cognitive repertoire in assigned tasks, and that play is a powerful way of mobilizing children's curiosity and motivation to learn. The potential of play as a resource for the fostering of literacy development in a classroom setting was demonstrated in Akintunde Morakinyo's (1995) doctoral dissertation research with a subsample of children in the Early Childhood Project. Drawing on the work of Neuman and Roskos (1990), Morakinyo recruited the participation of kindergarten teachers in eight classrooms, distributed across four schools, serving low-income African American and European American families. Each teacher agreed to set up in a suitable part of her classroom a play corner designed to simulate a post office. The play post office was equipped with a stock of assorted stationery, including envelopes, printed forms, stamps and ink pads, pens, pencils and markers, stickers, posters, play money, trays, a mailbox and a tote bag for mail. Children were periodically assigned a free play session of 20 to 40 minutes duration in this structured activity setting in groups of 3 to 5 children. Three of them at any one time were asked to wear a jacket with a small transmitter microphone installed in it so their speech could be tape-recorded. A hand-held camera was also used to make concurrent videotapes.

Morakinyo's analysis of the children's interactions in this setting focused on extended episodes of literacy-related play. Roskos (1990) proposed a theoretical taxonomy of increasing complexity for children's pretend play, with the simplest form of play centering on isolated categories (e.g., money, a postage stamp, a mailman), the next level incorporating several categories into a broader scheme (e.g., buying a stamp from the mailman), and the most complex level involving social interaction and language to integrate play into an extended episode. During episodes, children are actively involved in solving problems within schemes. Morakinyo reliably coded the children's videotaped free play sessions in the post office centers, and computed the amount of time spent in episodic play. Significantly more time was devoted to more complex, episodic play by the African American children in his sample than by the European American children, a finding that he attributed to the African American children's greater investment in negotiating roles and routines in their play sessions.

Turning to the development of communicative competence, Morakinyo adopted Halliday's (1973) pragmatic perspective that focuses on how the meaning of language is derived from the social context in which it is used. Halliday distinguished seven pragmatic functions of language: the personal function that expresses the theme of "here I come"; the interactional function ("me and you"); the informative function ("I've got something to tell you"); the heuristic function ("tell me why"); the imaginative function ("let's pretend"); the instrumental function (e.g., "I want", "see!", or "listen!"); and the regulatory function ("do as I tell you"). Morakinyo found that the children of European American heritage in his low-income kindergarten sample employed a greater proportion of the informative language function. He had also hypothesized that children of African American heritage would display a greater proportion of utterances expressing the personal and imaginative functions, but those hypotheses were not confirmed.

However, children of African American heritage more often used overlapping turns, which Morakinyo interpreted as an aspect of the cohesiveness of social interaction observed in their play. Overlapping turns are part of a cluster of expressive skills prioritized in the culture of low-income African American families, which also include the use of rhythm, intonation variation, and body language "to embellish and complement the informative mode of discourse" (Morakinyo, 1995, p. 120).

Children almost universally enjoyed playing in the post office corner, and teachers found that it was easy to integrate within the range of activities they had programmed for their classroom.

It was observed that teachers' enthusiasm about the post-office and their attitude to play-time in general was an important factor in the quality of the children's response to the play centers. Those teachers who perceived the post-office as a learning tool for their students or as a teaching tool for themselves were able to create an atmosphere in which children appropriated the post-office's props and materials and mastered the roles and routines associated with this literacy setting, and in general use the center effectively. (Morakinyo, 1995, p. 88)

Teachers who displayed this attitude often responded constructively to playful initiatives by a child, seizing the opportunity to fine-tune the child's interest in a literacy-related topic or activity.

The strategy of structuring an activity setting to afford particular types of learning opportunity for students is quite widely used in contemporary early childhood classrooms. By embedding the agenda of literacy learning in a play center, teachers are able to capitalize on the motivational power of play to capture children's interest and demystify the skills required. In other words, the entertainment perspective on learning to read has application in the classroom, just as it does in the context of children's homes.

Teachers' Perspectives on the Importance of Three Developmental Domains

Building on our interviews with parents about the importance of different developmental domains (discussed in Chapter 3), we asked prekindergarten, kindergarten, and first-grade teachers to rate on a 5-point scale the importance of social skills, academic skills, and self-esteem for the children in their classrooms. The three domains were typically rated as important; no one gave a rating lower than 3 on any domain. However, reflecting the shift in curricular emphasis between kindergarten and Grade 1, first-grade teachers more strongly endorsed the importance of academic skills for their students ($M = 4.32$) than did teachers of prekindergarten ($M = 3.64$) or kindergarten children ($M = 3.14$).[3] The ratings provided by the teachers did not differ with their ethnic heritage.

Teachers' stronger emphasis on self-esteem and social skills is consistent with parents' socialization goals for their children. As discussed in Chapter 3, most parents mentioned academic goals,

---

[3] $F (2, 38) = 7.26, p = .002$.

but such goals were included among several nonacademic goals. In contrast to parents, however, teachers tended to view social skills and self-esteem as enabling skills for children's academic development. For example, a kindergarten teacher at a low-income African American school stated, "If they don't know how to interact socially in this type of setting, they are not going to be successful in the classroom." A kindergarten teacher at a middle-income African American school noted, "I think self-esteem and social skills extremely important because without those you can't teach." Teachers' views on the importance of self-esteem and social skills are compatible with a current policy message arising from educational research: being successful in school is multidetermined (Raver, 2002).

The Nature of Individual Literacy and Its Early Development

Picking up the themes about the significance of literacy in early childhood that we derived from our interviews with parents of children when they were in prekindergarten, and described in Chapter 3, we included in our second and subsequent rounds of interviews with teachers a request for them to rate in importance the three themes of literacy as a set of skills to be learned, literacy as a source of entertainment, and literacy as an integral ingredient of everyday life. A total of 54 teachers over a 3-year period responded, and consistently rated all three themes as important. On a 5-point scale with 5 representing extremely important, the mean rating for the entertainment theme was 4.09, for the skills theme 4.28, and for the everyday life theme 4.63. Ratings did not differ across teachers of kindergarten, first, or second grade.

Teachers were asked to give examples of how they conveyed these themes in their classrooms. The most frequently cited examples for the entertainment theme were reading stories to the children (19%), modeling by the teacher of enjoyment of reading (9%), having books available all over the classroom (7%), and allowing children to choose what they want to read during silent reading periods (7%). For the skills theme, the most common response was that the teacher specifically teaches the skill (28%). For the everyday life theme, the most common responses were practice in filling out forms and reading menus (11%), incorporating reading and writing into everything (13%), and talking about and demonstrating the need for literacy (7%).

We also asked the teachers in Grades 1 and 2 to rank the three themes in order of importance for children in their school's neighborhood. Although there was quite high consensus on the greater importance of *literacy as an integral ingredient of everyday life* than the other two themes, this was significantly more pronounced among the European American teachers (88%) than among the African American teachers (52%). A substantial minority of the African American teachers (32%) ranked first in importance the theme of *literacy as a skill to be learned*, whereas only one European American teacher did so. Given that there was a preponderance of matches between the ethnicity of teachers and that of the population of their school's neighborhood, it is unclear whether this partial convergence with the findings reported in Chapter 3 represents evidence of a shared cultural perspective between low-income African American parents and middle-class teachers of the same ethnic origin or of a tendency for teachers to deliberately reflect in their answers to this question what they recognized to be the dominant opinion of parents in the neighborhood.

Teachers' Assessments of Children's Reading Skills

One facet of the expertise that teachers are expected to have is a capacity for accurate and insightful assessment of their students' strengths and needs as these relate to the agenda of schooling. Our data afforded an opportunity to gauge the degree to which this expectation was upheld. In our interviews with first- and second-grade teachers, we asked them to rate on a 5-point scale the reading competence of each of the cohort children in their class with reference to three different criteria: the child's own developmental trajectory ("How much progress would you say (*child's name*) has made in reading relative to how well he/she was reading at the beginning of the year?"); the distribution of such competencies within the class in which he/she was enrolled ("How would you rate (*child's name*) relative to the rest of your class?"); and national norms ("How would you rate (*child's name's*) present reading level relative to national standards for children at the end of first/second grade?"). We then compared the teachers' ratings with other indicators available to us for the same children.

For the child's growth relative to his or her own developmental trajectory, we looked at the child's score on the Basic Reading Skills measure of the Woodcock-Johnson Test at the end of Grade 2, controlling for the child's performance on the same test at the end of Grade 1. Teachers' ratings were moderately correlated with children's reading growth.[4] In other words, teachers were reasonably accurate at gauging children's individual progress. We asked the teachers to estimate how each child would rate his or her own reading skills, and also to tell us how often the child chose to read independently. Teachers estimated that the majority of the children believed they were good readers (33% would say they were excellent, 33% good, and only 15% below average or poor). How highly the teacher estimated the child would rate himself as a reader and how frequently the child reportedly read were both highly correlated with the teacher's other ratings of the child's literacy skills, as well as with the child's own reading scores on the Woodcock-Johnson.

Teachers' ratings with respect to the other two frames of reference did not differ greatly, suggesting that the distinction was not a strong and salient one for them. The distribution of teacher ratings relative to national norms for the 47 children they rated in Grade 1 was 35% low or seriously delayed (ratings of 1 or 2), 41% average (a rating of 3), and 24% high or exceptional (ratings of 4 or 5). In Grade 2, the corresponding percentages were 30%, 42%, and 28%. Yet, it is widely publicized in the Baltimore media that the reading levels of city students are well below national norms. Moreover, when we examined teachers' ratings relative to national norms, we found that although they were quite accurate with respect to relative standing within our cohort (correlating strongly with the child's Woodcock-Johnson Basic Reading Skills scores[5]), they tended to overestimate how well the child was reading relative to national norms. Thus, in Grade 1, 20 children rated by their teacher as average earned reading scores significantly below grade level, whereas in Grade 2, 13

[4] $r = .44, p. = .003$.
[5] Grade 1, $r = .56, p < .001$; Grade 2, $r = .76, p < .001$.

students who were rated by their teacher as average to high earned scores that were significantly below grade level.

These data suggest that teachers are quite sensitive to individual differences among their students and to the rate of improvement of their students' reading over time, but that they are less able to make accurate assessments of their students' reading levels relative to national norms, and tend systematically to overestimate how well their students are reading. As a result, the teachers we interviewed may have been in a position to offer parents accurate information about their child's rate of progress, but less accurate forecasts of how well their child was likely to fare on public examinations or in competitive access to jobs or entry into institutions of higher education. The significance of these strengths and limitations in teachers' assessments of their students' reading may be mediated by how their appraisals are communicated to the child and his or her parents.

Teachers' Perspectives on the Educational Futures of the Children in the Early Childhood Project

When the children in the study were completing second grade, we asked their teachers to speculate about how far each of the cohort children in their classes would go in school, "Realistically, do you think *(child's name)* will complete high school? Go on to college?" Seventy-eight percent of the children were predicted to complete high school and 52% percent were predicted to go on to college. An additional 13% were believed to have a chance of going to college if they received additional help with school from their parents. More middle-income children than low-income children were predicted to complete high school (100% vs. 62%, respectively) and to go on to college (100% vs. 38%, respectively).[6] Predictions did not differ in relation to children's ethnicity.

Teachers' predictions of the children's future education were significantly related to the children's second-grade reading scores on the Woodcock-Johnson test. Correlations between the children's reading

---

[6] High school: $F (1, 44) = 11.96, p = .001$; college: $F (1, 44) = 31.72, p = .000$.

scores and predictions of high school completion were moderate;[7] correlations between the reading scores and predictions of college attendance were strong.[8] These relations provide further evidence that teachers' assessments of their students' academic competencies accord with our independent assessments of those competencies.

SUMMARY

Our analysis in this chapter of the agenda and practices of schooling has examined the testimony of the teachers within multiple layers of context: the institutionalized structure of public basic schooling (an international model), the politics of educational opportunity (grounded in American history), and more specific features of the Baltimore schools in the 1990s, including a tendency for teachers to be cultural outsiders to the communities in which their students reside, and a school culture concerned with security and discipline. The organization of recurrent activities for children at school was constrained by these macrosystemic factors, and by the architecture of the buildings, the time table, and the officially prescribed curriculum. Yet within that framework, the individual teacher exercised considerable discretionary judgment on how best to cultivate individual literacy. This could be done, for instance, by prioritizing various options such as reading aloud a story to the class, or assigning time in a literacy activity center, or by placing relatively greater emphasis, when assisting a student to read, on the phonics of decoding words or on the broader meaning of the text.

The ethnic heritage of teachers in our sample accounted for significant variance in the relative emphasis they placed on the philosophical theme of universal educability (a high priority for African American teachers) relative to child centeredness and individualization of instruction (both high priorities for European American teachers). However, across the board, teachers attached great importance to social skills and self-esteem as dimensions of young children's development, and they strongly endorsed the significance of individual literacy for their students as a set of skills to be learned, as a source

[7] $r = .30, p = .05$.
[8] $r = .60, p = .000$.

of entertainment, and as an integral ingredient of everyday life. For the fine-tuning of instruction, every teacher needs to assess and track the growing competencies of her students.

In Chapter 7, we discuss some of the commonalities and differences between the perspectives of teachers and parents on literacy socialization, and their implications for the possibility of cooperative communication about the support and promotion of literacy development in the children for whose education they shared responsibility.

7

Relations Between Homes and Schools

Although most of the process of a child's formal education takes place within school, the child's family can and often does influence that process. Families and schools share a common goal of educating children. Sharing that goal does not necessarily mean, however, that families and schools hold the same beliefs about how to accomplish it. In Chapter 3, we presented information about the literacy-related ideas, beliefs, and practices of the parents of children in the Early Childhood Project. In Chapter 6, we discussed the beliefs about learning and schooling held by the children's teachers. In this chapter, we continue our discussion of parents' beliefs about children's learning and development by focusing in more detail on those beliefs most pertinent to children's academic development. We compare parents' and teachers' beliefs about the schooling process and consider how similarities and differences in beliefs may affect children's literacy development. We frame our discussion around two general questions: (1) Is there congruence between the intimate culture of children's homes and the agenda of schooling? In particular, do parents and teachers hold similar beliefs about children's academic development and one another's role in supporting it? and (2) Do parents and teachers hold similar views of the focal children as individuals? The information from parents comes from the seven parental ethnotheory interviews conducted during the 5 years of the Early Childhood Project, as well as from the ecological inventories that documented children's participation in various activities. Information from teachers comes from interviews conducted with children's prekindergarten through Grade 2 teachers.

This chapter is organized into four sections. The first section presents our theoretical perspective on home–school relations by expanding on material presented in Chapter 1. The second section considers the parents' and teachers' ideas about the schooling process and their respective roles in that process by documenting their general ideas about children's learning and development. The third section focuses on parents' beliefs about their own children and relates those beliefs to how the children's teachers view the children. In the final section, we discuss an intervention to improve communication between teachers and families. Because we were interested in commonalities and differences related to social address, we included sociocultural group as a factor in all our analyses. As it turned out, there were few differences across groups, but those that were found are discussed.

THEORETICAL APPROACHES TO UNDERSTANDING HOME–SCHOOL RELATIONS

Bronfenbrenner (1979) proposed that a child lives his or her life in several contexts that individually and synergistically impact development. Two important contexts for children growing up in the United States between the ages of 5 and 17 years are home and school. Although these two contexts can be viewed as autonomous, there is a necessary relation between the child's family and school due to the child's daily transitions between the two. Bronfenbrenner suggested that the optimal relation between home and school for a child's development was one that "encouraged the development of mutual trust, a positive orientation, goal consensus between settings . . ." (p. 216).

Current theories about children's academic development acknowledge the importance of involving parents in their children's education (e.g., Bruneau, Ruttan, & Dunlap, 1995; Pryor & Church, 1995; Swap, 1993). Parental involvement can be beneficial for at least three reasons: (1) It may increase the frequency of children's academically relevant experiences; (2) It may convey a message to the *child* about the importance of school; and (3) It may convey a message to the *teacher* that this parent cares about her child's schooling (Sonnenschein & Schmidt, 2000).

The importance of involving parents in their children's education is recognized by federal legislation, which states that "every school will promote parent involvement to support the social, emotional, and academic growth of children" (U.S. Department of Education, 1996; see also Goal 8 of Goals 2000, National Education Goals Panel, 1998). Parental involvement seems to have been implemented in most schools through what Swap (1993) has called a "School-to-Home Transmission Model." The aim of such an approach is to train parents to be involved in their children's education in ways that the school considers appropriate, and it stems from the notion that there is a deficit at home that needs correction. In contrast, Swap's preferred model of home–school relations is what she calls the "Partnership Model," a means of interaction that is more egalitarian in nature, and involves shared planning and decision making.

The establishment of linkages between the child's home and school has served as an important component of several nationally recognized intervention programs (e.g., School Development Program, Comer & Haynes, 1991; Success for All, Madden, Slavin, Karweit, Dolan, & Wasik, 1993; see also Connors & Epstein, 1995). These approaches have in common an outreach component to increase parental involvement in all aspects of the educational process. Such attempts stem from a largely untested set of assumptions about the nature of families' ideas, beliefs, and abilities. Although all families likely want their children to succeed in school, we cannot assume that schools and families share a set of beliefs about what success is and how best to foster it. Moreover, there may well be cultural differences in which beliefs are shared by parents and teachers. In a more recent review, Goldenberg (2001) stressed the need for teachers to understand how parents view various educational practices, such as learning to read, before attempting interventions with them. His views are in keeping with those we have expressed about the importance of understanding parental beliefs about children's learning (e.g., Baker et al., 1996; Serpell, 1997; Sonnenschein & Schmidt, 2000).

We next consider some examples of how a lack of consensus between parents' and teachers' expectations may result in misunderstandings, even when schools are making efforts to involve parents. Most elementary schools have a variety of activities to involve parents in their children's schooling, such as Back-to-School Nights and parent–teacher conferences (U.S. Department of Education, 1996). However, attendance at these activities varies with the percentage of low-income or minority children enrolled in the schools. Attendance tends to be lowest when minority or low-income families comprise the majority of a school's population.

Research by Catherine Snow and her colleagues with low-income children in the Boston, Massachusetts region illustrated how parents' beliefs about their role in their children's education may contribute to low parental attendance (Snow et al., 1991). These authors found that parents assumed that if their child was doing well, as indicated by report card grades or no negative messages from teachers, they need not be in contact with their child's teacher. Thus, parents' failure to attend parent–teacher conferences was due to being satisfied with how their children were doing rather than a lack of interest. Unfortunately, teachers misinterpreted the parents' absences at Back-to-School Night programs or their failure to sign up for routine parent–teacher conferences as a lack of interest in their children's education.

Valdes (1996), in an ethnographic study of school children growing up in a southwestern Mexican American community, discussed how the behaviors of children's families at a Back-to-School Night program at the start of the year may have given teachers a negative impression of parental interest in children's schooling. Because parental attendance at the program was typically low, the school made a special effort to increase the number of parents who attended. Their efforts were successful, but the low-income parents who attended the program spent little time in their children's classrooms and did not interact with their children's teachers. The behavior of the low-income parents contrasts with that typically displayed by middle-income parents. Lareau (1996) similarly observed that low-income parents were less likely than middle-income parents to initiate interactions with their children's teachers, even when they had concerns about how well children were doing.

CONGRUENCE OF CHILDREN'S HOME LIVES WITH THE
AGENDA OF SCHOOLING

Much of the research on the congruence of children's home and school lives has focused on activities and material resources available to children at home. Clearly, this is an important area of inquiry and one where we find sociocultural differences. For example, our ecological inventory data (presented in Chapter 3), as well as data from other studies, showed that low-income children generally have fewer story-books available at home than middle-income children and spend less time engaging in parent–child storybook reading (Goldenberg, 2001; Smith & Dixon, 1995). Adams (1990) suggested that the less frequent storybook reading experienced at home by low-income children puts them at a disadvantage upon entering school because they had fewer opportunities to acquire knowledge and skills that teachers take for granted.

Research by Goldenberg, Gallimore, and their colleagues, however, has shown that discontinuities between the worlds of home and school involve more than the availability of material resources and opportunities to interact with others (see Goldenberg, 2001, for a fuller review). Goldenberg and his colleagues (1992) investigated literacy practices in low-income Spanish-speaking families in Los Angeles, California. One question of interest was why these parents rarely read storybooks with their young children. Was this due to limited availability of Spanish storybooks at home? If so, providing parents with such books should increase the frequency of storybook reading. Accordingly, the research team supplied kindergarten children with Spanish language storybooks to bring home with them from school for their parents to read with them. Although parents did read these books with their children, direct observation suggested that they conceptualized learning to read as learning to decode because they did not focus on comprehension or motivational factors in their interactions with their children. In a subsequent study with different families from the same population, Reese and Gallimore (2000) found that parents believed that learning to read did not commence until children received formal instruction in school and they did not encourage children's earlier attempts to engage with print. Furthermore, the parents believed that once children began formal instruction they needed much practice, of a rote drill nature, to achieve proficiency.

We turn now to our own findings regarding the congruence between children's experiences at home and what teachers expect and desire. To preview our main findings, our data suggest that parents and teachers assumed they had much more knowledge about each others' beliefs and expectations than was actually the case. We organize our discussion around three topics: parental beliefs about literacy development, parents' views of their children's academic progress, and parents' and teachers' ideas about their roles in helping children learn.

Parental Views of Learning to Read

As we noted in previous chapters, theorists interested in children's reading development have turned from a reading readiness perspective, which conceptualized learning to read as a discontinuous process, to an emergent literacy perspective, which posits that reading development is a continuous process that may begin at home several years before formal instruction occurs (Whitehurst & Lonigan, 2001). Before a child is able to decode text, that child has become aware of the differences among the sounds of the language he or she hears, learned quite a lot about what books are, noticed print in the environment, and acquired an interest in reading. Such knowledge is typically acquired without formal instruction, but rather through engagement in everyday living activities with family and friends. This knowledge serves as an important foundation for the skills taught once the child enters school so children who lack this knowledge will be at a disadvantage.

We were interested in discerning parents' knowledge of children's early literacy development. Although educators urge parents to read storybooks with their children, parents may not know of the role that storybook reading plays. Moreover, parents may not realize that emergent literacy can be fostered by common daily living activities such as attending to print on grocery products.

As part of the second parental ethnotheory interview, conducted a few months after each family enrolled in the project, we asked parents, ". . . what signs does your child show that he is beginning to learn to read?" Although parents could give as many examples as they desired, most gave one or two. We categorized responses as focusing on (1) emergent literacy (showing an awareness of what books are and how they are used; showing an awareness of environmental print by recognizing or asking about print found in one's environment);

(2) decoding skills/word recognition (sounding out letters or words, word recognition or asking what a word is, attempting to read text); (3) motivation (showing an interest in reading or reading related activities, expressing/showing desire to read on one's own); and (4) general improvements in a child's reading. (This last category was mentioned by only a few parents so we do not discuss it further.)

The most common response type, provided by 71% of the parents, focused on decoding or word recognition skills. For example, a low-income European American mother (C11) responded, "... try to sound out words, he'll be reading what's coming on tv ... " A low-income African American mother (F3) said, " ... she'll break a word down. She can take a long word actually like that word there, experiences, and break it down. . . . If she can't quite get it then she'll spell it and ask me what does it mean ... "

Thirty-five percent of the parents talked about emergent literacy signs. For example, a low-income European American parent (E8) stated, "He'll sit there and look at (the book) and when I read to him he knows from the pictures what it's about." A low-income African American mother (B2) noted, "She good looking at the pictures ... she can basically tell you what's going on in the pictures." A middle-income European American mother (G3) reported: "I guess recognizing signs, would that come under there?"

Twenty-six percent of the parents talked about motivation for reading. A low-income European American mother (H7) said, "He wants you to read those books to him ... " Mrs. G, the middle-income European American parent introduced in Chapter 3, stated, "They want you to read to them."

Because parents often identified multiple signs, we can also look at the percentages of responses of each type that were given. Of the 120 responses, over one-half (56%) addressed aspects of decoding, 16% focused on a child's interest in reading, and 27% dealt with signs of emergent literacy (half focusing on knowledge of books and their uses and half on environmental print awareness).

It is not surprising that most of the responses about early signs of literacy focused on decoding. Given the pattern of parents' responses, a greater effort may be needed to increase parents' awareness of the importance of emergent literacy and motivation for learning to read, as well as activities to foster their development.

Parents' responses about early signs of literacy development were generally unrelated to either social address or the age of the focal child at the time of recruitment (Wave 1 vs. Wave 2). The one area where there were significant differences was in the mention of motivation as a sign.[1,2] More middle-income African American parents mentioned motivation (82%) than parents in the two low-income groups (African American = 13%, European American = 18%). The percentage of middle-income European American parents who mentioned motivation (42%) did not differ significantly from the other three groups.

Although more of the parents commented on children's attempts to decode print than on their children's emergent literacy knowledge, 35% did comment on such early signs of literacy development as recognizing a McDonald's logo or learning to turn the pages of a book appropriately. Furthermore, parents' reports in response to the ecological inventory evidenced sensitivity to changes with age in what are the most appropriate types of literacy-related experience. Thus (as we noted in Chapter 3), as the children grew older, their parents reported less frequent interaction with preschool books and storybooks, and more frequent use of chapter books. By the time children enter second or third grade, reading the more complex chapter books with adults may facilitate the development of more integrative information-processing strategies for higher-level story comprehension. As our analysis revealed in Chapter 5, the middle-income European American parents in our study reported a stronger shift with age in this regard. This suggests that this group was more committed to the theory of cognitive development that informed

---

[1] We analyzed differences among cultural groups in the number of motivation responses; Kruskal-Wallis chi square (3) = 8.00, $p = .046$.

[2] We compared the number of motivation responses given by Wave 1 and 2 parents. Significantly more of the Wave 2 parents mentioned motivation, Pearson chi square (2) = 8.52, $p = .01$. The difference in the number of motivation responses given by Wave 1 and 2 parents is probably explained by there being a greater number of middle-income African American parents in Wave 1 (two responses) than 2 (nine responses). Note that there were no significant differences related to cultural group in the pattern of responses between parents in Wave 1 and 2.

the training of their children's teachers, and thus provided a set of literacy-related experiences to their children at home that was more congruent with the schools' agenda.

Parents' responses to another interview question provide some additional evidence of sensitivity to developmental changes in optimal literacy-related experiences. When the children were in second grade, we asked their parents about reasons for reading with prekindergartners and second graders, "We are interested in the kinds of things parents do with children when they read. We will ask you first about reading at home with a pre-kindergartner, and then about reading with a second grader. What reasons do you think parents have for reading with their pre-kindergarten child? What reasons do you think parents have for reading with their children when they are in second grade?" Although parents could give as many reasons as they desired, many mentioned just one. The most common reasons given for reading with a prekindergartner were to get the child interested in reading (53% of parents mentioned this) and to help the child learn to read (46%). The most common reason given for reading with a second grader was skill development (65%). Although these responses do not provide information about the types of materials used or how the reading experience changed, they do show an awareness by parents that children's needs change with development.

Parental Views of Academic Success

As discussed in Chapter 3, almost all the parents in the Early Childhood Project indicated a desire for their young children to be successful in school. For parents to effectively assist their children with school, they need to have an understanding of how well their child is progressing. Unfortunately, children's report cards, the obvious means of communicating such information, do not necessarily present an easily interpretable picture for many parents. To illustrate, Snow et al. (1991) found with their sample of low-income elementary school children that most of the children in the early grades received As and Bs on their report cards. However, such grades did not correlate well with children's scores on standardized tests, perhaps because teachers often awarded grades based on nonacademic factors, such as motivation, and progress relative to presumed aptitude, or progress relative to classmates. The parents in the Snow et al. study assumed that grades of B and C indicated their child was making satisfactory progress, a view not necessarily shared by the teachers. Sixty-eight percent of the mothers thought their children were reading above grade level, but 40% of these children were not, according to their reading scores.

We asked parents when their children were in second grade and again in third, "How is your child doing this year in reading?"[3] Fifty of the parents responded on both occasions. Parents' responses were categorized as either doing well (which included positive responses, such as pretty well, shows much improvement, very well) or not doing well. Most parents reported that their children were doing well in reading (88% in second grade and 82% in third). Nevertheless, the average reading scores of the children in both years were about one-half a year below grade expectations when compared with norms from nationally standardized tests. Our findings, in keeping with those of Snow et al. (1991), suggest that parents are not necessarily fully aware of how well their children are reading. Nevertheless, parents responses were significantly correlated with their children's reading scores, indicating some sensitivity to their children's progress.[4]

Parents' and Teachers' Views of the Role of the Home and the School in Children's Learning

For parents and teachers to establish a partnership, they need consensus about their respective roles in a child's education. To achieve such consensus, they need to be knowledgeable about one another's expectations and beliefs. Over the course of the Early Childhood Project, we asked parents and teachers various questions about their expectations of each other. We start our discussion with a

---

[3] Included is the question asked in third grade. The wording of the question in second grade was, "Tell me how your child is doing in school. How is she doing in reading?"
[4] Relation between parents' judgments when child in second grade and word recognition score, r (48) $= .49, p = .00$. Relation between parents' judgments when child in third grade and word recognition score, r (47) $= .35, p = .02$. Relation between parents' judgments when child in third grade and reading comprehension, r (47) $= .33, p = .02$.

focus on their views of their roles in facilitating children's literacy development.

When children were in prekindergarten, we asked their parents about the roles of the home and school in helping children become literate. More specifically, we said, "I'm going to ask you to tell me now how you feel about the responsibilities of the school and the home for each of these parts of children's learning. Does one of these two worlds in which the child gains experience have more responsibility than the other, and do they have different responsibilities? Which is more important?" We asked the same questions of the children's prekindergarten, kindergarten, and first-grade teachers. Although we asked about the role of the home and school in several different domains, we limit our discussion here to responses for learning to read and write and responses to learning right from wrong. We classified responses as primarily emphasizing school, primarily emphasizing home, or emphasizing both. Many parents (53%) and most teachers (73%) stressed that both home and school played a role in children's learning to read. Thirty-one percent of the parents and 27% of the teachers believed that the school was primarily responsible for teaching children to read. Relatively few parents (16%) or teachers (14%) believed that the home was primarily responsible. None of the differences between the responses of parents and teachers were statistically significant. In all but seven cases, the responses of a child's parent and teacher about who bears the primary responsibility for teaching reading were in accord.

The attribution of responsibility for teaching children moral awareness was different from the domain of literacy. Thirty-nine percent of the parents and 60% of the teachers believed that both home and school were responsible for teaching children right from wrong. Sixty-one percent of the parents and 40% of the teachers believed the home was primarily responsible. No parent or teacher viewed the school as bearing primary responsibility. Again, none of the comparisons between the responses by parents and teachers yielded significant differences.

Although many parents and teachers may agree about the need to share responsibility for teaching a child to read, such consensus does not necessarily mean agreement on what roles each will play.

TABLE 7.1. *Questions from Third-Grade Parental Ethnotheory Interview*

When we met last year, we began to talk about how your child was doing in school. I'd like to continue with that topic:

1. Does the teacher ever contact you to let you know how well your child is doing?
2. Do you ever contact the teacher as opposed to her contacting you? (If parent responds yes) If you are not pleased about something, do you contact the teacher to discuss your concerns?
3. In the kind of conversation between teachers and parents that we've been discussing, one question that arises is: What do parents and teachers expect of each other? Do you have any clear idea of what your child's teacher expects of you as a parent?
4. What do you expect of her as a teacher?
5. What are your expectations of the school more generally?

We turn next to parents' responses to a series of questions focusing on what they expected of their children's teachers and schools, as well as what they believed was expected of them as parents. These questions, presented in Table 7.1, were part of the final parental ethnotheory interview conducted when children were in third grade. Coding categories for the open-ended questions were developed from the responses given by the parents. Parents tended to give more than one response to these questions.

In response to the question about what parents expected from their children's teachers (question 4), many parents (54%) gave a general response, such as they expected the teacher to "teach" or "do their job." Other common responses were that teachers should help facilitate their children's intellectual or academic development (32%), view children as individuals (21%), and communicate with the parents (23%). A majority of parents (76%) stated that teachers contacted them to let them know how their children were doing in school (question 1). About 25% of these parents noted that contact occurred as part of the normal daily routine (e.g., when picking a child up from school). Moreover, all the parents reported that they initiated discussion with their child's teacher when they were displeased or concerned about something, by purposely contacting the teacher (98% of the parents) or taking advantage of naturally occurring meetings (2% of the parents).

The most common responses from parents about what they expected of their children's school (question 5) focused on the school's providing an environment rich in resources (30%), where their children were safe (20%) and could learn (38%), and where the teachers in the school individualized the curriculum for the children (20%).

Did these parents have a clear understanding of what their children's teachers expected of them (question 3)? Sixty-seven percent of the parents responded that they had such an understanding; 33% said they did not. A greater percentage of low-income parents (28%) than middle-income parents (5%) were unsure exactly what their child's teacher expected of them. As we discussed previously, others have found that low-income parents tend to have less contact with their children's teachers than middle-income parents. Low-income parents generally have completed fewer years of education than middle-income parents, making them less familiar and/or comfortable with educational mores (Stevenson & Baker, 1987). Cultural differences in parental educational levels and amount of contact with teachers offer some possible explanations for why more low-income parents in the Early Childhood Project reported not knowing what their child's teacher expected.

Our finding that some parents do not receive sufficient guidelines from their children's teachers echos that of McNaughton and Parr (1992), who suggested that there may be a mismatch between the type or amount of information that teachers think they are giving parents and the information parents report receiving. In a study conducted in New Zealand, McNaughton and Parr investigated the guidelines that teachers gave when sending home books for children to read with their parents, a common practice with children starting school. All the teachers and parents supported the practice of having parents read with their children. Two-thirds of the teachers reported that they had given the parents guidelines for how to read with their children, but only one-third of the parents reported receiving such guidelines.

Let us turn now to what the teachers in the Early Childhood Project reported about their beliefs about parental involvement and what they did to communicate those beliefs to parents. Children's prekindergarten, kindergarten, and first-grade teachers were asked two open-ended questions about their expectations for parental involvement, "What expectations do you have for the families' involvement with their child's education or schooling? What do you do to foster this involvement?" Children's second-grade teachers were asked a reworded version of the first question as well as the second. Teachers also were asked about the kinds of feedback they gave to families about the children's progress.

Teachers' responses about what type of involvement they wanted from children's families fell into three general categories: (1) involvement at the school (attending school functions, communicating with teachers, volunteering in some capacity at school); (2) helping the child at home (checking or assisting with homework, reading with the child, taking the child on outings); and (3) just generally supporting a child's schooling (ensuring the child attended school and got to school on time, stressing to the child that school is important, stopping by the child's classroom to see what was going on). What few grade-related differences were found in the patterns of responses are noted as follows.

Forty-nine percent of the teachers mentioned wanting some form of parental involvement at children's schools. As articulated by one of the teachers, "Parents should attend school and/or class meetings and find out what is stressed this year . . . should come to class when they have class activities, programs . . . " (a first-grade teacher at a middle-income, predominantly African American school, J). Communication was the most frequently mentioned form of school-related involvement; 34% of the teachers expressed the desire that parents should communicate with them.

Fifty-nine percent of the teachers mentioned expecting parents to help their children at home. As articulated by one of the teachers, " . . . they should follow up closely their homework to make sure that the child really is understanding . . . " (a second-grade teacher at a middle-income, mixed ethnicity school, K). A first-grade teacher at a low-income, predominantly European American school (H) suggested parents: " . . . sit down and spend time with them, make sure that they're doing their homework . . . put forth what they need to do to have the child reading . . . " The home involvement mentioned most often, by 25% of teachers, was for parents to read with their children.

Surprisingly, however, given the well-publicized value of shared storybook reading to early literacy development, this was articulated by only one kindergarten teacher and none of the prekindergarten teachers.

Twenty-nine percent of the teachers noted that they expected parents to support the school. As teachers commented, "Come in more often and find out for yourself what is going on" (a second-grade teacher at a middle-income, mixed ethnicity school, K); and "I expect they will be interested in what the children are doing in school . . . I expect them to make school a big deal" (a kindergarten teacher at a low-income, predominantly African American school, B). Twenty percent of the teachers mentioned that parents should stop by the classroom to see what is going on.

Teachers' responses to our questions about the types of parental involvement they expected should be viewed as somewhat of a wish list. Few teachers noted that parents were involved in the ways they desired. Nevertheless, most parents in their interviews with us endorsed the importance of homework as a means for them to monitor their children's development, to hear about their children's experiences at school, and to communicate with teachers (Serpell et al., 2002). Regardless of whether parents were involved in the ways teachers desired, they parents clearly were engaged in their children's schooling.

Teachers rarely acknowledged that some families, especially low-income ones, may not know how to assist their children and may need special guidance. This type of comment, from a first-grade teacher at a low-income school (E), was very rare, "We've had different groups come in and . . . they'll do math themes with them and show them how to do that at home." The importance of giving parents explicit guidelines was stressed by Dauber and Epstein (1993), who noted that low-income parents were more likely to be actively involved in their children's day-to-day education, such as checking homework, if they believed that the teacher had provided such support.

Teachers reported using a variety of means of communicating with families. These included report cards, weekly progress letters, and other forms of written communication as well as phone calls and parent–teacher conferences. European American teachers were more likely to report using written forms of communication, whereas African American teachers were more likely to report using interactive means of feedback.[5]

The majority of the teachers (almost 90%) viewed themselves as responsible for initiating discussion with parents about their children's progress. The remaining teachers reported that the initiator varied across families. Although most teachers acknowledged that they were most often the initiators of discussions about progress, they expected parents to take the initiative in seeking assistance or guidance from them. A first-grade teacher at a low-income school (E) stated, "If they've come in and asked me, 'How can I help such and such with this problem,' I'll give them suggestions. I'll send home, I'll buy flash cards and give them to parents. . . . The school has parent meetings once a week to help parents know what to do . . . " This teacher talked about the guidelines and assistance available to parents who needed such help *if* the parent took the initiative and sought out help. A second-grade teacher at another low-income school (C) commented, "Parents should come in and find out what is going on and what skills are taught at school . . . " Again, it was up to the parent to take the initiative.

As illustrated in many of the previous quotes, teachers often spoke in generalities without specifying exactly what a parent should be doing. Invitations voiced in such general terms place considerable responsibility for interpretation and initiation on parents. This may be especially problematic for parents whose own educational histories make them uncomfortable in school settings. For example, a kindergarten teacher in a low-income mixed ethnicity school (E) responded to our question, "What do you do to foster parental involvement?" with: "I always tell them anytime that you want to come in, come in and volunteer. My door is always open. If you come in, you can help do something. You will see what their day is like." At first glance, the teacher's response seems very welcoming. However, it may be easier for parents to respond to a more structured invitation that specifies what they can or should do and when. In fact, this teacher noted that few of the parents accepted her invitation.

---

[5] We thank our colleague, Abdeljalik Akkari, for this compilation of the data, as well as his insights about the meaning of various remarks made by the teachers.

That teachers' requests for parental involvement were often stated in very general terms is consistent with results reported by Eccles and Harold (1996), who asked teachers of elementary students to note the frequency with which they made certain types of requests from parents or offered them specific guidelines for how to assist their children with schoolwork. Although teachers reported that they frequently encouraged parents to become involved in classroom activities or to monitor their children's work at home, they rarely offered specific suggestions for exactly what parents should do in monitoring or assisting children with homework. Does checking homework mean making sure the child has done the work, or does it include correcting errors? It is not surprising that some parents in the Early Childhood Project were unsure what teachers expected of them.

What Do the Parents and Teachers Think of Each Other?

Several interview questions asked the parent to give her opinion of her child's teacher and vice versa. Because respondents also revealed their opinions through spontaneous comments given at other times during an interview, we reviewed the entire written transcripts for relevant evaluative comments and incorporated them into our analyses. For each evaluative comment, we considered whether it was positive or negative in nature and the content of the comment. Because there was a great deal of variability in the number of comments given by different respondents, we converted the raw frequencies to proportional scores. The content of the evaluative comments was categorized as shown in Tables 7.2 (parents' comments) and 7.3 (teachers' comments).

Across all coding categories, parents were significantly more likely to make positive comments (73%) than negative ones (27%) when discussing their children's teachers or schools.[6] Regardless of evaluative tone, the topic most frequently mentioned by parents was communication, whether with their children's teachers (40%) or schools (29%; Table 7.2).

[6] $t(58) = 7.71, p = .000.$

TABLE 7.2. *Content of Parents' Evaluative Comments About Their Children's Teachers and Schools*

	Percentage of Comments
Comments about children's teachers	
Communication with parents	40
How teachers should interact with children	13
Differentiation of the educational program for child	17
What teachers should do to teach	18
Teacher as role model	1
General comments (e.g., teacher does job)	11
Comments about children's schools	
Available resources	10
Communication with parents	29
Interest in the needs of every child	12
Consistent discipline policy	4
A learning environment for children	23
How teachers and school should teach	14
Place of safety	1
General comments	6

Note: Percentages are based on the total number of parents comments, regardless of their evaluative tone, made about teachers or about schools. Percentages may not sum to 100 due to rounding.

TABLE 7.3. *Content of Teachers' Comments About Parents*

	Percentage of Teachers' Comments	
	Positive	Negative
Provides appropriate experiences	0	9
Communicates with teachers	0	10
Involved with the school	12	2
Involved in routine activities[a]	9	6
Cares about child	29	0
Knowledgeable about children's development	11	2
Problems at home interfere with children's learning	N/A	11

Note: Percentages are based on the total number of comments made about the parents. Percentage may not sum to 100 due to rounding.

[a] The category Involved in Routine Activities includes tasks such as gets child to school on time and check homework.

Let us now turn to what teachers thought of the children's families. When children in the Early Childhood Project were in prekindergarten, kindergarten, first and second grade, we asked their teachers several questions about their relations with the children's families. We began by asking, "Who in (child's name)'s family do you know?" Teachers typically mentioned parents as well as siblings and cousins in their responses. We next asked, "How well do you know them?" and asked the teachers to provide a rating on a scale ranging from 1 "do not know" to 5 "know extremely well." Teachers typically referenced the parents in their responses. The majority of the teachers (76%) believed they knew the children's families well, as indexed by ratings ranging from 3 to 5.

We then asked teachers what they thought of each of the parents (or other primary caregivers): "What do you think of them? How does their approach to the child's development relate to your goals for this child in school? How knowledgeable and wise are they? What do you see as their level of caring and commitment to their child?" Teachers talked about parents of a specific child in the class; they talked about groups of parents in the class, school, or community; and they also talked about how parents of the generic child should or do behave. Although some of the comments about the parents were nonevaluative or neutral, most were evaluative. Overall, teachers gave a greater number of positive evaluative comments (55%) than negative ones (35%).[7] Few of the comments were mixed (10%).

Teachers' responses to direct questions about a specific family were generally positive. That is, 82% of the teachers noted that the parents' goals seemed similar to their own, 91% stated that the parents appeared caring, and 73% indicated that the parents appeared fairly knowledgeable about children's development. Teachers used a different reference group for their positive and negative comments. Individual parents and families served as the recipients of positive comments (90% of all positive comments) but were less likely to be the recipients of negative comments (20% of all negative comments). The teachers talked more generally about "parents in the class, school, or community" when making negative remarks, probably out of

[7] $t (59) = 2.47, p = .02.$

a sense of tact or concerns with confidentiality, despite our assurances that we would not reveal any identifying information about participants.

Teachers working in low-income schools differed significantly from those working in middle-income schools with respect to positive comments (47% vs. 69%) and negative comments (42% vs. 23%).[8] This greater negativity by teachers in low-income schools contrasts with parents' responses. That is, low-income parents spoke as positively about their children's teachers as did middle-income parents.

The highest percentages of teachers' positive comments were about parents' commitment to their children, their assistance with school activities and their knowledge of children's development (29%, 12%, 11%; Table 7.3). The highest percentages of negative comments were about the failure of parents to provide their children with experiences that would be of educational benefit, their lack of communication with teachers, or the fact that problems at home spilled over into the classroom (9%, 10%, 11%). If we consider these comments in terms of the percentages of families referenced rather than the percentages of teachers' responses, 14% of the parents were viewed as not providing their children with beneficial experiences, 16% of the parents were noted as not communicating with the teachers, and 18% of the children were said to be impacted by problems at home that intruded into their learning at school.

DID PARENTS AND TEACHERS VIEW THE CHILDREN THEY DISCUSSED IN A CONSISTENT MANNER?

Research on the effects of parent involvement in children's education generally shows that it has a positive impact (e.g., Marcon, 1999; Rimm-Kaufman & Pianta, 1999; see Stevenson & Baker, 1987, for a review). Through being involved in the educational process, a parent may learn more about what the teacher expects of her child, what strengths and needs the child displays, and what kinds of experiences would be useful for the child. The involvement of parents in their children's schooling may give rise to increased communication

[8] $F (1, 58) = 5.95, 13.50, p = .02, .001$.

between parents and teachers that, in turn, may lead to consensus in how they view the child.

Several of the questions from the various parent and teacher interviews allowed us to directly compare and contrast their views of the children. We focus here on questions asked of parents and teachers when the children were in first grade. We began by asking each respondent to indicate several strengths the child had, "Can you tell me about some things that make you feel proud of (*child's name*), things that she is good at?" We next asked, "Can you tell me some things that you feel you need to pay particular attention to, things that you feel (*child's name*) needs to improve on?" We then asked about the perceived agreement between the parties. "How often, in general, do you think you and your child's teacher/parent agree about your child's needs and what to do about them?" Response options ranged from 1 (very often agree and very seldom disagree) to 5 (very often disagree and very seldom agree). Two final questions on the issue were, "What are some things you and (*child's name*) teacher/parent would agree about? Why?" and "What are some things you and (*child's name*) teacher/parent would disagree about? Why?"

We begin our discussion by considering whether parents and teachers viewed themselves as having similar views about the children in the Early Childhood Project and turn from there to examining how similar their views actually were. Overall, 84% of the parents believed they and the teachers agreed often or very often, and 83% of the teachers believed the same. Agreement was similar at the level of the individual parent–teacher dyads. Eighty-six percent of the dyads had similar ratings (within 1 point on the rating scale), suggesting that most of the parents and teachers believed they agreed with the other party. However, these ratings of agreement are not wholly consistent with parents' and teachers' responses to more specific questions.

Table 7.4 categorizes the areas of agreement and disagreement reported by parents and teachers. Bear in mind that the responses were given to open-ended questions and might have differed had respondents been asked to complete a structured checklist. However, we can view the responses as those that were uppermost in the minds of the parents and teachers. The most common areas of agreement noted by parents were academic strengths and problems, how a child's academic problems were handled, social/behavioral problems, and

TABLE 7.4. *Areas That Parents and Teachers Believed They Agreed with the Other Party*

	Respondent	
Topic Area	Parent (%)	Teacher (%)
Social/behavioral problems	22	22
How such problems were handled	7	3
Social/behavioral strengths	16	0
Encouraging such strengths	0	0
Social/behavioral issues (general)	0	8
Academic problems	20	18
How such problems were handled	20	8
Academic strengths	20	3
Encouraging such strengths	7	0
Academic issues (general)	4	7
Teacher's general philosophy	22	3
Agree about everything	7	7

Note: Responses are the percentages of parents (or teachers) who gave the response. As respondents could give more than one response, percentages do not equal 100%. A score of 0 means that no respondent (either party) gave such an answer. About 38% of the teachers and 4% of the parents did not answer the question about areas of agreement.

teachers' general teaching method or philosophy.[9] The most common areas of agreement reported by teachers were social/behavioral problems and academic problems. Areas of disagreement were seldom noted by either parents or teachers. In fact, 42% of the parents and 27% of the teachers reported no areas of disagreement.

Nevertheless, comparison of the responses of parents and teachers in Table 7.4 reveals several areas of discrepancy. For example, 16% of the parents believed that they agreed with their child's teacher about a social/behavioral strength but no teacher noted the same. Similar discrepancies were also evident for academic strengths, how academic problems were handled, and teaching philosophy. In general, parents were more likely to note areas of consensus than were teachers.

We next discuss parents' and teachers' independent reports of the children's strengths and needs. We first categorized responses

[9] There was a weak but significant relation between parents' and teachers' reported agreement about the nature of children's academic problems, $r(32) = .35, p = .045$.

TABLE 7.5. *Percentage of Comments About Children's Academic Strengths and Needs*

	Respondent	
	Parent	Teacher
Academic strengths		
Academic competencies	35	20
Behavior/personality traits	33	37
Cognitive traits	15	18
Motivation	13	22
Attendance	2	0
Improvement	2	4
Academic needs		
Academic competencies	29	32
Behavior/personality traits	40	29
Cognitive traits	26	29
Motivation	6	2
Attendance	0	7
Improvement (lack of)	0	0

into academic/intellectual, social/moral and personal domains (see Chapter 3 for examples of the domains) and then further categorized the academic/intellectual domain as follows: (1) child's academic competencies (e.g., strengths: doing well in school, being a good speller; weaknesses: not doing well in school, being a poor reader); (2) behaviors or personality traits necessary to achieve academic success (e.g., strengths: trying one's best, not afraid to fail at an attempt; weaknesses: needing to put more effort into school work); (3) cognitive traits (e.g., strengths: smart; weaknesses: having a learning disability or attention deficit/hyperactivity disorder); (4) motivation (e.g., strengths: wanting to do well, interested in learning; weakness: not being interested in or hating school); (5) attendance (e.g., strength: good attendance, weakness: absent a lot); and (6) improvement (e.g., strength: improvement in one of the previously mentioned categories, weaknesses: not mentioned).

As shown in Table 7.5, parents most commonly mentioned academic competencies and behaviors/personality traits when discussing academic strengths. Teachers most commonly mentioned behaviors/personality. Parents were more likely than teachers to focus on academic competencies, such as how well the child was doing in an area. Teachers focused more than parents on motivation. When discussing academic needs, both parents and teachers frequently mentioned academic competencies, behavior/personality, and cognitive traits. However, teachers were less likely than parents to consider needs in behaviors/personality.

We next examined consensus between parents and teachers about each child's strengths and needs. If the parent noted that the child had a certain academic strength or weakness, did the teacher of that child mention the same thing? This line of inquiry was developed by Danseco (1998), as part of her doctoral dissertation conducted in conjunction with the Early Childhood Project, in which she compared commonalities in parents' and teachers' ethnotheories for children receiving special education services and children receiving regular education services. To illustrate how we identified consensus, consider the following example. The parent of a low-income European American child (C4) and that child's teacher both mentioned that reading was a strength. We viewed this as congruence or consensus between the parent and teacher. That is, not only did both note a strength in an area categorized as academic, but also the actual type of academic strength noted was the same. The parent also mentioned that spelling was a strength and attention was a need, but the teacher did not mention either. The teacher noted that math was a need and that the child required a lot of praise to feel comfortable (viewed as a need). Neither issue was noted by the parent. Thus, in addition to the one issue on which both parent and teacher agreed, there were four issues where the parent and teacher did not match each other. There were no outright incongruences in the example; that is, issues where the parent viewed something as a strength and the teacher viewed it as a need.

Most parents and teachers mentioned at least one academic strength per child. About 30% of parents and 41% of teachers did not mention any academic needs when discussing a child. Consensus was limited on children's academic strengths and needs. Teachers and parents agreed on the nature of a child's academic strength 43% of the time and on a child's academic need 18% of the time. About 57% of the time a parent mentioned an academic strength that was not noted by the teacher. Similarly, about 57% of the time a teacher mentioned an academic strength not mentioned by the parent. About 70% of the time an academic need noted by a teacher was not mentioned by the child's parent, and 75% of the time an academic need noted by the parent was not mentioned by the child's teacher. Fourteen percent of the time an area that one respondent (parent or teacher) viewed as a strength, the other viewed as a need. For example, Mrs. G noted that her child, Amina, was having difficulty "learning numbers," but Amina's teacher noted that math was one of her strengths.

IMPROVING RELATIONS BETWEEN HOMES AND SCHOOLS

The goal of improved relations between home and school is based on the belief that such relations will positively impact children's academic success. Attempts to increase parental involvement in children's education have taken different routes. Some involve the entire school community (e.g., Comer & Haynes, 1991; Madden et al., 1993), whereas others involve a teacher and the parents of children in her class (Baker et al., 1996). Some investigators have focused on empowering parents by drawing on their stores of knowledge (Moll & Greenberg, 1990), whereas others have asked parents to perform activities at home with their children, such as reading with them, and have even provided the supplies (e.g., books; Goldenberg et al., 1992).

The various attempts to increase parents' involvement in their children's education have met with differential success. Several factors may interfere with teachers' desire to increase parental involvement. Hoover-Dempsey and Sandler (1997) suggested that a parent's decision to be involved in her child's education is based on the parent's beliefs about the parental role, the parent's sense of efficacy for helping the child succeed in school, and the general invitations and demand for involvement from the child and school. Even when teachers welcome parental involvement, they may erroneously assume that parents have the necessary background or skills. In addition, they may expect parents to accommodate to the school without the school similarly accommodating to the parents' interests and needs (MacLeod, 1996). For example, many parents who want to be more involved with their children's schooling are typically unavailable to assist in the class during school hours because they work during the day. As

McCarthey (1997) noted, "An interest in making home–school connections is not enough – it is imperative for teachers to understand the complexity of students' lives, especially of those students whose backgrounds are different from their own" (p. 176).

In this section, we summarize our findings from a complementary project, "Cooperative Communication Among Parents and Teachers About Children's Emergent Literacy," conducted during the 1994–1995 academic year with funding from the National Reading Research Center. The major goal of the project was to improve communication between teachers and parents by seeking ways for teachers to learn more about and, hence, adapt their instructional programs to the culture of the children's homes. A secondary goal was to explore how research findings could be translated by teachers into action projects.

We invited prekindergarten and kindergarten teachers in the schools enrolled in the Early Childhood Project to participate. The children in the project were in first grade at this time, so participation by teachers at these levels would not compromise our ongoing study. We arranged with the school system to have the Cooperative Communication Project serve as a continuing education course for which participants could earn academic credit. We sent invitations to 15 teachers at eight schools; of those, 6 teachers at three schools accepted our invitation. Two withdrew after a few weeks for personal reasons. The remaining four teachers taught at two schools located in low-income communities populated by both African American and European American families. Two of the teachers were African American and two were European American, one of each ethnicity at each school (see Serpell et al., 1996, for a fuller description of the project).

The four teachers who completed the course shared certain similarities, including their teaching at low-achieving schools serving children from low-income neighborhoods. The teachers were all sufficiently interested in the course and their projects to devote their time for an entire academic year (24 hours of class time as well as time out of class to design and implement a project). All had been teaching for more than a few years. At the outset of the course, however, the teachers differed in the tone of remarks about parents in their schools, with some expressing a more critical stance than others.

The project began with four group seminars at the university on Saturday mornings during a 6-week period from September through

November 1994. Each meeting lasted 4 hours. During the seminars we presented findings from the Early Childhood Project, as well as findings or approaches from other researchers and theorists. We also discussed several means of intervention. At one of the meetings, a graduate student showed a video filmed during data collection for his doctoral dissertation within the larger project (Morakinyo, 1995). As discussed in Chapter 6, Morakinyo established a "play" post office in several prekindergarten classrooms as a means of increasing children's literacy-related play experiences at school. The teachers were active participants in the seminars, engaging in animated discussion at each meeting. They often stayed after the formal aspect of the class ended to continue ongoing discussions. What teachers liked and commented on was the opportunity to engage with other professionals, something they found missing in their daily lives.

During the third meeting, each teacher was asked to begin developing a project designed to improve communication with parents in her class that she would implement during the academic year. We spent some time assisting in the development and implementation of the projects. In addition to attending the group seminars, each teacher met monthly with a graduate assistant and experienced prekindergarten teacher, Linda Gorham, who provided support with the teachers' projects. We met as a group two additional times during the winter and spring, once to discuss progress and address any difficulties teachers were having with their projects and once, at the end of the school year, for presentations of the projects. Teachers also submitted a written report. Although we provided guidance, the initial choice or idea originated with the teacher. Most of the projects were adapted from ones that the teachers had learned about during our discussions of relevant research. We provided modest funding to support the teacher's efforts. Following is a brief description of each project.

An African American kindergarten teacher (teacher 1) decided to implement in her classroom a play version of a corner store, a neighborhood store that serves as a mini-food market in many areas of Baltimore. The teacher's interest in establishing a play corner store was sparked by Morakinyo's study using play post offices. Teacher 1 chose her project to help parents understand that, "their children were already readers and that they had begun long before they entered my class.... My purpose was to show writing and reading as an integrated part of the emergent literacy process and to provide a center where the children would be encouraged to explore writing and reading as a means of self-expression and communication" (from Serpell et al., 1996).

A European American prekindergarten teacher (teacher 2) was interested in improving the quantity and quality of homework assignments turned in by the children. When children are in prekindergarten, such assignments often involve their families. Thus, the project, if successful, would increase parents' involvement in their children's education and perhaps, indirectly, serve to improve the quality of the teacher's relationships with her students' parents. For her project, teacher 2 decided to alter the nature of her homework assignments: "I typically receive a poor and untimely response to nightly home assignments for a variety of reasons. I hoped to increase the number of returns by changing the nature of the homework. I wanted learning to be a shared activity between the family and the teacher. I wanted parents to realize how discussion and developing verbal skills are prerequisite to the development of early reading skills" (from Serpell et al., 1996). Each month, teacher 2 asked the parents to assist their children with a different seasonally appropriate assignment. Each assignment was written in a composition book that was brought home by the child, along with any needed materials. For example, in December the children and families co-authored a book, "Our families prepare for winter." Each child was asked to talk with the family about what they did to prepare for winter. The parent and child were asked to complete their assignments in the composition book, which would be used as the basis for discussion during circle time at school. Eventually, the completed assignments were made into displays that were put on the bulletin boards and in hallways for parents to view.

Teacher 3 (an African American kindergarten teacher) was interested in learning whether increased communication between a child's family and herself would lead to improvement in the child's classroom performance. She implemented an interactive journal writing project involving herself and the children's parents. In one typical task, the child was asked to read a story, previously read in class, to his or her parent. Parents were asked to assist their children in responding in the journal (either kept in written/notebook or oral/taped format) to some questions about the reading. The teacher then responded in writing to the journal entries.

Teacher 4, a European American kindergarten teacher, was interested in starting a classroom lending library because she was concerned that the children in her class never went to the local public library and thus missed opportunities to engage in storybook reading. She noted, "as a kindergarten teacher, I am aware of the importance of the home environment in young children's beginning reading." Children served as librarians in the lending library, in charge of checking books in and out. Each day several children would choose books from the library to take home and read. After a child completed reading a book at home, the child, was asked to briefly evaluate the book with assistance from a family member.

Our original intention had been to assess the impact of the projects on the children and families, but because so few teachers participated, we decided to forego an evaluation. The informal feedback we received from the teachers suggested that the families were very positive about the projects. The teachers themselves were also quite positive, as we illustrate. Although all the teachers noted how much work the projects had been, all stated that they would do some version of the project the following year. We present here the outcomes of the projects, as reported by the teachers. As we listened to the teachers give their reports, we perceived two complementary positive results: enhanced involvement by the families, and growth of insight and empathy by the teachers.

At the end of the year, teacher 1 talked about the corner store she implemented in her classroom:

I think that this was a wonderful project for my class. . . . I have always been aware of the importance of the home environment in young children's beginning reading and writing experiences. . . . Parents rarely thought what their children did before entering school was important. . . . My parents were very pleased with the project and all said that they saw a big difference in their children's writing. I especially liked the way the parents volunteered in the store from time to time. They added new aspects to the store that I didn't think of, such as giving the children packaged items so they could copy the words off the packaging. . . . They would role play right along with the children. Several of the parents let their children help them with the shopping. (Serpell et al., 1996, p. 25)

Teacher 2 reported: "I did succeed in getting more parents to come into our room casually to chat, to view some of our projects and work." Not only was there more positive interaction between the teacher and parents, but this teacher reported learning things about the families that she had not known before.

Our families have a lot to share with their children and the school.... Many of our families have complicated and dependable structures of family support. While one member works, another takes over child care duties.... I learned that there are a lot of reasons why homework did not get done on a regular basis. Many children live in a chaotic situation.... Often with the flux of babysitters during the evening, the homework loses priority to eating, bathing and family recreational activities.... Many parents value education as a vehicle to take their children further into the world than they have been able to go. (Serpell et al., 1996, p. 29)

Teacher 3, in discussing the interactive journals, concluded:

The journals and tapes show the parental interest, as well as the children's, in reading and the child doing their best. I feel teachers should begin journal writings with parents because it seems to be more personal and many parents, I think, will respond to their writings. If the child sees that there is a positive relationship between their teacher and parent they will do better in class. (Serpell et al., 1996, p. 31)

Thus, this teacher commented on both the quality of parent–teacher relationships and the resulting academic outcomes for the children.

Teacher 4 was perhaps the most expressive about the positive benefits of her project, the lending library. She noted improvement in parents' attitudes and involvement, children's interest and learning, and most eloquently, in her own attitudes. She concluded:

I believe this research project has allowed me to know more about children's storybook reading experiences in the home and how their parents feel about reading to their children.... The lending library proved to be an exciting vehicle which fostered communication between the child's home and school. But the rich interaction that was taking place transcended the lending library: the rapport between parents, children and school was improving in other areas than the library. I observed increased participation on class trips, parties, perfect attendance assemblies and closing activities. I also experienced much more parental involvement in the day to day activities in the classroom. When the children saw their parents and others participating in their education, it gave them support, led to a much more positive attitude towards learning and made school a very important place.... Involving the

parents more closely fostered a group cohesion.... During the last week of
school, the parents put on a group surprise luncheon which they had worked
on for weeks.... I felt more appreciated than in many years before. I feel that
the reason this happened was a closeness developed between home and
school because of the interaction that occurred this year through the lending
library.... I too had a more positive attitude this year. When a parent came in
with a suggestion or complaint, I tried to view the concern from the parent's
and child's perspective as well as my own. I had more patience because I had
so much emotional and physical support. I was enjoying my job; this feeling
of joy motivated me to teach.... (Serpell et al., 1996, p. 21)

Teacher 4 had initially expressed concerns about implementing the
lending library in case books got lost, stolen, or ruined. In fact, 20 of
the original 118 books were not returned. However, she concluded
that "the benefits of the project far outweighed any loss that occurred"
(Serpell et al., 1996, p. 22; see Britt & Baker, 1997, for additional information about this project).

   Our own appraisal of the Cooperative Communication Project was
similarly positive. We attribute the program's success to several factors: (1) Teachers self-selected; thus, those that participated wanted to
do something to improve their relationships with the families of the
children in the class. However, it seemed that what may have started
with an expectation that it would be the parents who changed often evolved, by the end of the project, into an acknowledgment of
change on both sides. (2) The seminar meetings allowed teachers a
welcome format to meet with professionals interested in discussing
ideas about teaching, something all noted was missing in their daily
professional lives. One kindergarten teacher mentioned that she was
not even in the same building as teachers of older students. As noted
by Tharp and Gallimore (1988), teachers have too few opportunities
to meet with more skilled teachers to discuss ideas about teaching.
(3) Teachers received ongoing guidance in implementing their
projects and acknowledgment from their peers for successful completion. After the initial seminar meetings during the fall, ongoing
guidance was provided by our graduate research assistant. Consider
her reflections on the need for such assistance, as well as the limited
time teachers have to fulfill all their daily demands:

The on-site visits were always scheduled according to the teachers' preferences, which was always at the end of the school day. However, each

time I arrived, I found teachers harried and exhausted. I soon discovered that my support role involved large doses of reassurance. Teachers needed to hear that they were indeed progressing nicely on their research ... that I would help them develop strategies for collecting, recording, and evaluating data ... and that they could successfully complete the task they had set for themselves.... Teachers would obviously benefit from having administrators who understand the level of commitment required to complete an action research project in addition to teachers' daily responsibilities. (Gorham, 1995)

SUMMARY

In this chapter, we addressed relations between home and school, comparing and contrasting perspectives of teachers and parents on several relevant issues. Even parents who themselves may not have been highly successful in school want such success for their children and have some understanding of the role of the home and school in helping children do well in school. However, they appear to lack a full awareness of the importance of exposure to language and environmental print for early literacy development. At least two-thirds of the families we interviewed did not mention emergent literacy when asked about early signs of reading. A similar proportion did not mention child interest in reading, suggesting an area that deserves emphasis by teachers is helping parents realize the importance of children's motivation and ways to foster it.

We found it encouraging that the parents and teachers generally thought well of each other. Holding positive views may be a necessary precondition for putting forth the effort to improve pathways of communication. Although many parents believed they and their child's teacher already communicated well, teachers viewed effective communication as a desire, not a reality. One of our most striking findings is that parents and teachers believed they agreed in their views of individual children, but consensus in reality was not that high. Teachers frequently mentioned the importance of parents being aware of what was expected, but too often they did not make these expectations explicit. We recognize that teachers are overworked, but part of their professional role is to communicate effectively with parents. Improved communication could lead to parents, particularly low-income parents, becoming more aware of teacher expectations, more knowledgeable about ways to assist their children, and better informed about their children's progress.

The Cooperative Communication Project focused explicitly on improving the channels of communication between home and school. We do not want to overstate the findings from the Cooperative Communication Project given the limited number of participants and the lack of an outcomes assessment. Nevertheless, our findings make us optimistic about the possibilities for improving communication between parents and teachers, which should result in improved educational experiences for children.

8

Conclusions and Implications for Policy and Practice

The longitudinal study of early literacy socialization presented in this book followed a cohort of Baltimore children in prekindergarten in 1992 through completion of third grade in 1997. The children and their families came from four broadly different social addresses, reflecting two levels of income and two types of ethnic heritage. Much of the focus of our study was on the intimate culture of children's homes; that is, the confluence of parental beliefs, recurrent activities, and interactive processes that inform children's literacy development. In this concluding chapter, we consider the broader implications of our findings for policy and practice.

We begin by summarizing and integrating the key findings of the research reported in the preceding chapters. Our account transcends the organizational structure of the preceding chapters to demonstrate how our broadly framed inquiry yields new insights into the socialization and appropriation of the cultural practice of literacy. We conclude this section with a discussion of why so many of the children in our study struggled to learn to read.

In the subsequent sections of the chapter we offer recommendations for teachers, parents, and policy makers. We discuss how parents, teachers, and children stand to benefit if teachers learn about the intimate culture of the family; we illustrate how the ecological inventory can serve as a tool for initiating productive home–school connections. We discuss how findings from the Early Childhood Project complement and extend recommendations offered to parents by professional organizations for promoting children's literacy development. We also address policy implications in terms of the value of moving beyond social address in analyses of historical patterns of underachievement on the part of children of poor families or from ethnic minority groups.

SALIENT CONCLUSIONS OF THE EARLY CHILDHOOD PROJECT

The Intimate Culture

Children should not be defined by their ethnicity or socioeconomic status because the influence of cultural heritage is filtered through the distinctive intimate culture of their family. To be sure, some aspects of parents' implicit theoretical perspectives are informed by broad themes publicized by the media and/or passed on from one generation to the next within ethnocultural groups. However, in addition to the structure derived from such broad sociohistorical influences, each family co-constructs its own unique, intimate culture, blending the specifics of the individual personalities it includes, its particular ecological niche, and its own history of shared events.

A major contribution of the Early Childhood Project lies in its demonstration of the value of the construct of intimate culture. In our analyses of various predictors of literacy developmental outcomes, we found that when indices of particular aspects of the family's intimate culture were entered first, only a small proportion of the variance remained to be accounted for by family income, a popular index of social class, and no significant additional variance was accounted for by ethnic heritage. Moreover, the various indices we designed of potentially relevant dimensions of family culture attested to their relevance and coherence. For instance, the degree to which a family was rated by a parent as invested in reading aloud as a regular, valued tradition was significantly correlated with the frequency with which she reported that the focal child engaged in shared literacy-related activities at home. Furthermore, we found that a parents' emphasis on the significance of literacy as a source of entertainment was negatively correlated with an emphasis on literacy as a set of skills to be acquired.

Particular features of intimate family culture that seem to be more or less conducive to the early appropriation of literacy are unevenly distributed in Baltimore society across the four social addresses that we systematically sampled in our study. For instance, a much higher proportion of middle-income families than low-income families reported that their prekindergarten children interacted with at least one type of book at home every day. When the children were in second grade, middle-income families reported engaging in a range of literacy-related activities more frequently than low-income families. Middle-income parents were more likely to mention that their child enjoyed the routine of reading than were low-income parents. More generally, the entertainment theme was more often emphasized by middle-income families in our sample than by low-income families, whereas the latter often placed relatively greater emphasis on the theme that literacy constitutes a set of skills to be learned.

Parents, even if they had little formal education, often held elaborate theories that informed their socialization practices, albeit those theories were at best informal and often only implicit. Most of the parents we interviewed derived intrinsic satisfaction from articulating their child-rearing ethnotheories for us. Indeed, transcribing some of the interviews required substantial effort by our administrative assistant because the parents had so much to say! During the final home visit at the end of the project, parents were asked about their perceptions of our research process, and many responded that they appreciated having their views carefully documented in one interview and reflected back to them in subsequent interviews.

Literacy was an important socialization goal for most parents of young children in Baltimore in this period of history. However, literacy was not of paramount importance to parents in the Early Childhood Project when their children were in pre-kindergarten; rather, it was one of several goals they cited. Indeed, parents generally ranked social or moral goals higher than academic goals, and this pattern was apparent regardless of social address. Had we not cast a wide net in our interviews and characterized the focus of our study as the broad domain of early childhood development, parents might have focused on literacy goals simply because they perceived literacy as our primary concern. Parents of children making the transition to formal schooling quite rightly recognize that developmental goals need to extend beyond the purely academic. In this regard, they are in consensus with early childhood educators, including the teachers we interviewed in the Early Childhood Project.

Families that aspired to foster a child's enjoyment of reading (the entertainment orientation) were more effective in supporting the child's early appropriation of literacy than those that focused more directly on the fostering of literacy skills. Parents differed in terms of whether they emphasized enjoyment of reading as a way to help children learn to read and write, or whether they emphasized drills and practice. The opportunities they made available to their children were consistent with these perspectives. For example, parents who endorsed an entertainment orientation reported that their children engaged in storybook reading and that they played word games or board games. In contrast, parents who endorsed a skills orientation were unlikely to report that their children read storybooks; instead, their children reviewed flash cards and workbooks or read preschool books. These findings support the theoretical contention by Super and Harkness (1997) that the recurrent activities in a child's developmental niche are largely organized and driven by parents' implicit theoretical perspectives on child development and socialization.

We also obtained evidence of the enduring importance of pleasurable interactions around literacy in the intimate culture of the child's home (discussed further as follows). For example, children's reading comprehension at the end of Grade 3 was jointly predicted by how often they engaged with printed material on their own in earlier years and their parents' endorsement of an entertainment orientation.

The entertainment orientation was more frequently found in middle-income families, but also featured in some low-income families, and was predictive of literacy development within each of those broad social addresses. It became clear to us within the first year of the Early Childhood Project, when children were still in prekindergarten, that middle-income families were more likely to adopt a playful approach to the socialization of literacy than low-income families. These differences remained salient throughout the 5 years of the study. In the diaries collected at the outset of the project, middle-income parents' reports indicated that their children were more likely to use literacy as a source of entertainment and they had more book-reading experiences on a daily basis than lower-income children. In contrast, low-income parents reported more frequent literacy activities undertaken for the purpose of teaching/learning literacy than did middle-income parents.

We speculated (Baker et al., 1995) that middle-income parents may prefer to provide their children with opportunities that enable them to construct their own understandings of literacy, through ready availability of literacy materials for independent use. We further speculated that low-income parents, in contrast, may believe they need to provide more structured opportunities for their children that involve direct instruction and practice. These speculations received considerable support through follow-up interviews with the parents over the years, both in terms of continued endorsement of entertainment or skills perspectives, and in terms of their preferred intervention strategies for fostering learning to read and write. For example, low-income parents were more likely than middle-income parents to cite forms of proactive intervention, such as deliberate instruction. The fact that we were able to verify our initial interpretations through the subsequent development of focused questions and structured rating scales, and the systematic analysis of how these features of the intimate culture related to children's literacy competencies, is a particular strength of the mixed-method longitudinal approach we adopted in the Early Childhood Project.

Different ways of interacting with children around books have correlates with, and may have reliable causal influences on, the child's forms of literacy competence and attitudes. Our findings extend the existing literature in demonstrating the importance of the affective, as well as the cognitive aspects of shared reading. The affective quality of reading interactions when children were entering kindergarten was related to children's motivation for reading in first and second grade. In addition, children who experienced early enjoyable interactions when reading with an adult member of their family subsequently read more frequently. The affective atmosphere was not directly related to subsequent reading test scores, but rather appeared to have an indirect influence; affective quality was related to reading frequency, which in turn was related to reading achievement. Parents' beliefs about the approach to take in facilitating their children's reading development were related to the affective quality of subsequent reading interactions. An emphasis on the importance of entertainment was associated with positive affective quality, whereas an emphasis on skills was not. Pleasant reading interactions and ones where children were highly engaged were more likely when parents and children talked about the content of the story and its illustrations. Talk about print or word recognition, however, detracted from the pleasant atmosphere.

Families differ considerably in terms of who interacts with children around literacy events, and this has implications for what children take away from those experiences. Low-income children were less likely to experience shared storybook reading with an adult than were middle-income children, as reflected in information collected in our ecological inventories. Our observations of shared storybook reading revealed that there were clear differences in both the cognitive and affective quality of reading interactions due to the proficiency level of the reader. Pre-adolescent siblings were less fluent readers than the children's parents, and they were less skilled at maintaining the interest of their listeners or refocusing their wandering attention. In addition, the affective quality of the interaction was poorer, with less enjoyment exhibited by reader and listener alike. Furthermore, middle-income families obtained higher scores than low-income families on a composite index of frequency of participation in reading, writing, and drawing activities with adults or adolescents. These differences ultimately may have contributed to the stronger literacy attainments of the middle-income children in our sample.

Parents typically do not use shared storybook reading as an explicit opportunity for teaching children how to read. Our observations of shared reading when children were in kindergarten and first grade confirmed previous research showing that parents do not spend much time discussing print when reading storybooks to their children. Such discussion occurred mainly when children made reading errors, and parents frequently simply stated the word for their child. Such an approach takes less time away from the meaning of the text and is less likely to disrupt children's enjoyment of the story than providing decoding assistance.

Children's Literacy Competencies

Children may arrive at the same level of competence in a particular domain of literacy through markedly different routes, tied to differences in the intimate cultures of their home. Low-income African American children and middle-income European American children displayed comparable strengths in story retelling. However, differences in the patterns of correlations with reading comprehension suggested that this competency may have different origins. The middle-income European American children likely performed well on the story retelling task as a result of their frequent access to shared storybook reading with adults, which fosters familiarity with the narrative genre. These experiences would promote reading comprehension and listening comprehension. The strong performance on the retelling task by the low-income African American children probably arose from the greater emphasis on oral expression and rhetorical skills in their homes, a strength that would not give them an advantage when dealing with print.

An important methodological contribution of the Early Childhood Project is its demonstration of the value of using measures tailored to individual children's home experiences and that draw on knowledge acquired outside of school. Children in the project demonstrated many emergent literacy competencies by the time they were in prekindergarten, competencies that might have been missed had only standardized assessments been used. For the most part, they did better when asked to perform tasks that more directly related to what they might encounter at home. Thus, during prekindergarten they did better on tasks requiring them to recognize products found at home or logos from those products, and even when the children could not identify an item, their answers showed that they usually knew that the item contained print. When asked to identify the functions of various printed materials, the majority of the children's responses were reasonable. For example, stating that a calendar is something you use to recall birthdays is one use that many people make of calendars. In addition, children were more frequently able to identify letters of the alphabet that appeared in their own names than letters that did not.

These findings illustrate the importance of considering the context within which development occurs and is assessed. The majority of children growing up in the United States have many and varied exposures to literate activities, but the specific experiences to which a child is exposed differ with social class and cultural background (Heath, 1983; Neuman & Celano, 2001; Taylor & Dorsey-Gaines, 1988). By testing children's emerging competencies using materials that the children used and saw used at home, we were able to demonstrate that even in prekindergarten the majority of the children had an awareness and an understanding about various forms of print.

We drew on measures linked more directly to the children's own experiences and backgrounds as they progressed through the primary grades as well. Completing coupons to send away for prizes, going through family mail to identify recipients, and looking up dates on a calendar are literacy activities that many children experience at home. These functional print tasks, reflecting orientations to print that could be acquired at home, were stronger predictors of basic reading skills than a well-established phonemic awareness measure. This is an important finding, given the national focus on phonological awareness as the critical contributor to early reading development. Recall, too, that children performed well when they were asked to write about a typical visit to McDonald's restaurant). Even though the low-income children did not fare as well as the middle-income children in mastering basic reading skills, their cognitive and linguistic skills served them well on this measure that drew more heavily on out-of-school experience.

A major source of difficulty for low-income children as they learn to read appears to be mastery of the skills needed to decode the text rather than comprehension per se. Comprehension of narrative did not differ across income levels, as long as it was presented in the oral modality. However, as early as first grade, income-related differences were apparent in children's letter knowledge, word identification, decoding, and phonological awareness. These foundational skills were predictors of reading comprehension in third grade, but they were not related to oral language competencies. Why did the low-income children have more difficulty mastering decoding? Although many of the children from low-income homes were being raised by parents who strongly endorsed a skills approach to fostering their children's literacy development, they had less frequent engagement than middle-income children with materials pertinent for such skill development.

Home experiences and emergent literacy competencies prior to formal schooling are important foundations for subsequent literacy growth, but a child's developmental potential is not fixed at school entry. What children do at home, and with whom they do it, makes a difference in whether children will overcome a slow start on the pathway to literacy. We were able to identify two groups of children who had comparably low emergent literacy profiles at the beginning of first grade, but who had divergent literacy outcomes at the end of third grade, with one group continuing to perform poorly and the other now achieving at grade level. Conversely, the fact that children get off to a good start in aspects of emergent literacy does not necessarily guarantee that they will continue on that pathway. Each of the four children who had high letter knowledge in prekindergarten ended up with third-grade word recognition scores at least 1 year below grade level. Their parents reported providing extensive opportunities for their children to learn the letters, but this early knowledge did not "protect" them from later difficulties. Indeed, one child who had among the highest scores on letter knowledge, rhyme sensitivity, nursery rhyme knowledge, and alliteration detection in prekindergarten was described by her second-grade teacher as having serious difficulties with reading, an observation that was borne out by the child's low scores on the Woodcock-Johnson reading tests.

Children's appropriation of literacy involves not only appropriation of the cognitive skills, but also appropriation of literacy motivation and recognition of the value literacy serves in their lives. When parents reported that their children liked being read to and that they took an active interest in learning to read on their own, the children subsequently earned higher scores on a task assessing motivation to read. Appropriation of a positive view of reading comes about, at least in part, from parental beliefs about reasons for reading. Children whose parents identified pleasure as a reason for reading had higher motivation scores than children of parents who did not. Similarly, parents who demonstrated that they took pleasure in reading during the shared storybook readings we observed had children who were subsequently more motivated for reading and chose to read more frequently on their own.

As early as first grade, children exhibited fairly elaborate ethnotheories about reading. They described how to teach a child to read in terms quite consistent with their own experiences, and they identified shared storybook reading as a major avenue for teaching/learning. They provided many different reasons for reading that paralleled those expressed by parents in the Early Childhood Project. Almost one-third of the low-income children indicated that people read in order to learn to read, providing evidence of cultural transmission of ideas about literacy given that many of their parents endorsed the cultural theme that literacy is a set of skills to be deliberately cultivated.

Teachers' Beliefs and Home–School Connections

Teachers bring to their professional role a variety of beliefs and attitudes that reflect different sociocultural traditions within American society, and these have a bearing on how they teach and how they relate to their students' families. Teachers of African American heritage, for example, tended to articulate the ideological principle of universal educability more frequently than teachers of European American heritage, reflecting perhaps a greater concern with equal opportunity and access. Many teachers appeared reluctant or found it difficult to reach out beyond the scope of their traditional classroom duties to their students' parents. As a result, they probably were inaccessible to many of the parents, especially those with limited education. It is precisely those parents who may be most in need of guidance and assistance from their children's teachers. In fact, approximately one-third of the parents in the Early Childhood Project reported that they did not know what their children's teachers expected of them. Although teachers expressed a desire to have parental involvement, they may have placed too much of the actual burden of initiating such involvement on the parents. Teachers often incorrectly mistook a failure of parents to assist or make an appearance in the classroom as a lack of interest in their children's academic progress or an unwillingness to assist at home. Other researchers have documented that teachers make less effort to contact parents they view as difficult to contact.

Teachers and parents tended to believe that they agreed much better about a given child's strengths and needs than was actually the case. The majority of parents and teachers (84%) viewed themselves as agreeing with each other about children's progress and difficulties. However, on closer examination, this was not the case. Far too often there was little consensus between a parent and her child's teacher on the child's progress. That is, what a parent noted as a strength or need of her child was not one mentioned by the teacher. This illustrates the need for closer communication between parents and teachers, at a level that goes beyond generalities.

*Some teachers are receptive to efforts to promote a socioculturally produc-
tive interaction between schools and the communities they aspire to serve.*
Our Cooperative Communication Project served both as an intervention designed to foster the practical application of our research
findings and as an opportunity to learn about the potential of teacher
inquiry/action research projects for bridging theory and practice. The
program was not set up as a typical inservice course, a half-day work-
shop where the "experts" come in to tell teachers what they should
be doing based on the latest findings. Rather, teachers were invited in
as colleagues, as collaborators, who have important knowledge and
insights, to identify and generate questions about children's early literacy and home–school relationships, and to design and test ways of
forging stronger links between home and school. The opportunities
these teachers had to involve parents more meaningfully in the school
lives of their children stimulated a desire to implement similar efforts
in subsequent years, and to share their knowledge and insights with
colleagues at their schools.

Why So Many Children Struggled Learning to Read

Forty-seven percent of the third graders in our study scored at least
1 year below grade level on the Woodcock-Johnson Basic Skills composite. The high percentage of poor readers was not unique to our
study; it is endemic to the Baltimore City Public Schools and, indeed, to many urban school systems. Becoming literate depends on
coordination of effort in a child's home and school. Significant differences existed in the frequency and nature of the home reading experiences of the skilled readers and those who scored below grade level.
Skilled readers engaged in frequent, usually daily, age-appropriate
reading activities. They progressed from reading storybooks in first
grade to chapter books in second and third grades. They engaged frequently with preschool books in prekindergarten and kindergarten,
but stopped doing so by the time they were in first grade, presumably because they had already developed the skills such books were
designed to promote (e.g., knowledge of the alphabet). Moreover,
skilled readers engaged with more types of printed material on a
daily basis than did the less skilled readers. Far fewer of the less
skilled readers had daily reading experiences with age-appropriate

text. Our data further showed that even when children entered first grade with less than optimal early literacy skills compared with their peers in the study, frequent engagement in reading activities apparently helped them overcome their earlier difficulties and develop more grade appropriate skills.

What makes one child engage in frequent reading experiences and another child not? One way young children develop an interest in reading is by the quality of their interactions with others surrounding text. Parents who sought to make this an enjoyable or engaging experience for their children had children who became better readers. Parents who created a pleasant atmosphere during shared reading had children who were more motivated to read and, in fact, read more frequently, and what they chose to read were more challenging texts (i.e., chapter books). Such activity, in turn, fostered reading development.

Although what happens at home is important, what occurs in school is equally important. In fact, one often expects teachers to compensate for weaknesses children experience when they enter school. The limitations of such reasoning is shown in research by Snow et al. (1991), who investigated how the quality of children's home and school environments jointly affected growth in reading comprehension. Snow and her colleagues interviewed and observed parents and teachers of a sample of low-income elementary school children. Each child's home and class were rated as high or low in literacy-promoting quality. A home with a high rating was found to compensate for 1 but not 2 years of low-rated school experiences. Two years of high-rated schooling compensated for a low-rated home, but 1 year of high and 1 year of low school experiences did not. Thus, neither a strong home nor a strong school could independently buffer a child for the long term against significant weaknesses from the other environment.

In the Early Childhood Project, our interviews with the teachers suggested that there were several areas of potential weakness in many of the children's school environments. It appeared that the teachers often lacked sufficient knowledge of current research findings showing how best to foster children's literacy development. Teaching children to read requires a highly skilled teacher (National Reading Panel, 2000), and it is possible that the teachers in the schools serving low-income neighborhoods were not as well prepared to teach phonics.

We know that many of the teachers completed their training during a time when the whole language approach was the predominant means of reading instruction. In addition, many teachers complained that they had insufficient supplies with which to augment their curriculum. Another significant limitation was that many teachers lacked an accurate set of standards against which to judge their students' performance. Thus, teachers often considered students to be excellent readers when, in fact, they were below grade level.

Most of the teachers stressed the important roles that families played or should play in their children's school success. Nevertheless, many teachers, particularly those in schools serving low-income families, were disappointed in the role that parents played. We found, consistent with what has been noted by others (e.g., MacLeod, 1996), that teachers often misjudged the willingness or capabilities of the neediest families to assist their children. Thus, insufficient efforts were made to reach out to these families, and insufficient guidance was offered to enable them to effectively assist their children with their schooling.

Far greater outreach efforts need to be made to parents of preschool children. Parents need to be made aware, much earlier than is customary, of the importance of encouraging their children's interest in reading. It is true that children need to develop skills. However, a direct emphasis on skill development is often counterproductive, at least during the early years. Parents should be made aware of informal opportunities to foster children's knowledge and how they can best foster such knowledge.

IMPLICATIONS FOR TEACHERS: HOW LEARNING ABOUT THE INTIMATE CULTURE OF A CHILD'S FAMILY CAN ENHANCE CONNECTIONS BETWEEN HOME AND SCHOOL

Teachers and parents do not necessarily agree on the best ways to help children learn to read. However, "training" parents to interact with their children in prescribed ways may not be effective. Goldenberg et al. (1992) argued that, instead, "... parent involvement efforts in the area of early literacy might be more effective, and possibly more sustainable, when they build on parents' understandings and beliefs about how children learn to become literate" (p. 530).

For such an approach to be effective, teachers need to understand something of the intimate culture of the children's families. Interviews with prekindergarten teachers at the beginning of the Early Childhood Project gave us the idea that our ecological inventory, although developed for research purposes, could be a valuable resource for teachers. Several of the teachers expressed a desire to know more about the home experiences of the children in their classes. Accordingly, we prepared a document that explained to teachers how to use this tool (Sonnenschein, Baker, & Serpell, 1995). We provided a copy of the ecological inventory (as implemented during the first home visits), along with detailed descriptions of the diary procedure and follow-up interviews with parents. Among the applications recommended for teachers were the following:

1. *Negotiating a shared understanding between the teacher and the parent.* The ecological inventory provides the basis for beginning discussion with the parent about his or her child, beliefs about his or her child, and goals for the child. Because parental beliefs or ethnotheories differ, teachers need to be aware of the potential for a mismatch between home and school beliefs and practices. The teacher can begin discussion with the parents by asking about the parent's views of recurrent activities. For example, what is the parent's opinion about the amount or type of television watching, pretend playing, or storybook reading the child is doing? Do the teacher and the parent share similar views? What goals does the parent have for his or her child? How are the activities that the child engages in related to the parent's goals? How do the child's experiences at school relate to the goals that the parent may have for the child? The teacher also can offer his or her own goals for the child and indicate how these goals are being implemented at school. Parents and teachers often have different perspectives and understandings so establishing intersubjectivity is a valuable first step in strengthening connections between home and school.

2. *Identifying recurrent activities outside of school in which children engage.* By documenting the range of activities and experiences familiar to the child, the teacher can more readily find productive

topics of discourse with the child. For example, a shy child might be drawn out if a teacher knew that the child liked to read Dr. Suess books or liked to watch Sesame Street on television.

Teachers can also note which particular literacy-related activities are more frequent at home and use those productively within the classroom. For example, if a teacher knows that many of the children in her class frequently play hand-clapping games at home, she might incorporate this activity into the lesson plans for promoting children's phonological awareness. By inviting the children to suggest rhymes for the class to recite, the teacher may build up their self-confidence, help to promote the legitimacy of activities rooted in the local neighborhood culture and, at the same time, increase her own professional repertoire of instructional routines.

Similarly, teachers can use commonly occurring home activities to create a bridge to the less common. For example, a child may have many home experiences with oral language activities such as pretend play and rhyming games, but fewer opportunities with print. A teacher may decide to use the child's facility to make up rhymes as a basis for exposure to print by creating "books" consisting of the child's own rhymes as text.

3. *Identifying socialization agents in the child's home.* The ecological inventory also affords an opportunity to document who in a child's family interacts with that child in specific activities. By looking at the participants in the activities, teachers will gain a better understanding of the social organization of the home learning experiences available to their students. For example, in many middle-income families in our sample, parents read to their young children. However, this was not the norm in the low-income families, where older siblings were at least as likely as parents to serve as primary co-participants. Teachers can use this information to design participant structures at school that are complementary with the children's home experiences, such as cross-age tutoring or cooperative learning. Knowing which individuals serve as socialization agents in the home may provide the foundation for bridging home and school.

IMPLICATIONS FOR PARENTING: RECOMMENDED PRACTICES
FOR PROMOTING CHILDREN'S LITERACY DEVELOPMENT

In 1998, the International Reading Association (IRA) and the National
Association for the Education of Young Children (NAEYC) published
a joint position statement on developmentally appropriate practice
in literacy instruction. Although its major focus was on classroom
instruction, the position statement also identified what parents and
family members could do to promote children's development in early
reading and writing. It included a listing of recommended practices
in each of five phases from preschool to Grade 3. Our 5-year longitudinal study encompassed the same developmental phases, affording
us an opportunity to compare the actual practices documented in
the Early Childhood Project with those recommended in the position statement. Moreover, in many cases we were able to document
the effectiveness of the recommended practices in fostering literacy
development. In an analysis prepared for a 1999 symposium on developmentally appropriate literacy practices (Baker, Sonnenschein,
& Serpell, 1999), we organized the recommended practices into eight
underlying themes. With the increased national emphasis on early
literacy development, such recommendations are becoming increasingly common. For example, the National Research Council has
also prepared a set of recommendations for parents that correspond
closely to those included in the position statement (Burns, Griffin, &
Snow, 1999). In the discussion that follows, we refer to the NAEYC
and IRA recommendations as an expert consensus. (See Baker et al.,
1999, for supporting data and details regarding what follows.)

Theme 1: Engage in Shared Book Reading

Like much of the widely publicized advice to parents on how to
foster children's literacy development, expert consensus highlights
the value of shared book reading. Our project examined this activity
from several angles. Our findings are consistent with other research
in supporting the recommendation that parents engage in shared
storybook reading, and they afford some additional relevant insights.

The consensus recommendation to engage in shared book reading in the position statement dropped out in Grade 3. Parents might

take this to mean that the activity should no longer occur. Shared storybook or chapter book reading may be a valuable opportunity for the promotion of children's literacy development even in Grade 3 and beyond, provided that the adults engaging in it are sensitive to the shifting literacy interests and cognitive needs of children as they grow older. Sharing with older children may beneficially include some analysis of style and vocabulary in comparison with other texts, whereas at earlier ages a focus is best maintained on the context of the story and linking it to the child's lived experience. Moreover, shared reading can continue to be a pleasant experience even for older children. Parents in the Early Childhood Project did report less frequent shared storybook reading in Grade 3 than in earlier years. This drop-off was most dramatic for middle-income European American families, where there was a concomitant increase in children's independent reading of chapter books.

The expert consensus guidelines were silent as to whether parents should read books with an explicit skills-building focus; the only types that were mentioned were stories with predictable text and informational stories. The Early Childhood Project does provide evidence that educational books are of value in the early years. Experience with preschool (ABC) books during prekindergarten was a strong predictor of word recognition in the primary grades, more so than shared storybook reading.

This genre difference can be understood by considering our observations of shared storybook reading when the children were in kindergarten. One of the categories used for coding speech that occurred in this context was a focus on print, such as "N is also in your name," and "What's that word? Spell it." This kind of talk occurred very infrequently. However, it was more common with certain types of books, including alphabet books, as well as rhyming and predictable language books. It may be that books with a more explicit educational focus are more useful for fostering the skills involved in word recognition than conventional storybooks.

The consensus statement recommended that, for first and second graders, children should read to their parents and parents should read to their children. We have a word of caution to offer in this regard based on our analysis of shared storybook reading when the children were completing Grade 1. During this session either the child read to the parent or the parent read to the child, or they shared responsibility, as they chose. When the child served as reader, there was more talk about reading the words on the page; usually the parent simply supplied the word if the child hesitated or stumbled. The more the parent tried to provide specific help with letters and sounds, the less positive the affective atmosphere. If the child is a struggling reader, needing considerable help in recognizing words, he or she may find the experience stressful rather than rewarding. As we documented, affective quality was related to subsequent reading activity at home, which in turn related to reading achievement.

Theme 2: Provide Frequent and Varied Oral Language Experiences

Expert consensus gives considerable emphasis to the importance of oral language development to reading and writing. One recommendation in the position statement was to: "Have conversations with children during mealtimes and throughout the day." Conversation plays a key role in young children's vocabulary development, and it provides them with the opportunity to learn how to talk about experiences that were not shared with the listener. Being able to go beyond the immediate context is an important academic language skill. Across several years, the majority of the parents in the Early Childhood Project reported that their child engaged in mealtime conversations with them on a daily basis. In addition, many, especially middle-income, parents perceived mealtime conversation to be an important family ritual.

Another recommendation was to: "Encourage children to recount experiences and describe ideas and events that are important to them." Across the years, about more than one-half of the families in our study reported daily or at least weekly engagement in oral storytelling, an activity likely to foster narrative competence in particular. Frequent participation in storytelling and other activities with a storyline was indeed related to kindergarten children's narrative production.

Another type of oral language competence of concern in the Early Childhood Project was phonological awareness. One of the ecological inventory activities with the potential to foster phonological awareness was playing word games, which often involve rhyme or alliteration. The position statement recommended that teachers of preschoolers engage children in language games, but language games were not mentioned in the recommendations for parents. Nevertheless, many other research-based recommendations to parents do include this activity, such as those presented by the National Research Council. Although language games were not a daily occurrence for most families in the Early Childhood Project, about one-half reported at least weekly engagement across the years. Home experiences such as these appear to influence the development of phonological awareness and early reading competencies. Prekindergarten knowledge of nursery rhymes was a strong predictor of rhyme sensitivity, as was frequency of engagement in word games and language play at home. Nursery rhyme knowledge also predicted word recognition in the primary grades.

Theme 3: Encourage Self-Initiated Interactions With Print

Literacy development depends on children choosing to engage with print on a regular basis. The expert consensus document included several recommendations related to this point, ranging from "Provide opportunities for children to draw and print, using markers, crayons, and pencils" at the preschool level to "Engage children in activities that require reading and writing" at the Grade 2 level. This was a topic of particular interest in the Early Childhood Project, with many ecological inventory activities and parental ethnotheory questions explicitly focused on it.

In our early interviews with parents, many spontaneously described their children playing school. We asked parents when the children were in first grade to describe the kinds of activities that took place. Most of these play-school activities included writing letters and words. We asked specifically about the frequency of playing school in Grades 2 and 3, and more than one-half of the parents reported daily or weekly play. That many children chose to play school during their free time indicates the degree to which they had appropriated the concept of schooling as a valued cultural practice.

In the ecological inventories, parents were asked to distinguish whether children's reading occurred with others or alone.

Self-initiated interactions with print are clearly important to later literacy development. For example, children who frequently engaged in independent reading or writing had better word identification and reading comprehension in Grades 1 and 2. Among children who scored low on our composite measure of orientation to print in kindergarten/Grade 1, those who went on to become good readers had more frequent independent experiences with a breadth of print materials (involving both reading and writing) in Grades 2 and 3 than those who subsequently were poor readers.

The expert consensus on the value of engaging children in activities that require reading and writing does not necessarily imply that all children will respond in similar ways to such activities. Compare these comments, the first from a parent of a successful third-grade reader, the second from a parent of a struggling third-grade reader: (1) "... we'll have books lying all over the kitchen and she'll just pick one up and sit at the table like while she reads," and (2) "to get him to pick up a book is asking a lot." These quotations illustrate the complex challenge of nurturing the child's reading motivation. For child 1, the mere provision of materials was enough, whereas child 2 needed more focused guidance and enticement. This suggests an interaction between parental strategies for the socialization of literacy and individual differences in motivation. That is, for a child who is already eager to read, laissez-faire enrichment may be optimal, whereas for a child who shows little spontaneous interest in reading, a more proactive intervention approach may be optimal (see also Baker, 2003).

Theme 4: Visit the Library Regularly

A large body of research attests to the importance of the library in promoting literacy development. The expert consensus document recommended that parents of preschoolers "visit the library regularly" and that parents of third graders "continue to support children's learning and interests by visiting the library and bookstores with them." In the Early Childhood Project, the mean ratings for visiting the library remained stable across time, but consistent with other studies, low-income families visited the library less often than middle-income families. In an analysis of the relation of early home experiences to the development of word recognition, frequency of visits to the library when children were in prekindergarten predicted word recognition in the primary grades.

It is not going to the library per se that directly impacts word recognition and other literacy competencies, but rather all that going to the library entails. For example, going to the library reflects parental valuing of books and reading. It exposes children to a place that exists almost entirely for the purpose of making large numbers of books widely accessible, demonstrating the importance of books and reading in the larger society. It gives children an opportunity to make choices about what they would like to read or have read to them. Intrinsic interest is critical to self-initiated interactions with print. Public libraries in Baltimore, as elsewhere in the western world, have introduced over the second half of the twentieth century a rich variety of display and service features designed to cater to the tastes of young children and to foster their emergent reading motivation. Frequent visits to the library make it more likely that a broad range of print materials will be available at home.

Theme 5: Demonstrate the Value of Literacy in Everyday Life

The expert consensus document emphasized that young children need to see the functional value of reading and writing. Activities should be meaningful and purposeful, whether they involve reading a story, writing a letter to a grandparent, or using print to accomplish a task or goal of everyday life. Several recommendations addressed this latter function of literacy, such as "Allow children to participate in activities that involve writing and reading (for example, cooking, making grocery lists)" for kindergartners and "Encourage children to use and enjoy print for many purposes (such as recipes, directions, games, and sports)" for third graders.

Many of the activities included in our ecological inventory were intended to capture children's experiences with print as a component of everyday life or in the service of accomplishing another goal. About two-thirds of the parents reported daily or at least weekly participation of their prekindergarten and kindergarten children in food preparation, which at least on occasion involves reading recipes and package directions. Parents often reported their children playing a role in picking out food items at the grocery store as early as prekindergarten, again paying attention to the print. As children's literacy skills increased over the years, participation in board games became more frequent. By Grade 3, almost three-fourths played board games on a daily or at least a weekly basis. Parents' diary reports also indicated that their children were exposed to print as a part of daily routines, and they held the perspective that literacy was an essential ingredient of everyday life. The children themselves were aware of this fact when we asked them in first grade why people read and why it is important to learn to read. Teachers in the Early Childhood Project also saw this as an important theme, as reflected in their interview responses.

Theme 6: Promote Children's Motivation for Reading

The expert consensus document did not address this important component of literacy development directly. However, key phrases in other recommendations refer to constructs that are related to motivation: building a *love* of language, supporting children's learning and *interest*, encouraging children to *enjoy* print. All three of these recommendations were made for the first time at the level of third grade, which appears to us to be rather late along the continuum of literacy development.

Many parents in the Early Childhood Project placed considerable emphasis on the importance of building children's motivation for reading. They conceptualized reading as an enjoyable activity and sought to increase children's interest in it. As discussed earlier in the chapter, children whose parents displayed such an emphasis attained higher scores on tests of comprehension and word recognition in the primary grades than children whose parents had stronger endorsement of a skills perspective. In addition, children who experienced reading in a comfortable and supportive social context at age 5 were more likely to recognize the value of reading, show interest in reading, and have positive concepts of themselves as readers in subsequent years.

The evidence is clear that motivation is critical to independent reading and that frequent independent reading is critical to reading development. In our study, children's self-reported motivation for reading was correlated with parental reports of the frequency with which their second graders chose to read material not assigned by their teachers. Children whose parents emphasized the importance of enjoying reading scored higher on the motivation scale in first grade, demonstrating again the contribution of parental beliefs.

Theme 7: Foster a Sense of Pride and Perceptions of Competence in Literacy

The theme of fostering pride and perceived competence is closely related to the previous one. The expert consensus document did not explicitly recommend to parents that they help children develop a sense of pride in their literacy accomplishments, but several of the recommendations have the potential to do so. For example, a recommendation at the third-grade level was, "Find ways to highlight children's progress in reading and writing." In their diaries and responses to various interview questions, parents in the Early Childhood Project often indicated such practices. Displays of children's work on the refrigerator or elsewhere were common.

The instrument we developed to assess motivation for reading included items dealing with children's sense of themselves as readers. Most of the children, even those who had not gotten off to a strong start, had positive views of their competencies in Grades 1 and 2. Our findings are consistent with a large body of research showing that most children start off with optimism and interest in learning to read. However, those who experience difficulties soon come to develop a concept of self as poor reader, and their motivation for reading declines. They read less, both in school and out, than children who are succeeding. The amount that children read influences further growth in reading. Consistent with the systems perspective on literacy development that underlies the Early Childhood Project, how parents respond when their children are struggling to read interacts with teachers' responses and the child's own developing self-system (see Baker, 2003, for further discussion).

Theme 8: Communicate With Teachers and Be Involved With School

The final expert consensus theme goes beyond the family to focus on home–school connections, emphasizing the importance of communication with teachers and school involvement. For example, a recommendation at the first-grade level was: "Bring to a parent–teacher's conference evidence of what your child can do in writing and reading." A recommendation at the third-grade level was: "Stay in regular contact with your child's teachers about activities and progress in reading and writing." All the parents in our study reported behaviors consistent with the recommendation; they said that they initiated discussion with their child's third-grade teacher when they were displeased or concerned about something.

We were struck by the fact that home–school connections were not given attention at the earlier levels. The absence of a recommendation could be misinterpreted to mean that it does not matter if parents are uninvolved in prekindergarten and kindergarten. Or perhaps it was assumed that parents would be heavily involved in the early years, and so explicit recommendations were only included when drop-off might occur. Evidence of a drop-off in involvement was indeed obtained in the Early Childhood Project. Second-grade teachers reported considerably less involvement by the same parents who were rated as heavily involved when their children were in prekindergarten and kindergarten.

An Overlooked Practice: Promote Children's Knowledge of the World

Overall, the themes derived from the expert consensus document are those we agree are of primary importance for parents in their efforts to promote their children's early literacy development. The activities we chose to include in our ecological inventory, selected on the basis of research evidence for their value, fall quite closely within the same themes. There is one area to which we gave some emphasis, however, that was not apparent in the recommendations to parents: exposure to opportunities to acquire knowledge of the world. The statement did not explicitly mention the value of such experiences, except to note that preschool children need "firsthand experiences that expand children's vocabulary, such as trips in the community and exposure to various tools, objects and materials." Books, particularly informational text, can serve as a valuable source of vocabulary.

Television can be an important tool for acquiring knowledge, which in turn promotes reading comprehension and interest in reading. Television was not mentioned, either positively or negatively, in the expert consensus guidelines. In the Early Childhood Project, television viewing was the most common recurrent activity. It was engaged in on a daily basis by almost all children, regardless of income level or ethnicity, across all 5 years of the study.

The variety of experiences to which children are exposed by their families plays an important role in expanding the child's knowledge base. Trips to stores and libraries, visits with friends and relatives, participation in organized activities, and informal play all provide knowledge and experience that will serve children well in reading. Evidence of the value of first-hand experience comes from an analysis of third-grade data in the Early Childhood Project: the more frequently children engaged in these activities, the better their reading comprehension, even after taking into account their earlier reading skills (Mackler & Baker, 2001).

GOING BEYOND SOCIAL ADDRESS: IMPLICATIONS FOR POLICY

The Early Childhood Project has documented the range of home experiences children bring with them to school. All too often people say that children living in poverty do not engage in activities conducive to literacy development that are commonplace in middle-income homes. Although we did find income-related differences in the frequency of engagement in several of the activities in our ecological inventory, we did not find such differences in many more. In some activities, ethnicity differences were more apparent than income differences (Baker et al., 1999). For example, across all years, the African American children more frequently played word games and engaged with educational toys than the European American children. Early experience with drawing and writing was more frequent among African American children than European American children. Oral storytelling across all years was most frequent among the middle-income African American families. It seems clear that there are some cultural differences that guide the choices parents make for their children. However, overall, variations within groups in the intimate cultures of the children's homes were more salient than differences between groups related to social address.

In the everyday discourse of contemporary American society, the concept of culture is often deployed as a way of referring to widely recognized contrasts between large self-identifying social groups. In our usage, however, its primary significance is to characterize a dimension of behavior and experience that is shared among co-participants in joint activity and that endures over time. Thus, families are equally legitimate repositories of a distinctive culture as are larger social groups.

Social addresses can be construed as offering a simplistic typology of intimate cultures based on superficial features. An extensive psychological and educational literature in the 1950s and 1960s invoked the concept of cultural deficiency as an explanation for the prevalence of educational failure among children of certain stigmatized sectors of society, such as the poor, immigrants, or historically oppressed ethnic groups (e.g., Bereiter & Englemann, 1966; Lewis, 1966). This type of deficiency formulation has, however, been thoroughly critiqued on the grounds that it confounded correlation with causation and blended popular stereotypes into purportedly scientific reasoning (Cole & Bruner, 1971; Ginsburg, 1972; Guttierez & Rogoff, 2003; Howard & Scott, 1981).

Whatever their origins, such stereotypes necessarily overgeneralize, and are therefore likely to be weaker predictors of parental behavior and of child developmental outcomes than a finer-grain analysis of the patterns of activity, meanings, and technology that characterize particular families. Thus, from the perspective of literacy development, psychosocial features of a family's intimate culture are much more informative than economic indices of the family's material resources.

Why do we pay so much attention to getting beyond social addresses? First, we have seen that the correlations are not perfect. Cases abound in which a particular family departs from the modal pattern for their social address. For instance, Mrs. A, the mother discussed in Chapter 3 who coined the epigrammatic formulation of the entertainment theme, "Why make reading boring?" was a low-income parent who had grown up herself in conditions of poverty.

Second, even when the correlation is impressively strong, we contend that it is important to look beyond appearances to the underlying mechanisms or processes through which some families succeed in cultivating early literacy development, while others seemingly do not. Knowing the social class or ethnicity of a family might enable a researcher to predict with a certain degree of confidence how many of the beneficial conditions of literacy socialization will be found within the home. However, to intervene to change the situation for the better, policy makers and professionals need an account of characteristics that are open to change through advocacy, education, or guidance. In the language of Epstein and Weikart (1979) and Kagitcibasi (1996), we need to know how to set in motion a "virtuous cycle" of mutually supportive processes that will generate long-term gains in children's developmental opportunities.

CLOSING COMMENTS

During the time period of the Early Childhood Project, Baltimore advertised itself as the "City That Reads." Mayor Kurt Schmoke stated in his 1987 inaugural speech: "Of all the things I might be able to accomplish as mayor of our city, it would make me the proudest if one day it could simply be said that this is a city that reads, this is a city that waged war on illiteracy." Unfortunately, too many of its younger residents did not read well by the end of his term, and 38% of the city's adults still read below the sixth-grade level as of 2001. Despite the importance accorded to schooling by the families, teachers, and civic leaders of Baltimore, more than one-half of the children in our study were struggling to achieve basic literacy at the end of third grade. All too often, the children who came from homes in which there was less support for literacy development attended schools that were unsuccessful in building upon the skills the children possessed when they arrived at school. If, in the language of the current national educational policy, we are to "leave no child behind," more effective ways need to be found for bridging between home and school.

References

Adams, M. (1990). *Beginning to read: Thinking and learning about print*. Cambridge, MA: MIT Press.

Akkari, A. (1999). African American educators' perspectives about teaching and learning. *Negro Educational Review, L*, 29–42.

Akkari, A., Serpell, R., Baker, L., & Sonnenschein, S. (1998). An analysis of teacher ethnotheories. *The Professional Educator, 21*, 45–61.

Anderson, A., & Stokes, S. (1984). Social and institutional influences on the development and practice of literacy. In H. Goelman, A. Oberg, & F. Smith (Eds.), *Awakening to literacy* (pp. 24–37). Portsmouth, NH: Heinemann.

Astatke, H. (1996). *Older playmates' contribution to preschoolers' acquisition of emergent literacy skills*. Unpublished master's thesis, University of Maryland, Baltimore County.

Auletta, K. (1982). *The underclass*. New York: Random House.

Baine, D. (1988). *Handicapped children in developing countries: Assessment, curriculum and instruction*. Edmonton, Alberta, Canada: University of Alberta.

Baker, L. (2000). Building the word-level foundation for engaged reading. In L. Baker, M. J. Dreher, & J. T. Guthrie (Eds.), *Engaging young readers: Promoting achievement and motivation* (pp. 17–42). New York: Guilford.

Baker, L. (2003). The role of parents in motivating struggling readers. *Reading and Writing Quarterly, 19*, 1–20.

Baker, L., Allen, J., Shockley, B., Pellegrini, A. D., Galda, L., & Stahl, S. (1996). Connecting school and home: constructing partnerships to foster reading development. In L. Baker, P. Afflerbach, & D. Reinking (Eds.), *Developing engaged readers in school and home communities* (pp. 21–41). Mahwah, NJ: Erlbaum.

Baker, L., Dreher, M. J., & Guthrie, J. T. (2000). Why teachers should promote reading engagement. In L. Baker, M. J. Dreher, & J. T. Guthrie (Eds.),

Engaging young readers: Promoting achievement and motivation (pp. 1–16). New York: Guilford.

Baker, L., Fernandez-Fein, S., Scher, D., & Williams, H. (1998). Home experiences related to the development of word recognition. In J. Metsala & L. Ehri (Eds.), *Word recognition in beginning literacy* (pp. 263–288). Mahwah, NJ: Erlbaum.

Baker, L., Garrett, A., & Morse, F. (2003, April). *Eating at McDonalds: Relations between children's written scripts and their reading development.* Paper presented at the meeting of the Society for Research in Child Development, Tampa.

Baker, L., Mackler, K., Sonnenschein, S., & Serpell, R. (2001). Parents' interactions with their first-grade children during storybook reading and relations with subsequent home reading activity and reading achievement. *Journal of School Psychology, 39,* 415–438.

Baker, L., Mackler, K., Sonnenschein, S., Serpell, R., & Fernandez-Fein, S. (1998, April). *Early home experience and emergent literacy skills as contributors to children's word recognition in the primary grades.* Paper presented at the meeting of the American Educational Research Association, San Diego.

Baker, L., & Scher, D. (2002). Beginning readers' motivation for reading in relation to parental beliefs and home reading experiences. *Reading Psychology, 23,* 239–269.

Baker, L., Scher, D., & Mackler, K. (1997). Home and family influences on motivations for reading. *Educational Psychologist, 32,* 69–82.

Baker, L., Serpell, R., & Sonnenschein, S. (1995). Opportunities for literacy-related learning in the homes of urban preschoolers. In L. Morrow (Ed.), *Family literacy: Connections in schools and communities* (pp. 236–252). Newark, DE: International Reading Association.

Baker, L., Sonnenschein, S., & Gilat, M. (1996). Mothers' sensitivity to their competencies of preschoolers on a concept learning task. *Early Childhood Research Quarterly, 11,* 405–424.

Baker, L., Sonnenschein, S., & Serpell, R. (1999, April). A five-year comparison of actual and recommended practices for promoting children's literacy development. In K. Roskos & A. G. Bus (Chairs), *Early literacy at the crossroad: Policy, practices and promise.* Symposium presented at American Educational Research Association, Montreal, Canada. (ERIC Document Reproduction Services No. ED435466.)

Baker, L., Sonnenschein, S., Serpell, R., Fernandez-Fein, S., & Scher, D. (1994). *Contexts of emergent literacy: Everyday home experiences of urban prekindergarten children* (Research Report # 24). Athens, GA: University of Georgia and University of Maryland, National Reading Research Center. (ERIC Document Reproduction Services No. ED396266.)

Baker, L., & Wigfield, A. (1999). Dimensions of children's motivation for reading and their relations to reading activity and reading achievement. *Reading Research Quarterly, 34,* 452–477.

Baltimore City Public School System (BCPSS). (1999). *Study of the Baltimore City Public School System.* (www.bcps.k12.md.us/facts/history. htm).

Baltimore City Public School System (BCPSS). (2001). Performance on the Maryland Functional Testing Program: 1996–97 to 2000–01. A report prepared for the new Board of School Commissioners, October 9, 2001, by the BCPSS, Division of Research, Evaluation, and Accountability. (www.bcps.k12.md.us/htm).

Baltimore City Public School System (BCPSS). (2002). Master Plan II. (www.bcps.k12.md.us/board/masterplan)

Bereiter, C., & Engelmann, S. (1966). *Teaching disadvantaged children in the preschool.* Englewood Cliffs, NJ: Prentice-Hall.

Bourdieu, P. (1974). The school as a conservative force: Scholastic and cultural inequalities. In J. Eggleston (Ed.), *Contemporary research in the sociology of education* (pp. 32–46). London: Methuen.

Bourdieu, P., & Passeron, J. C. (1964). *Les Heritiers.* Paris: Minuit.

Britt, G., & Baker, L. (1997). *Engaging parents and kindergartners in reading through a class lending library.* (Instructional Resource Report No. 41). Athens, GA: University of Georgia and University of Maryland, National Reading Research Center. (ERIC Document Reproduction Services No. ED405553.)

Bronfenbrenner, U. (1979). *The ecology of human development.* Cambridge, MA: Harvard University Press.

Bronfenbrenner, U. (1989). Ecological systems theory. In R. Vasta (Ed.), *Annals of child development: Vol. 6. Six theories of child development: Revised formulations and current issues* (pp. 187–251). Greenwich, CT: JAI Press.

Bronfenbrenner, U., & Crouter, A. C. (1983). The evolution of environmental models in developmental research. In P. H. Mussen (Series Ed.) & W. Kessen (Vol. Ed.), *Handbook of child psychology: Vol. 1. History, theory and methods* (3rd ed., pp. 357–414). New York: Wiley.

Browne, E. (1991). *Where's that bus?* New York: Simon & Schuster.

Bruce, L. J. (1964). The analysis of word sounds by young children. *British Journal of Educational Psychology, 34,* 158–174.

Bruneau, B., Ruttan, D., & Dunlap, S. K. (1995). Communication between teachers and parents: Developing partnerships. *Reading and Writing Quarterly: Overcoming Learning Difficulties, 11,* 257–266.

Bruner, J. S. (1986). *Actual minds, possible worlds.* Cambridge, MA: Harvard University Press.

Bryant, P. E., Bradley, L., MacLean, M., & Crossland, J. (1989). Nursery rhymes, phonological skills and reading. *Journal of Child Language, 16,* 407–428.

Bryant, P. E., MacLean, M., Bradley, L., & Crossland, J. (1990). Rhyme and alliteration, phoneme detection, and learning to read. *Developmental Psychology, 26,* 429–438.

Burns, M. S., Griffin, P., & Snow, C. E. (Eds.) (1999). *Starting out right: A guide to promoting children's reading success.* Washington, DC: National Academies Press.

Bus, A. G. (2001). Joint caregiver–child storybook reading: A route to literacy development. In S. B. Neuman & D. K. Dickinson (Eds.), *Handbook of early literacy research* (pp. 179–191). New York: Guilford Press.

Bus, A. G., Leseman, P. P. M., & Keultjes, P. (2000). Joint book reading across cultures: A comparison of Surinamese-Dutch, Turkish-Dutch, and Dutch parent–child dyads. *Journal of Literacy Research, 32,* 53–76.

Bus, A. G., & van IJzendoorn, M. H. (1988). Mother–child interactions, attachment, and emergent literacy: A cross-sectional study. *Child Development, 59,* 1262–1272.

Bus, A. G., & van IJzendoorn, M. H. (1999). Phonological awareness and early reading: A meta-analysis of experimental training studies. *Journal of Educational Psychology, 91,* 403–414.

Bus, A. G., van IJzendoorn, M. H., & Pellegrini, A. D. (1995). Joint book reading makes for success in learning to read: A meta-analysis on intergenerational transmission of literacy. *Review of Educational Research, 65,* 1–21.

Caldwell, B., & Bradley, R. H. (1984). *Home observation for measurement of the environment.* Little Rock: University of Arkansas at Little Rock.

Cannella, G. S. (1997). *Deconstructing early childhood education: Social justice and revolution.* New York: Peter Lang.

Chaney, C. (1994). Language development, metalinguistic awareness, and emergent literacy skills of 3-year-old children in relation to social class. *Applied Psycholinguistics, 15,* 371–394.

Chapman, J. W., & Tunmer, W. E. (1995). Development of young children's reading self-concepts: An examination of emerging subcomponents and their relationship with reading achievement. *Journal of Educational Psychology, 87,* 154–167.

Christelow, E. (1992). *Don't wake up Momma! Another five little monkeys story.* New York: Clarion Books.

Clark, K. B. (1965). *Dark ghetto: Dilemmas of social power.* New York: Harper & Row.

Clay, M. M. (1979). *Reading: The patterning of complex behavior* (2nd ed.). Auckland, New Zealand: Heinemann.

Cohen, J. (1987). *Statistical power analysis for the behavioral sciences.* Hillsdale, NJ: Erlbaum.

Cole, M. (1996). *Cultural psychology: A once and future discipline.* Cambridge, MA: The Belknap Press of Harvard University Press.

Cole, M., & Bruner, J. (1971). Cultural differences and inferences about psychological processes. *American Psychologist, 26,* 867–876.

Cole, M., & Griffin, P. (1980). Cultural amplifiers reconsidered. In D. Olson (Ed.), *Social foundations of language and thought.* New York: Norton.

Cole-Henderson, B., & Serpell, Z. (1998). *Successful schools and their character-istics: A bibliography.* Washington, DC: Howard University, CRESPAR.

Comer, J., & Haynes, N. (1991). Parent involvement in the schools: An eco-logical approach. *Elementary School Journal, 91,* 271–277.

Connors, L. J., & Epstein, J. L. (1995). Parent and school partnerships. In M. H. Bornstein (Ed.), *Handbook of parenting, Vol. 2* (pp. 437–458). Hillsdale, NJ: Erlbaum.

D'Andrade, R. G. (1984). Cultural meaning systems. In R. A. Shweder & R. A. Levine (Eds.), *Culture theory: Essays on mind, self and emotion* (pp. 88–119). Cambridge, UK: Cambridge University Press.

D'Andrade, R. G. (1990). Some propositions about the relations between cul-ture and human cognition. In J. W. Stigler, R. A. Shweder, & G. Herdt (Eds.), *Cultural psychology: Essays on comparative human development* (pp. 65–129). Cambridge, UK: Cambridge University Press.

Danseco, E. (1998). *Building bridges: African American mothers' and teachers' ethnotheories on children's development, children's problems and home-school relations for children with and without disabilities.* Unpublished doctoral dis-sertation, University of Maryland, Baltimore County.

Dauber, S. L., & Epstein, J. L. (1993). Parents' attitudes and practices of in-volvement in inner-city elementary and middle schools. In N. F. Chavkin (Ed.), *Families and schools in a pluralistic society* (pp. 2–71). Albany: State University of New York Press.

DeBaryshe, B. D. (1995). Maternal belief systems: Linchpin in the home read-ing process. *Journal of Applied Developmental Psychology, 16,* 1–20.

Delpit, L. (1988). The silenced dialogue: Power and pedagogy in educating other people's children. *Harvard Educational Review, 58,* 280–298.

Dickinson, D. K., & Keebler, R. (1989). Variation in preschool teacher's style of reading books. *Discourse Processes, 12,* 353–376.

Dickinson, D. K., & Smith, M. W. (1994). Long-term effects of preschool teach-ers' book readings on low-income children's vocabulary and story com-prehension. *Reading Research Quarterly, 29,* 104–122.

Dickinson, D. K., & Tabors, P. O. (Eds.). (2001). *Beginning language with literacy: Young children learning at home and school.* Baltimore: Brookes Publishing.

Duke, N. K. (2000). 3.6 minutes per day: The scarcity of informational texts in first grade. *Reading Research Quarterly, 35,* 202–225.

Eccles, J. S., & Harold, R. D. (1996). Family involvement in children's and adolescents' schooling. In A. Booth & J. F. Dunn (Eds.), *Family-school links: How do they affect educational outcomes?* (pp. 3–34). Mahwah, NJ: Erlbaum.

Ehri, L. C. (1998). Grapheme-phoneme knowledge is essential for learning to read words in English. In J. Metsala & L. Ehri (Eds.), *Word recognition in beginning literacy* (pp. 3–40). Mahwah, NJ: Erlbaum.

Elley, W. B. (1989). Vocabulary acquisition from listening to stories. *Reading Research Quarterly, 24,* 174–187.

Elliott, J., Bridges, D., Ebbutt, D., Gibson, R., & Nias, J. (1981). *School account-ability*. London, UK: Grant MacIntyre.

Epstein, A. S., & Weikart, D. P. (1979). *The Ypsilanti-Carnegie Infant Education Project: Longitudinal follow-up*. Ypsilanti, MI: High/Scope Press.

Evans, M. A., Shaw, D., & Bell, M. (2000). Home literacy activities and their influence on early literacy skills. *Canadian Journal of Experimental Psychology, 54,* 65–75.

Fernandez-Fein, S. (1995). *Rhyme and alliteration in preschoolers from differ-ent sociocultural backgrounds*. Unpublished master's thesis, University of Maryland, Baltimore County.

Fernandez-Fein, S., & Baker, L. (1997). Rhyme sensitivity and relevant ex-periences in preschoolers from diverse backgrounds. *Journal of Literacy Research, 29,* 433–459.

Fiese, B. H., Hooker, K. A., Kotary, L., & Schwagler, J. (1993). Family rituals in the early stages of parenthood. *Journal of Marriage and the Family, 55,* 633–642.

Fiese, B. H., & Kline, C. A. (1993). Development of the Family Ritual Ques-tionnaire (FRQ): Initial reliability and validation studies. *Journal of Family Psychology, 6,* 290–299.

Fitzgerald, J., Spiegel, D. L., & Cunningham, J. W. (1991). The relationship be-tween parental literacy level and perceptions of emergent literacy. *Journal of Reading Behavior, 23,* 191–210.

Foorman, B. R., & Francis, D. J. (1994). Exploring connections among read-ing, spelling, and phonemic segmentation during first grade. *Reading and Writing: An Interdisciplinary Journal, 6,* 65–91.

Fordham, S. (1996). *Blacked out: Dilemmas of race, identity and success at Capital High*. Chicago: Chicago University Press.

Forman, E. A., & McPhail, J. (1993). Vygotskian perspective on children's collaborative problem-solving activities. In Forman, E. A., Minick, N., & Stone, C. A. (Eds.), *Contexts for learning sociocultural dynamics in children's development* (pp. 213–229). New York: Oxford University Press.

Freund, L. (1990). Maternal regulation of children's problem-solving behav-ior and its impact on children's performance. *Child Development, 61,* 113–126.

Furman, L. N., & Walden, T. A. (1990). Effect of script knowledge on preschool children's communicative interactions. *Developmental Psychology, 26,* 227–233.

Gadamer, H. G. (1975). *Truth and method*. London: Sheed & Ward.

Galdone, P. (1969). *The monkey and the crocodile*. New York: Houghton Mifflin.

Gallimore, R., Weisner, T. S., Kaufman, S. Z., & Berneheimer, L. P. (1989). The social construction of ecocultural niches: Family accommodation of developmentally delayed children. *American Journal on Mental Retardation, 94,* 216–230.

Geertz, C. (1983). *Local knowledge: Further essays in interpretive anthropology.* New York: Basic Books.

Gersten, R., Fuchs, L. S., Williams, J. P., & Baker, S. (2001). Teaching reading comprehension strategies to students with learning disabilities: A review of research. *Review of Educational Research, 71,* 279–320.

Gibson, E. J. (1982). The concept of affordances: The renascence of functionalism. In A. Collins (Ed.), *The concept of development: The Minnesota Symposia on Child Development* (Vol. 15, pp. 55–81). Hillsdale, NJ: Erlbaum.

Gibson, J. J. (1979). *The ecological approach to visual perception.* Boston: Houghton-Mifflin.

Ginsburg, H. (1972). *The myth of the deprived child: Poor children's intellect and education.* Englewood Cliffs, NJ: Prentice-Hall.

Goldenberg, C. (2001). Making schools work for low-income families in the 21st century. In S. B. Neuman & D. K. Dickinson (Eds.), *Handbook of early literacy research* (pp. 211–231). New York: Guilford.

Goldenberg, C., Reese, L., & Gallimore, R. (1992). Effects of literacy materials from school on Latino children's home experiences and early reading achievement. *American Journal of Education, 100,* 497–536.

Goodnow, J. J. (2002). Parents' knowledge and expectations: Using what we know. In M. C. Bornstein (Ed.), *Handbook of parenting, Vol. 3. Being and becoming a parent* (2nd ed., pp. 444–460) Mahwah, NJ: LEA.

Goodnow, J. J., & Collins, A. W. (1990). *Development according to parents: The nature, sources and consequences of parents' ideas.* Hillsdale, NJ: Erlbaum.

Gorham, L. (1995). *Cooperative communication inservice seminar for preschool teachers.* Unpublished manuscript, University of Maryland, Baltimore County.

Goswami, U., & Bryant, P. (1992). Rhyme, analogy, and children's reading. In P. B. Gough, L. C. Ehri, & R. Treiman (Eds.), *Reading acquisition* (pp. 49–63). Hillsdale, NJ: Erlbaum.

Grice, H. P. (1975). Logic and conversation. In P. Cole & J. Morgan (Eds.), *Syntax and semantics: Vol. 3. Speech acts* (pp. 41–58). New York: Academic Press.

Guittierez, K. D., & Rogoff, B. (2003). Cultural ways of learning: Individual traits or repertoires of practice. *Educational Researcher, 32,* 19–25.

Guthrie, J. T., & Greaney, V. (1991). Literacy acts. In R. Barr, M. L. Kamil, P. Mosenthal, & P. D. Pearson (Eds.), *Handbook of reading research* (Vol. 2, pp. 68–96). New York: Longman.

Hale, J. E. (1982). *Black children, their roots, culture and learning style.* Provo, UT: Brigham Young University Press.

Hallden, G. (1991). The child as project and the child as being: Parents' ideas as frames of reference. *Child and Society, 5,* 334–346.

Halliday, M. A. K. (1973). *Explorations in the functions of language.* London, England: Edward Arnold.

Harris, A. J., & Sipay, E. R. (1980). *How to increase reading ability* (7th ed.). New York: Longman.

Harste, J. C., Burke, C. L., & Woodward, V. A. (1982). Children's language and world: Initial encounters with print. In J. A. Langer & M. T. Smith-Burke (Eds.), *Reader meets author/Bridging the gap* (pp. 105–131). Newark, DE: International Reading Association.

Haynes, B., Baker, L., Serpell, R., & Sonnenschein, S. (2003, April). *Story retelling and reading comprehension among ethnically diverse second graders.* Paper presented at the meeting of the Society for Research in Child Development, Tampa.

Heath, S. B. (1983). *Ways with words: Language, life and work in communities and classrooms.* Cambridge, UK: Cambridge University Press.

Hecht, S. A., Burgess, S. R., Torgesen, J. K., Wagner, R. K., & Rashotte, C. A. (2000). Explaining social class differences in growth of reading skills from beginning kindergarten through fourth grade: The role of phonological awareness, rate of access, and print knowledge. *Reading & Writing: An Interdisciplinary Journal, 12,* 99–127.

Hill, S. (1994). *Culture, context and personal narrative.* Unpublished master's thesis, University of Maryland, Baltimore County.

Hoover-Dempsey, K. V., & Sandler, H. M. (1997). Why do parents become involved in their children's education? *Review of Educational Research, 67,* 3–42.

Howard, A., & Scott, R. A. (1981). The study of minority groups in complex societies. In R. H. Munroe, R. L. Munroe, & B. B. Whiting (Eds.), *Handbook of cross-cultural human development* (pp. 113–152). New York: Garland.

Huston, A. C., Wright, J. C., Marquis, J., & Green, S. B. (1999). How young children spend their time: Television and other activities. *Developmental Psychology, 35,* 912–925.

Jahoda, G. (1982). *Psychology and anthropology: A psychological perspective.* London: Academic Press.

Jensen, A. R. (1969). How much can we boost IQ and scholastic achievement? *Harvard Educational Review, 39,* 1–123.

Jordan, L. C., Bogat, G. A., & Smith, G. (2001). Collaborating for social change: The black psychologist and the black community. *American Journal of Community Psychology, 29,* 599–620.

Kagitcibasi, C. (1996). *Family and human development across cultures: A view from the other side.* Mahwah, NJ: Erlbaum.

Kamil, M. L., Mosenthal, P. B., Pearson, P. D., & Barr, R. (Eds.). (2000). *Handbook of reading research* (Vol. III). Mahwah, NJ: Erlbaum.

Kasarda, J. D. (1986). Transforming cities and employment for displaced workers. In E. Bergman (Ed.), *Local economic transition* (pp. 286–307). Durham, NC: Duke University Press.

Kasza, K. (1987). *The wolf's chicken stew.* New York: G. P. Putnam's Sons.

Laosa, L. (1984). Social policies toward children of diverse ethnic, racial, and language groups in the United States. In H. W. Stevenson, & A. E. Siegel (Eds.), *Child development research and social policy* (Vol. 1, pp. 1–109). Chicago: Chicago University Press.

Lareau, A. (1996). Assessing parent involvement in schooling: A critical analysis. In A. Booth & J. F. Dunn (Eds.), *Family-school links: How do they affect educational outcomes?* (pp. 54–64). Mahwah, NJ: Erlbaum.

Lave, J., & Wenger, E. (1991). *Situated learning: Legitimate peripheral participation*. Cambridge, UK: Cambridge University Press.

Leont'ev, A. N. (1981). The problem of activity in psychology. In J. V. Wertsch (Ed.), *The concept of activity in Soviet psychology* (pp. 37–71). Armonk, NY: M. E. Sharpe.

Leseman, P. P. M., & de Jong, P. F. (1998). Home literacy: Opportunity, instruction, cooperation and social-emotional quality predicting early reading achievement. *Reading Research Quarterly, 33*, 294–318.

Levinson, B. A. (1996). Social difference and schooled identity at a Mexican secundaria. In B. A. Levinson, D. E. Foley, & D. C. Holland (Eds.), *The cultural production of the educated person: Critical ethnographies of schooling and local practice* (pp. 211–238). Albany, NY: SUNY Press.

Lewis, O. (1966). The culture of poverty. *Scientific American, 215*, 19–25.

Lightfoot, C., & Valsiner, J. (1992). Parental belief systems under the influence: Social guidance of the construction of personal cultures. In I. E. Sigel, A. V. McGillicuddy-DeLisi, & J. J. Goodnow (Eds.), *Parental belief systems: The psychological consequences for children* (2nd ed., pp. 393–414). Hillsdale, NJ: Erlbaum.

Loh, M. J. (1988). *Tucking Mommy in*. New York: Orchard Books.

Lomax, R. G., & McGee, L. M. (1987). Young children's concepts about reading: Toward a model of word reading acquisition. *Reading Research Quarterly, 15*, 237–256.

Lomnitz-Adler, C. (1992). *Exits from the labyrinth: Culture and ideology in the Mexican national space*. Berkeley: University of California Press.

Lonigan, C. J., Burgess, S. R., & Anthony, J. L. (2000). Development of emergent literacy and early reading skills in preschool children: Evidence from a latent variable longitudinal study. *Developmental Psychology, 36*, 596–613.

Mackler, K. (2001). *Relations between television viewing and reading achievement*. Unpublished master's thesis, University of Maryland, Baltimore County.

Mackler, K., & Baker, L. (2001, April). *Relations between third graders' television viewing and home literacy experiences and their reading achievement*. Paper presented at the meeting of the Society for Research in Child Development, Minneapolis.

MacLean, L., Bryant, P., & Bradley, L. (1987). Rhymes, nursery rhymes, and reading in early childhood. *Merrill-Palmer Quarterly, 33*, 255–281.

MacLeod, F. (1996). Integrating home and school resources to raise literacy levels of parents and children. *Early Child Development and Care, 117,* 123–132.

Madden, N. A., Slavin, R. E., Karweit, N. L., Dolan, L. J., & Wasik, B. A. (1993). Success for all: Longitudinal effects of a restructuring program for inner-city elementary schools. *American Educational Research Journal, 30,* 123–148.

Marcon, R. A. (1999). Positive relationships between parent school involvement and public school inner-city preschoolers' development and academic performance. *School Psychology Review, 28,* 395–412.

McCarthey, S. J. (1997). Connecting home and school literacy practices in classrooms with diverse populations. *Journal of Literacy Research, 29,* 145–182.

McLane, J. B., & McNamee, G. D. (1990). *Early literacy.* Cambridge, MA: Harvard University Press.

McNaughton, S., & Parr, J. (1992). Beginning reading and sending books home to read: A case for fine tuning. *Educational Psychology: An International Journal of Experimental Educational Psychology, 12,* 239–247.

Mehan, H. (1979). *Learning lessons.* Cambridge, MA: Harvard University Press.

Meyer, L. A., Wardrop, J. L., Stahl, S. A., & Linn, R. L. (1994). Effects of reading storybooks aloud to children. *Journal of Educational Research, 88,* 69–85.

Michaels, S. (1981). "Sharing time": Children's narrative styles and differential access to literacy. *Language in Society, 10,* 423–442.

Miller, S. A. (1988). Parents' beliefs about children's cognitive development. *Child Development, 59,* 259–285.

Miller, P. J., & Sperry, L. L. (1988). Early talk about the past: The origins of conversational stories of personal experience. *Journal of Child Language, 15,* 293–315.

Moll, L. C., & Greenberg, J. B. (1990). Creating zones of possibilities: combining social contexts for instruction. In L. C. Moll (Ed.), *Vygotsky and education: Instructional implications and applications of sociohistorical psychology* (pp. 319–348). Cambridge, UK: Cambridge University Press.

Morakinyo, A. (1995). *Discourse variations among African-American and European-American kindergartners' literacy-related play.* Unpublished doctoral dissertation, University of Maryland, Baltimore County.

Morrow, L. M. (1988). Young children's responses to one-to-one story readings in school settings. *Reading Research Quarterly, 23,* 89–107.

Moynihan, D. P. (1965). *The Negro family: The case for national action.* Washington, DC: Office of Policy, Planning and Research, U.S. Department of Labor.

Munsch, R. (1987). *Moira's birthday.* Toronto: Annick Press.

Munsterman, K. (1996). *An examination of home storybook reading and its contribution to kindergartners' emergent literacy skills and reading motivation.* Unpublished master's thesis, University of Maryland, Baltimore County.

National Association for the Education of Young Children (NAEYC). (1998). Learning to read and write: Developmentally appropriate practices for young children. A joint position statement of the IRA and NAEYC. *Young Children, 53*, 3–46.

National Education Goals Panel. (1998). *Ready for school*. Washington, DC: National Education Goals Panel.

National Reading Panel. (2000). *Teaching children to read: An evidence-based assessment of the scientific research literature on reading and its implications for reading instruction*. National Institute of Child Health and Human Development, Bethesda, MD.

Nerlove, S. B., & Snipper, A. S. (1981). Cognitive consequences of cultural opportunity. In R. H. Munroe, R. L. Munroe, & B. B. Whiting (Eds.), *Handbook of cross-cultural human development* (pp. 423–474). New York: Garland.

Neuman, S. B. (1988). The displacement effect: Assessing the relation between television viewing and reading performance. *Reading Research Quarterly, 23*, 414–440.

Neuman, S. B., & Celano, D. (2001). Access to print in low-income and middle-income communities. *Reading Research Quarterly, 36*, 8–27.

Neuman, S. B., & Dickinson, D. K. (Eds.) (2001). *Handbook of early literacy research*. New York: Guilford.

Neuman, S. B., & Roskos, K. (1990). Play, print & purpose: Enriching play environments for literacy development. *The Reading Teacher, 44*, 214–221.

Ninio, A., & Bruner, J. S. (1978). The achievement and antecedents of labeling. *Journal of Child Language, 5*, 1–15.

Ogbu, J. U. (1990). Cultural model, identity, and literacy. In J. W. Stigler, R. A. Shweder, & G. Herdt (Eds.), *Cultural psychology: Essays on comparative human development* (pp. 520–541). Cambridge, UK: Cambridge University Press.

Okagaki, L., & Sternberg, R. J. (1991). Cultural and parental influences on cognitive development. In L. Okagaki & R. J. Sternberg (Eds.), *Directors of development: Influences on the development of children's thinking* (pp. 101–120). Hillsdale, NJ: Erlbaum.

Olofson, A., & Niedersoe, J. (1999). Early language development and kindergarten phonological awareness as predictors of reading problems: From 3 to 11 years of age. *Journal of Learning Disabilities, 32*, 464–473.

Olson, D. R. (1977). Oral and written language and the cognitive processes of children. *Journal of Communication, 27*, 10–26.

Olson, D. R. (1994). *The world on paper*. Cambridge, UK: Cambridge University Press.

Olson, K. (1991). Old West Baltimore: Segregation, African-American culture, and the struggle for equality. In E. Fee, L. Shopes, & L. Zeidman (Eds.), *The Baltimore book: New views of local history* (pp. 57–78). Philadelphia: Temple University Press.

Orser, W. E. (1991). Flight to the suburbs: Suburbanization and racial change on Baltimore's west side. In E. Fee, L. Shopes, & L. Zeidman (Eds.), *The*

Baltimore book: New views of local history (pp. 203–225). Philadelphia: Temple University Press.

Padak, N. D., Vacca, R. T., & Stuart, D. (1993). Rethinking reading for children at risk. *Reading and Writing Quarterly: Overcoming Learning Difficulties, 9*, 361–368.

Pellegrini, A. D., Perlmutter, J. C., Galda, L., & Brody, G. H. (1990). Joint reading between Black Head Start children and their mothers. *Child Development, 61*, 443–453.

Phillips, G., & McNaughton, S. (1990). The practice of storybook reading to preschool children in mainstream New Zealand families. *Reading Research Quarterly, 25*, 196–212.

Piaget, J. (1971). *The construction of reality in the child*. New York: Ballantine.

Pressley, M. (2002). *Reading instruction that works: The case for balanced teaching* (2nd ed.). New York: Guilford Press.

Pressley, M., & Afflerbach, P. (1995). *Verbal protocols of reading: The nature of constructively responsive reading*. Hillsdale, NJ: Erlbaum.

Pressley, M., Wharton-McDonald, R., Allington, R., Block, C. C., Morrow, L., Tracey, D., Baker, K., Brooks, G., Cronin, J., Nelson, E., & Woo, D. (2001). A study of effective first-grade literacy instruction. *Scientific Studies of Reading, 5*, 35–58.

Pryor, E., & Church, B. (1995). Family–school partnerships for the 21st century. *Reading and Writing Quarterly: Overcoming Learning Difficulties, 11*, 257–266.

Purcell-Gates, V. (1996). Stories, coupons, and the TV guide: Relationships between home literacy experiences and emergent literacy knowledge. *Reading Research Quarterly, 31*, 406–428.

Purcell-Gates, V. (2000). Family literacy. In M. L. Kamil, P. B. Mosenthal, P. D. Pearson, & R. Barr (Eds.), *Handbook of reading research* (Vol. 3, pp. 853–870). Mahwah, NJ: Erlbaum.

Raver, C. C. (2002). Emotions matter: Making the case for the role of young children' emotional development for early school readiness. *Social Policy Report, 16*(3), 1–19.

Raz, I. T., & Bryant, P. (1990). Social background, phonological awareness and children's reading. *British Journal of Developmental Psychology, 8*, 209–225.

Reese, L., & Gallimore, R. (2000). Immigrant Latinos' cultural model of literacy development: An evolving perspective on home–school discontinuities. *American Journal of Education, 108*, 103–134.

Resnick, D., & Resnick, L. (1977). The nature of literacy: An historical exploration. *Harvard Educational Review, 47*, 370–385.

Rimm-Kaufman, S. E., & Pianta, R. C. (1999). Patterns of family–school contact in preschool and kindergarten. *School Psychology Review, 28*, 426–438.

Rodrigo, M. J., & Triana, B. (1995). Parental beliefs about child development and parental inferences about actions during child-rearing episodes. *European Journal of Educational Psychology, 11*, 55–78.

Rogoff, B. (1990). *Apprenticeship in thinking: Cognitive development in social context*. New York: Oxford University Press.

Rogoff, B. (1993). Children's guided participation and participatory appropriation in sociocultural activity. In R. Wozniak & K. Fischer (Eds.), *Development in context: Acting and thinking in specific environments* (pp. 121–153). Hillsdale, NJ: Erlbaum.

Rogoff, B. (1998). Cognition as a collaborative process. In W. Damon (Gen. Ed.) & D. Kuhn & R. S. Siegler (Vol. Eds.), *Handbook of child psychology: Vol. 2. Cognition, perception, and language* (5th ed., pp. 679–744). New York: Wiley.

Roskos, K. (1990). A taxonomic view of pretend play activity among 4- and 5-year-old children. *Early Childhood Research Quarterly, 5*, 495–512.

Sadker, M., & Sadker, D. (1994). *Failing at fairness: How America's schools cheat girls*. New York: Scribner.

Salomon, G. (Ed.). (1993). *Distributed cognition: Psychological and educational considerations*. New York: Cambridge University Press.

Sameroff, A. J. (1983). Developmental systems: contexts and evolution. In P. H. Mussen (Series Ed.) & W. Kessen (Vol. Ed.), *Handbook of child psychology: Vol. 1. History, theory and methods* (pp. 237–294). New York: Wiley.

Sameroff, A. J., & Fiese, B. H., (1992). Family representations of development. In I. E. Sigel, A. V. McGillicuddy-DeLisi, & J. J. Goodnow (Eds.), *Parental belief systems: The psychological consequences for children* (2nd ed., pp. 347–369). Hillsdale, NJ: Erlbaum.

Scarborough, H. S. (1998). Early identification of children at risk for reading disabilities: Phonological awareness and some other promising predictors. In B. K. Shapiro, P. J. Accardo, & A. J. Capute (Eds.), *Specific reading disability: A view of the spectrum* (pp. 77–121). Timonium, MD: York Press.

Scarborough, H. S., & Dobrich, W. (1994). On the efficacy of reading to preschoolers. *Developmental Review, 14*, 245–302.

Scardamalia, M., & Bereiter, C. (1986). Research on written composition. In M. C. Wittrock (Ed.), *Handbook of research on teaching* (3rd ed., pp. 778–803). New York: Macmillan.

Scher, D. (1996). *Attitudes toward reading and children's home literacy environments*. Unpublished master's thesis, University of Maryland, Baltimore County.

Schieffelin, B. B., & Eisenberg, A. R. (1986). Cultural variations in children's conversation. In R. L. Schiefelbusch & J. Pickar (Eds.), *The acquisition of communicative competence* (pp. 377–420). Baltimore: University Park Press.

Schmidt, D. C. (1998). *The relation between children's narrative production and literacy across differing socio-economic groups*. Unpublished manuscript, University of Maryland, Baltimore County.

Scott-Jones, D. (1991). Black families and literacy. In S. B. Silvern & B. A. Hutson (Eds.), *Advances in reading/language research: Literacy through family, community, and school interaction* (Vol 5., pp. 173–200). Greenwich, CT: JAI Press.

Scribner, S., & Cole, M. (1981). *The psychology of literacy*. Cambridge, MA: Harvard University Press.

Senechal, M., LeFevre, J., Hudson, E., & Lawson, E. P. (1996). Knowledge of storybooks as predictors of young children's vocabulary. *Journal of Educational Psychology, 88*, 520–536.

Serpell, R. (1976). *Culture's influence on behavior*. London: Methuen.

Serpell, R. (1977). Estimates of intelligence in a rural community of Eastern Zambia. In F. M. Okatcha (Ed.), *Modern psychology and cultural adaptation* (pp. 179–216). Nairobi: Swahili Language Consultants and Publishers.

Serpell, R. (1979). How specific are perceptual skills? A cross-cultural study of pattern reproduction. *British Journal of Psychology, 70*, 365–380.

Serpell, R. (1982). Measures of perception, skills, and intelligence: The growth of a new perspective on children in a Third World country. In W. W. Hartup (Ed.), *Review of child development research* (Vol. 6, pp. 392–440). Chicago: University of Chicago Press.

Serpell, R. (1990). Audience, culture and psychological explanation: A reformulation of the emic-etic problem in cross-cultural psychology. *Quarterly Newsletter of the Laboratory of Comparative Human Cognition, 12*, 99–132.

Serpell, R. (1991). Exaggerating the significance of text. *Curriculum Inquiry, 21*, 353–362.

Serpell, R. (1993a). *The significance of schooling: Life-journeys in an African society*. Cambridge, UK: Cambridge University Press.

Serpell, R. (1993b). Interaction of context with development: Theoretical constructs for the design of early childhood intervention programs. In L. Eldering & P. Leseman (Eds.), *Early intervention and culture* (pp. 23–43). Paris: UNESCO Publishing.

Serpell, R. (1994). Negotiating a fusion of horizons: A process of cultural validation in developmental psychology. *Mind, Culture, and Activity, 1*, 43–68.

Serpell, R. (1997). Literacy connections between school and home: How should we evaluate them? *Journal of Literacy Research, 29*, 587–616.

Serpell, R. (1999). Theoretical conceptions of human development. In L. Eldering & P. Leseman (Eds.), *Effective early intervention: Cross-cultural perspectives* (pp. 41–66). New York: Falmer.

Serpell, R. (2001). Cultural dimensions of literacy promotion and schooling. In L.Verhoeven & C. Snow (Eds.), *Literacy and motivation* (pp. 243–273). Mahwah, NJ: Erlbaum.

Serpell, R., Baker, L., Sonnenschein, S., Gorham, L., & Hill, S. (1996). *Cooperative communication among parents and teachers about children's emergent literacy*. (ERIC Document Reproduction Services No. ED414566.)

Serpell, R., & Hatano, G. (1997). Education, literacy and schooling in cross-cultural perspective. In J. W. Berry, P. R. Dasen, & T. M. Saraswathi (Eds.),

Handbook of cross-cultural psychology (Vol. 2, (2nd ed., pp. 345–382). Boston: Allyn & Bacon.

Serpell, R., Sonnenschein, S., Baker, L., & Ganapathy, H. (2002). The intimate culture of families in early socialization of literacy. *Journal of Family Psychology, 16,* 391–405.

Serpell, R., Sonnenschein, S., Baker, L., Hill, S., Goddard-Truitt, V., & Danseco, E. (1997). *Parental ideas about development and socialization of children on the threshold of schooling* (Reading Research Report No. 78). Athens, GA: University of Georgia and University of Maryland, National Reading Research Center. (ERIC Document Reproduction Services No. ED405568.)

Sigel, I. E. (Ed.) (1985). *Parental beliefs systems: The psychological consequences for children.* Hillsdale, NJ: Erlbaum.

Silver, H. (1994). *Good schools, effective schools, judgements and their histories.* New York: Cassell.

Smith, S. S., & Dixon, R. G. (1995). Literacy concepts of low- and middle-class four-year-olds entering preschool. *Journal of Educational Research, 88,* 243–253.

Smitherman, G. (1977). *Talkin' and testifyin': The language of black America.* Boston: Houghton Mifflin.

Snow, C. E. (1991). The theoretical basis of the Home-School Study of Language and Literacy Development. *Journal of Research in Childhood Education, 6,* 1–8.

Snow, C. E. (1994). Enhancing literacy development: Programs and research perspectives. In D. K. Dickinson (Ed.), *Bridges to literacy: Children, families, and schools* (pp. 267–272). Cambridge, MA: Basil Blackwell.

Snow, C. E., Barnes, W. S., Chandler, J., Goodman, I. F., & Hemphill, L. (1991). *Unfulfilled expectations: Home and school influences on literacy.* Cambridge, MA: Harvard University Press.

Snow, C. E., Burns, M. S., & Griffin, P. (Eds.) (1998). *Preventing reading difficulties in young children.* Washington, DC: National Academy Press.

Snow, C. E., & Dickinson, D. K. (1990). Social sources of narrative skills at home and at school. *First Language, 10,* 87–103.

Sonnenschein, S., Baker, L., & Serpell, R. (1995). *Documenting the child's everyday home experience: The ecological inventory as a resource for teachers* (Instructional Resources, #11). Athens, GA: University of Georgia and University of Maryland, National Reading Research Center. (ERIC Document Reproduction Services No. ED384860.)

Sonnenschein, S., Baker, L., Serpell, R., Scher, D., Fernandez-Fein, S., & Munsterman, K. A. (1996). *Strands of emergent literacy and their antecedents in the home: Urban preschoolers' early literacy development* (Reading Research Report #48). Athens, GA: University of Georgia and University of Maryland, National Reading Research Center. (ERIC Document Reproduction Services No. ED392019.)

Sonnenschein, S., Baker, L., Serpell, R., Scher, D., Goddard Truitt, V., & Munsterman, K. (1997). Parental beliefs about ways to help children learn to read: The impact of an entertainment or a skills perspective. *Early Child Development and Care, 127–128,* 111–118.

Sonnenschein, S., Baker, L., Serpell, R., & Schmidt, D. (2000). Reading is a source of entertainment: The importance of the home perspective for children's literacy development. In K. A. Roskos & J. F. Christie (Eds.), *Play and literacy in early childhood: Research from multiple perspectives* (pp. 125–137). Mahwah, NJ: Erlbaum.

Sonnenschein, S., Katenkamp, A., Tenowich, P., & Serpell, R. (2003, April). *Frequency of engagement in literacy-related activities at home and reading development.* Paper presented at the meeting of the Society for Research in Child Development, Tampa.

Sonnenschein, S., & Munsterman, K. (1996, April). *The Early Childhood Project: Aspects of the social nature of becoming literate.* In C. Daiute & A. D. Pellegrini (Chairs), *The role of relationships in the development of literacy.* Symposium conducted at the meeting of the American Educational Research Association, New York.

Sonnenschein, S., & Munsterman, K. (2002). The influence of home-based reading interactions on 5-year-olds' reading motivation and early literacy development. *Early Childhood Research Quarterly, 17,* 318–337.

Sonnenschein, S., & Schmidt, D. (2000). Fostering home and community connections to support children's reading. In L. Baker, M. J. Dreher, & J. T. Guthrie (Eds.), *Engaging young readers: Promoting achievement and motivation* (pp. 264–284). New York: Guilford.

Sonnenschein, S., Schmidt, D., & Mackler, K. (1999, April). *The role of the home in improving children's reading during early elementary school.* Paper presented at the meeting of the Society for Research in Child Development, Albuquerque, NM.

Sonnenschein, S., Schmidt, D., Pringle, B., Baker, L., & Scher, D. (1996, June). Personal narrative and its relation to other aspects of literacy development. In M. Benson (Chair), *Emerging narrative abilities among low-income children: Influence of practices in the home, intervention, and relationship to social competence.* Symposium presented at the Third National Head Start Research Conference, Washington, DC.

Sonnenschein, S., Williams, H., & Schmidt, D. (1997, April). How parental socialization practices and ideas about literacy are related to children's appropriation of literacy competencies. In R. Serpell, S. Sonnenschein, & L. Baker (Chairs), *Patterns of emerging competence and sociocultural context in the early appropriation of literacy.* Symposium presented at the Society for Research in Child Development, Washington, DC.

Stahl, S. A., & Murray, B. A. (1998). Issues involved in defining phonological awareness and its relation to early reading. In J. Metsala & L. C. Ehri (Eds.), *Word recognition in beginning literacy* (pp. 65–88). Mahwah, NJ: Erlbaum.

Stanovich, K. E., West, R. F., Cunningham, A. E., Cipielewski, J., & Siddiqui, S. (1996). The role of inadequate print exposure as a determinant of reading comprehension problems. In C. Cornoldi & J. Oakhill (Eds.), *Reading comprehension difficulties: Processes and interventions* (pp. 15–32). Mahwah, NJ: Erlbaum.

Stevenson, D. L., & Baker, D. P. (1987). The family–school relation and the child's school performance. *Child Development, 58*, 1348–1357.

Stevenson, H. W., Chen, C., & Uttal, D. H. (1990). Beliefs and achievement: A study of black, white, and Hispanic children. *Child Development, 61*, 508–523.

Stevenson, H. W., & Newman, R. S. (1986). Long-term prediction of achievement and attitudes in mathematics and reading. *Child Development, 57*, 646–659.

Stewart, J. (1992). Kindergarten students' awareness of reading at home and in school. *Journal of Educational Research, 86*, 95–104.

Street, B. (1984). *Literacy in theory and practice.* Cambridge, UK: Cambridge University Press.

Sulzby, E. (1985). Children's emergent reading of favorite storybooks: A developmental study. *Reading Research Quarterly, 20*, 458–481.

Sulzby, E., & Teale, W. H. (1991). Emergent literacy. In R. Barr, M. L. Kamil, P. Mosenthal, & P. D. Pearson (Eds.), *Handbook of reading research* (Vol. 2, pp. 727–758). New York: Longman.

Sulzby, E., Teale, W. H., & Kamberelis, G. (1989). Emergent writing in the classroom: Home and school connections. In D. S. Strickland & L. M. Morrow (Eds.), *Emergent literacy: Young children learn to read and write* (pp. 63–79). Newark, DE: International Reading Association.

Super, C. M., & Harkness, S. (1986). The developmental niche: A conceptualization at the interface of child and culture. *International Journal of Behavioral Development, 9*, 545–569.

Super, C. M., & Harkness, S. (1997). The cultural structuring of child development. In J. W. Berry, P. R. Dasen, & T. S. Saraswathi (Eds.), *Handbook of cross-cultural psychology, Vol. 2: Basic processes and developmental psychology* (2nd ed., pp. 1–39). Boston: Allyn & Bacon.

Swap, S. (1993). *Developing home–school partnerships.* New York: Teachers College Press.

Taylor, D., & Dorsey-Gaines, C. (1988). *Growing up literate: Learning from inner city families.* Portsmouth, NH: Heinemann.

Teale, W. H. (1986). Home background and young children's literacy development. In W. H. Teale & E. Sulzby (Eds.), *Emergent literacy: Writing and reading* (pp. 173–206). Norword, NJ: Ablex.

Tharp, R. G., & Gallimore, R. (1988). *Rousing minds to life: Teaching, learning, and schooling in social context.* Cambridge, UK: Cambridge University Press.

Treiman, R. (1991). Phonological awareness and its roles in learning to read and spell. In D. J. Sawyer & B. J. Fox (Eds.), *Phonological awareness in reading: The evolution of current perspectives* (pp. 159–189). New York: Springer-Verlag.

Treiman, R. (1998). Why spelling? The benefits of incorporating spelling into beginning reading instruction. In J. L. Metsala & L. C. Ehri (Eds.), *Word recognition in beginning literacy* (pp. 289–314). Mahwah, NJ: Erlbaum.

U.S. Department of Education. (1996). *Parents and schools: Partners in student learning (NCES 96-913)*. Washington, DC: Superintendent of Documents.

U.S. Department of Education. (2001). *The Nation's report card: Fourth grade reading 2000* (NCES 2001-499). Washington, DC: U.S. Government Printing Office.

Valdes, G. (1996). *Con respeto: Bridging the distances between culturally diverse families and schools: An ethnographic portrait.* New York: Teachers College Press.

Valsiner, J., & Lawrence, J. (1997). Human development in culture across the life span. In J. W. Berry, P. R. Dasen, & T. S. Saraswathi (Eds.), *Handbook of cross cultural psychology. Volume 2. Basic processes and human development* (pp. 69–106). Boston: Allyn & Bacon.

Vechiotti, S. (2003). Kindergarten: An overlooked educational policy priority. *Social Policy Report, 17*(2), 3–19.

Verhoeven, L., & Snow, C. (Eds.). (2001). *Literacy and motivation.* Mahwah, NJ: Erlbaum.

Vygotsky, L. S. (1978). *Mind in society: The development of higher psychological processes.* Cambridge, MA: Harvard University Press. London, England: Springer Verlag.

Watson, R. (2001). Literacy and oral language: Implications for early literacy acquisition. In S. B. Neuman & D. K. Dickinson (Eds.), *Handbook of early literacy research* (pp. 43–53). New York: Guilford.

Weisner, T. S. (1989). Comparing sibling relationships across cultures. In G. P. Zukow (Ed.), *Sibling interaction across cultures: Theoretical and methodological issues* (pp. 79–105). London: Springer Verlag.

Wells, G. (1986). *The meaning makers: Children learning language and using language to learn.* Portsmouth, NH: Heineman.

Wells, G. (1990). Talk about text. *Curriculum Inquiry, 20,* 370–405.

Westat. (2001). *Report on the final evaluation of the city–state partnership, presented to the Board of School Commissioners and the Maryland State Department of Education.* (www.bcps.k12.md.us/admin/westat.htm).

Whitehurst, G. J., & Lonigan, C. J. (1998). Child development and emergent literacy. *Child Development, 68,* 848–872.

Whitehurst, G. J., & Lonigan, C. J. (2001). Emergent literacy: Development from prereaders to readers. In S. B. Neuman & D. K. Dickinson (Eds.), *Handbook of early literacy research* (pp. 11–29). New York: Guilford.

Whitehurst, G. J., Zevenbergen, A. A., Crone, D. A., Schultz, M. D., Velting, O. N., & Fischel, J. E. (1998). Outcomes of an emergent literacy intervention from Head Start through second grade. *Journal of Educational Psychology, 91,* 261–272.

Williams, H. (1999). *Storybook readings in first grade classrooms.* Unpublished master's thesis, University of Maryland, Baltimore County.

Williams, H., & Baker, L. (1998, April). *Differences in teachers' approaches to storybook readings in first grade classrooms.* Paper presented at the meeting of the American Educational Research Association, San Diego.

Wilson, W. J. (1987). *The truly disadvantaged: The inner city, the underclass, and public policy.* Chicago: Chicago University Press.

Woodcock, R. W., & Johnson, M. B. (1989/1990). *Woodcock-Johnson Psycho-Educational Battery – Revised.* Allan, TX: DLM Teaching Resources.

Yopp, H. K. (1988). The validity and reliability of phonemic awareness tests. *Reading Research Quarterly, 23,* 159–177.

Zukow, P G. (1989). Siblings as effective socializing agents: Evidence from Central Mexico. In P. G. Zukow (Ed.), *Sibling interaction across cultures: Theoretical and methodological issues* (pp. 79–105). London: Springer-Verlag.

Name Index

Subject Index